DATE DUE

GAYLORD			PRINTED IN U.S.A.

D1442816

☆

JERRY BROWN
THE PHILOSOPHER-PRINCE

☆

JERRY BROWN

THE PHILOSOPHER-PRINCE

ROBERT PACK

𝔰𝔡

STEIN AND DAY/*Publishers*/New York

First published in 1978
Copyright © 1978 by Robert Pack
All rights reserved
Designed by Barbara Huntley
Printed in the United States of America
Stein and Day/*Publishers*/Scarborough House
Briarcliff Manor, N.Y. 10510

Library of Congress Cataloging in Publication Data

Pack, Robert Irving, 1942–
Jerry Brown: a biography.

1.-Brown, Edmund Gerald, Jr., 1938-   2.-California—Governors—Biography.
3.-California—Politics and government—1951-
4.-United States—Politics and government—1974-1977.
F866.2.B732P33   979.4'05'.0924 [B]   77-16251
ISBN 0-8128-2437-7

All quotations from E. F. Schumacher's *Small Is Beautiful*
are reprinted by permission of Harper & Row.

☆ CONTENTS

Photographs follow page 140

☆ ACKNOWLEDGMENTS

I want to thank all those I interviewed during the course of my research for their time and help. Some of the people I talked to are not referred to in the book or are mentioned only in passing, but each interview helped contribute to my knowledge of Jerry Brown. In particular I would like to express my gratitude to Marc Poché for his guidance at the start of my research and for his understanding that whatever feelings he might have about Governor Brown, my purpose was to present an objective profile. Thus Marc, while making clear his high regard for the Governor, steered me to a number of people, several of whom he knew would be as uncomplimentary as he had been complimentary. For that he has not only my thanks but my respect.

Elisabeth Coleman, Barbara Metzger, and the rest of Governor Brown's press staff were most helpful. Anna Michael, the librarian of the *Sacramento Bee,* graciously tolerated my intrusions into her files, which were extremely well organized, thorough, and most valuable. Isie Ramirez of the *Bee's* public relations department helped me gain access to photographs.

My editor, Michaela Hamilton, and my friend, Mary Ann Seawell, worked hard to help turn my original manuscript into a finished product. Two other friends of mine, Bill Keiser and Greg Movsesyan, contributed their political savvy.

Last but not least, my thanks to my wife Jane for her advice from the perspective of someone who is not involved in either politics or journalism. And to the late Clinton Rossiter, my teacher.

☆ FOREWORD

WHY JERRY BROWN?

The popular press has given extensive coverage to the current governor of California, Edmund G. Brown, Jr., better known as Jerry Brown. Much has been written and broadcast about Brown's three and a half years as a seminarian studying to be a Catholic priest; his love-hate relationship with his father, former Governor Pat Brown; his bachelor status; his preference for a modestly furnished apartment over the $1.5 million Governor's Mansion commissioned by his predecessor, Ronald Reagan; his penchant for asking philosophical questions instead of providing practical answers; and his triumphs over Jimmy Carter in the 1976 presidential primaries. Yet to date there have been few serious attempts to go beyond the surface in depicting both the personality and the politics of the man acknowledged by critics and supporters alike as America's most unusual elected official.

Who is Jerry Brown? Where has he been, and where is he going? These questions will serve as a starting point for a more detailed examination of this colorful and controversial figure. The answers are based on interviews with about 150 people, including Jerry Brown himself, which provided the source of all quoted statements that are not otherwise attributed.

Jerry Brown marches to the beat of a different drummer. Aside from personal traits that would brand him as unique even if he had not decided to enter politics, he is totally his own kind of politician: apparently beholden to no one, whether it be the voters who put him in office, the Democratic party, with which he is identified, the political heavyweights who have given their money and time to his campaigns, or even his father, who provided what was the younger Brown's most valuable political asset, at least through his election as governor in 1974: his name.

Throughout his earlier campaigns, if not while he was running for president in 1976, Jerry Brown seemed to be saying to the public, "Take it or leave it. If you don't like what I have to say, don't vote for me. But at least you know where I stand." And even after his successes in the 1976 primaries, Brown was still attracting attention with moves considered nonpolitical, such as his 1977 veto of legislation restoring the death penalty in California. Brown was well aware that capital punishment had the support of most of California's electorate and the vast majority of its elected officials. As it turned out, the governor's veto was overridden by the required two-thirds majority in each of the two houses of the state legislature; yet Brown maintained the unpopular position dictated by his conscience.

Brown also represents a break with traditional liberal policies like the New Frontier and the Great Society, which see money as the solution to all social ills. He combines a genuine concern for the downtrodden with a Reagan-like reluctance to spend money or to rely on government programs.

And so it is not surprising that Brown, who offers something to both liberals and conservatives, is an extremely popular politician. His name has appeared on the ballot in California seven times: twice in 1969, when he was elected to the Los Angeles Community College Board; twice in 1970, when he was elected secretary of state; twice in 1974, when he was elected governor; and most recently in June 1976, when he received almost 60 percent of the vote in a ten-way race in the state's presidential primary, compared to 20 percent for the closest runner-up, Jimmy Carter.

Jerry Brown's popularity has remained consistently high throughout his term as governor, with about 80 percent of California residents approving of his conduct in office. A poll released in March 1978 showed his popularity still strong, with leads ranging from 14 to 37 percentage points over his five potential Republican opponents.

Brown has repeatedly refused to comment on what role he might play in the 1980 presidential election. He appears to be trying to keep all his options open. But it is hard to forget that the first political campaign in which he was extensively involved, that of Eugene McCarthy in 1968, was an attempt from within the Democratic party to oust an incumbent Democratic president and that it was successful. As Jimmy Carter's term in office draws on, he seems increasingly vulnerable to criticism; perhaps most damaging, there have been frequent references to Carter in the media as a possible one-term president, and such prophecies have a way of influencing the public to such an extent as to become self-fulfilling.

A little more than two years before the two major parties would select their presidential nominees for 1980, it seemed clear that no one, whether Democrat or Republican, had a better chance of taking over from Carter than did Jerry Brown. As governor of the largest state, he had the largest constituency of any elected official except the president. If nominated, Brown could expect to win his own state, which would give him 10 percent of the nation's electoral votes before he even got warmed up. He showed his out-of-state appeal during his 1976 campaigns in Maryland, New Jersey, Rhode Island, Nevada, and Oregon, proving to be a formidable candidate in each.

Although publicly Brown and Carter have taken pains to play down any differences, it is clear that in private the reserved, grinning Carter and the reserved, poker-faced Brown have little use for one another. Meanwhile, Brown, who many people believe would have won the Democratic nomination in 1976 if he had entered the race a month or two sooner, is going out of his way to make sure he does not repeat that mistake in the future. During 1977, Brown made two trips to Canada and one each to England, Japan, and Mexico, each time adding to his credentials in foreign policy. While he was in London in late November and a month earlier, when Britain's Prince Charles visited Sacramento, Brown met privately and established a personal friendship with the future English monarch. While in New York in October 1977, Brown met with Jewish leaders and told them he would have a much stronger commitment to Israel than Carter does. During the same visit, Brown held discussions with the editors of the *New York Times* and the major weekly news magazines. The scope of such activities does not indicate that his aspirations are limited to the governorship.

Should Brown decide to seek the presidency in 1980, his biggest problem might turn out to be not Carter but other Democratic politicians Brown has offended with his frank, no-nonsense manner. During his first two years as governor, Brown avoided conferences with his fellow governors on the grounds they were a waste of his time. After attending his first governors' meeting in early 1977, Brown's reaction was, "I think it is interesting from an anthropological viewpoint," which might be true, but is not necessarily politic. A few days later, at a meeting of Western governors discussing the drought, Brown criticized what he called "the Cowboy Ethic," which he defined as "taking everything out and never putting anything back . . . everybody doing his or her own thing, without regard to the earth as a spaceship." Many of the governors present at that meeting in Denver, including the host, Governor Richard Lamm of Colorado, who was sitting next to Brown, were wearing cowboy boots as they listened to his remarks. Brown also did not endear himself to Frank Church and Morris Udall when, having trounced Carter in the Maryland primary in May 1976, Brown refused to agree to a division of the remaining primary states so that the three would not run against each other but could present a united front against Carter.

Brown's plan seems to be to appeal directly to the voters. If he does not ignore politicians and political organizations, he certainly pays much less attention to them than other candidates have. Minimal reliance on the Democratic party and vigorous attempts to reach the voters via the news media have clearly been the history of Brown's campaigns in California.

His appeal is also due in part to his age. Brown was three months short of his thirty-seventh birthday when he took the oath of office as governor on January 6, 1975, becoming the state's youngest chief executive since Frederick Low, who was thirty-five years, ten months old when he took over as governor on December 10, 1863. Low, who had gone to California to join the Gold Rush in 1849, symbolized the frontier spirit of his constituents in much the same way Brown represents the questing spirit of Californians today.

To many, Brown represents a new generation in politics. He is literally young enough to be the son of many of the major political figures on the national scene, including Reagan and Ford. In 1980, Brown will be forty-two, or a year younger than John F. Kennedy was when he was elected president in 1960. As the average voter's age goes down, the electorate is becoming much closer in years to Brown than to members of the generation that includes Carter, Church, Udall, Reagan, and Ford.

In dealing with Jerry Brown's political future, there is one possibility that cannot be ignored: He might decide he does not want to be a politician any longer and walk away from it all. According to one of Brown's closest associates over the years, he "just might decide to go build a cabin in the hills. His mind doesn't work like other people's minds. He's truly unique. He's not a linear thinker. Anyone else his age and in his position would be thinking, 'What should I do next? Run for the Senate or president?' But that's not at all as probable with Brown as it would be with any other politician."

That possibility in itself sets Brown apart as a member of a rare breed, politically speaking.

☆
_____

JERRY BROWN

THE PHILOSOPHER-PRINCE

CHAPTER ONE

THE SEMINARIAN

The three youths approached the imposing building at the top of the hill. It "scared the hell out of you," said one of them, Frank Damrell, Jr. "You didn't know what to expect in that thing."

"That thing" was the Scared Heart Novitiate in Los Gatos, California, 40 miles south of San Francisco. The date was August 15, 1956. In the car with Damrell were Peter Finnegan, who had recently graduated from St. Ignatius High School in San Francisco, and Edmund G. Brown, Jr., eighteen, whose father, Edmund G. "Pat" Brown, the former district attorney of San Francisco, was then the attorney general of California and two years away from being elected governor. Brown, Jr., known as Jerry, had been Finnegan's best friend in high school and Damrell's roommate the previous year when both Damrell and Brown were freshmen at the University of Santa Clara.

The driver of the car, Dave Dawson, and another passenger, Bart Lally, were giving their friends, Brown, Finnegan, and

1

Damrell, a ride to the seminary, where the trio would begin the study that leads to the priesthood. "It was a memorable ride, very memorable," Dawson recalled in his San Francisco law office more than two decades later. "They took their vows of poverty prematurely by emptying their pockets, saying, 'We don't need it,' " and throwing their money into the streets of Los Gatos, which Spanish explorers and missionaries had named for the large cats, or mountain lions, that roamed the hilly, heavily wooded area.

Jerry Brown was born in San Francisco on April 7, 1938. He was the third of four children, preceded by Barbara and Cynthia and followed by Kathleen. His mother, Bernice Layne Brown, is the daughter of a San Francisco police captain. Pat Brown, like his son, had a Catholic father and a Protestant mother, but there the parental similarities end. Pat Brown's father, Edmund Joseph Brown, was a gambler and theater operator who owned a legal poker hall in San Francisco's Tenderloin district. Pat's mother, Ida Schuckman Brown, apparently disapproved of her husband's occupation and the late hours his work forced him to keep, and according to Pat Brown, the couple split up in 1917 when Pat was twelve, although the elder Brown continued to live at home for a number of years. "My father dominated the scene until I was twelve and then they kind of separated, so my mother took over," said Pat Brown. "She really affirmatively avoided Catholicism." Nevertheless, Pat Brown has been a practicing Catholic throughout his adult life, and his wife agreed that their children would be raised as Catholics in spite of her own Protestant upbringing.

Pat Brown and Bernice Layne met in a history class at Lowell High School in San Francisco. Exceptionally bright, she was nearing the end of her junior year at the age of thirteen when she first got to know her future husband. Mrs. Brown must have been strikingly attractive even then, judging from her appearance as she approached seventy. She has the same heavy eyebrows and piercing eyes as her only son, although her eyes are lighter.

Shortly after Pat Brown and Bernice met, he invited her to a dance, and she accepted. There was only one problem, she recalled almost sixty years later: Her parents had raised her very strictly and in view of her tender age had thus far refused to allow her to date. But the prom Pat Brown had invited her to was several weeks away, and she was confident that during that period she could convince her parents to permit her to go. Also, she was embarrassed to admit to Pat when he asked her that she had never dated.

Unfortunately, the Laynes would not be persuaded, and at the last minute Bernice had to break the date. She was still ashamed to tell Pat the real reason, so she offered no explanation, and the whole incident caused him to suffer extensive baiting from his contemporaries, many of whom were no doubt jealous of his success in making a date with the previously unapproachable Bernice Layne. About a year later, the Laynes finally decided that their daughter, who was about to graduate from high school, was old enough to go out with boys, and she began dating Pat.

Pat Brown received his law degree from the old San Francisco Law School in 1927 and the next year he sought office for the first time, as a Republican candidate for the state assembly. Ironically, Pat Brown, who switched from Republican to Democrat in 1934, was ultimately ousted from the job of governor by Republican Ronald Reagan, who was originally a Democrat. Pat Brown was also the last statewide candidate in California to run as the candidate of both parties, when he ran for a second term as attorney general in 1954 as the nominee of both Republicans and Democrats. Until then, state law permitted a candidate to seek the nominations of the two major parties.

Pat Brown's first try for office was unsuccessful, but Bernice Brown later retrieved one of the campaign cards he handed out, framed it, and put it on display in the living room of the couple's home in Beverly Hills. The card reads: "Elect Edmund G. (Pat) Brown, Republican candidate for Assemblyman, 26th district. Rid the state of bossism and elect an independent and progressive young attorney."

Pat Brown and Bernice were married October 30, 1930, and he practiced law in San Francisco until 1943, when he was elected district attorney after an unsuccessful bid for that office in 1939. He spent the next twenty-three years as an elected official, seven years as district attorney and eight each as attorney general and governor, until he returned to private law practice in Beverly Hills after his loss to Reagan in 1966.

Jerry Brown was raised on Magellan Avenue in the Forest Hill section of San Francisco. He attended public schools until the fourth grade, when he entered the new St. Brendan's parochial school near his home. He went on to St. Ignatius High School.

Barbara Brown Casey, who is seven years his senior, still remembers Jerry Brown as the "bratty little brother that plagued my existence" until she talked him into moving into a room downstairs next to the kitchen so that sleeping arrangements in the upstairs bedrooms could be shifted and Barbara could have her own room. The new setup also worked well for Edmund G. Brown, Jr., because of the proximity of his new room to the kitchen and also because, as the only member of the family living downstairs, he could come and go at any hour with little chance of his parents finding out.

When Jerry was about twelve, Joe Kelly started to date Cynthia Brown, who is four and a half years older than her brother. Kelly, who was then a student at the University of San Francisco, met Cynthia by virture of being basketball coach at the Catholic girls' school she attended. Kelly got a little more than he had bargained for, however, when the younger brother of the object of his affection discovered that Kelly had graduated from St. Ignatius, which Jerry was planning to attend. When Kelly would arrive to call on Cynthia, "Jerry would hang around just to talk about St. Ignatius and ask questions. A lot of times my mind was on other things, and I'd give him a dismissal answer, but that would never do for Jerry. He wanted to get to the answer that he wanted."

If Joe Kelly was not available, there was Dr. John McGuinness, who lived a few doors from the Browns and whose son, Mark, born several weeks before Jerry Brown, has been a lifelong friend of Brown. Dr. McGuinness, who died in 1975, was a very conservative Republican, and Brown "would argue with my father all the time," according to Mark McGuinness. In fact, young Brown would often be in the McGuinness house carrying on his debates with Dr. McGuinness while Mark and the other neighborhood youngsters were playing basketball in the back yard. Mrs. Anne McGuinness remembers that Brown would be prepared with about a dozen questions a night for her husband. "And he would keep arguing until Dr. John would say, 'Jerry, come on.' Jerry always had to argue about every subject he could think about. There were so many times I'd hear my husband say, 'Jerrrry, go home.' " Mark McGuinness said his father would frequently declare, "I'm going to vote for Pat and get Jerry out of the neighborhood," but both Mrs. McGuinness and her son agree that Dr. McGuinness made such remarks in jest and was extremely fond of Jerry Brown.

In spite of his own political philosophy, Dr. McGuinness consistently voted for his neighbor and had no objection to his young son's accompanying Jerry Brown on election days to march outside the local voting precinct with signs that urged the voters to choose Pat Brown.

As Pat Brown rose on the political ladder, his work consumed more of his time. While he was district attorney of San Francisco, Bernice Brown had a standing rule that the family would not eat dinner until Pat came home, which meant he either had to be home relatively early or face four hungry children and his formidable wife. As a result, he tended to arrive at Magellan Avenue at reasonable hours most nights during his seven years as district attorney. But campaigning for attorney general and serving in that office required Pat Brown to travel extensively; the attorney general divides his time among Sacramento, Los Angeles, and San Francisco. By the time Pat Brown became attorney general in 1951, Barbara Brown was a student at Berkeley, and Cynthia Brown was seriously dating Joe Kelly. When Bernice Brown accompanied her husband, twelve-year-old Jerry Brown tended to spend much of his time in the McGuinness household or in the home of his other close friend at the time, Bart Lally, who also lived nearby. Lally, an only child, said his parents gave equal attention to him and Brown, and his mother "supported us in terms of our gastronomical needs." Brown often spent the night at the Lally home.

Mrs. McGuinness related, "Oh, my goodness! Jerry lived here. He knew where everything was, especially in the food line. He was a free thinker and a free soul and completely uninhibited. If he wanted something, he just went ahead and made sure he got it. If I was giving my children their lunch and dinner, he'd just sit down. So I got used to having him here all the time. During the day he was here more than he was home. Bernice was not home, and she wanted her children to be independent. Well, I'm not like that. I would make a point of being here and of fixing them meals." She added, "Jerry was just like one of my children."

When Mark McGuinness got married in 1962, Jerry Brown was an usher and caught the bride's garter. Twelve years later, at a party in honor of Brown's election as governor, Brown asked McGuinness, who had gone into the carpet business, "Have you put your application in yet?"

"For what?" responded McGuinness.

BROWN: "The Carpet Commission."

MCGUINNESS: "There is none."

BROWN: "We'll create one."

Brown also showed his affection for Mrs. McGuinness at the last Christmas party Pat and Bernice Brown hosted at the old Governor's Mansion in Sacramento. Mrs. McGuinness recalled proudly, "I saw Jerry standing on the stairs, just surveying the crowd, and he finally came down and walked over to me and asked me to dance. It was such a surprise."

According to Barbara Brown, the worst thing about having a father who was a politician was that she must give "command performances," posing for the happy-family-of-the-candidate photographs and making occasional public appearances with the rest of her family at political functions. "I turned off with my father," she says. "I felt like I was just kind of an ornamentation." She said she grew weary of being introduced when Pat Brown went out on the campaign trail. On such occasions, each member of the family would stand up, everyone would clap, "and my father would make some inane remarks. I prefer my anonymity."

As for the pictures, Barbara said, "I guess I resented the lack of identity for myself. I want to be identified as myself, not as someone's daughter or someone's sister. I've always tried to blend right into the neighborhood. It's kind of hard when your father comes driving up in a big limousine with state police and blows the siren. He thought that was funny."

Barbara Brown has always had an independent streak. While she was a student at Berkeley and living at International House, where her brother would live after he left the seminary, she worked as a reporter for the *Daily Cal*, the student newspaper, and sometimes covered meetings of the Young People's Socialist League. This was in the McCarthy era, and Pat Brown was attorney general. The last thing he needed was for it to become known that his daughter was engaged in such activities. When she told her mother about her assignments for the *Daily Cal*, Bernice Brown's reaction was, "You can't," but Barbara insisted,

"Yes, I can." She later reminisced, "I was probably the only society girl who did that kind of thing." She also remembers applying for jobs at which the interviewer would ask, "What does your father do?" "There would be a big picture of him on the wall, and I would say he's an attorney and works for the state."

On the other hand, Cynthia Brown enjoyed being in the spotlight and having a father who was a celebrity. "I always thought everything my father did was great," she said. Cynthia thinks her brother, like Barbara, resented being on stage. However, she believes that having a father like Pat Brown was a big plus for Jerry in at least one respect: "Jerry got a lot of experience debating right here," said Cynthia, who still lives in the home where she was raised.

Brown remembers, "Even as a young kid I think I had a little of the feeling that most voters have—that politicians are a little dubious."

Politics may have occupied much of Pat and Bernice Brown's time, but according to Mark McGuinness, it was hard for anyone to be lonely in the neighborhood where he and Jerry Brown grew up. "There were forty-two kids on our block. We were good, mischievous children, but we didn't cause any trouble for anybody. We were normal kids. We went every place we wanted to without any problems at all."

Brown was a year younger than most of his classmates, and as a result was smaller. He graduated from high school at seventeen and was about 5′ 8″ tall at the time, almost four inches shorter than his height as an adult. Nevertheless, he didn't let anyone push him around, and he was considered a respectable, if undersized, athlete. When Brown was in the ninth or tenth grade, he collided during a pickup football game with McGuinness, who was much bigger than he was. Brown suffered a broken collarbone and a split lip.

The apex of Brown's athletic career occurred on the traditional Fight Night at St. Ignatius, when seniors donned boxing gloves and fought before a crowd of several hundred people. Brown's opponent, who was a better athlete, took Brown lightly, but "Jerry worked out very, very hard for that fight. I guess it was the only disciplined exercise he ever did," said Baxter Rice, McGuinness's cousin, who was Brown's manager for the event and

strutted around the ring with a derby hat and a cigar. McGuinness served as trainer for the occasion. "Jerry bloodied his
opponent's nose pretty good," said Rice. Frank Damrell, who was
not present but who heard about the fight many times, said
Brown "used to like to tell about it, and it was always a big story.
Jerry Brown came out of his shell and just pounded this guy into
the ground."

Damrell first met Brown during debate contests between
Modesto High School, which he attended, and St. Ignatius.
Damrell said Brown was not a star debater, and "the only reason
you would probably be aware of Jerry at that time is he was the
son of the attorney general." However, Brown won prizes for his
debating and oratorical skills at St. Ignatius, where he was also a
cheer leader, a part of Brown's youth that prompted Damrell to
remark, "It's hard to believe, isn't it?"

Peter Finnegan enrolled as a freshman at St. Ignatius in 1952.
Like Brown, who was a sophomore, Finnegan was fourteen, and
the two soon became friends as well as debate partners. Finnegan
would usually speak first and Brown second, and "we were set up
even then for this great Jesuitical thinking, argue either side of
any subject at any time," according to Finnegan. "And no matter
what the debate topic was, no matter which side we were on, he
[Brown] would always end up by saying, 'What we need is a
flexible plan for an ever-changing world,' " laughed Finnegan.
"That's the great quote, 'a flexible plan for an ever-changing
world.' And I'll tell you, by God, he's got a flexible plan."

In high school, as in later life, Brown had a reputation for
being tardy. "Jerry Brown would never show up on time," said
Finnegan, who told the story of one trip to a debate tournament:
"Everybody was out in the fog at St. Ignatius at five A.M.,
everybody except Jerry. The debate coach calls the home, Jerry's
still in bed, so the bus proceeds out to his house on Magellan
Avenue and Jerry has to come on, no tie, stinky shirt. You got to
remember, he was the guy that you never knew if he was going to
show up. He'd walk in with one sock red, one sock blue, he was a
bumbler. Jerry's no longer a bumbler. And Jerry never had much
energy. Jerry was lazy. He's gotta be hyped up being governor."

Brown was also known then, as he is now, for being tight with
a dollar. "Jerry learned his frugality from his mother," according
to McGuinness, who said that when the Browns would buy a new
car, they would pick it up in Detroit and drive it to San Francisco

to save money. Finnegan says that by his accounting, Brown "still owes me seventy-four dollars plus two pairs of cufflinks and two ties, stemming from coming to my house and borrowing some clothes. He did, however, bring my father [now dead] a Christmas present a few years ago. It was very significant. Jerry arrived at my house at Christmas, and he brought a bottle for my father, and we all almost fell over. He's cheap."

Part of the sum Finnegan has put on Brown's tab over the years is the result of one of the many trips the two youths and their friends made to the Russian River resort area north of San Francisco, where Finnegan's family owned a cabin. On one such excursion, Finnegan said, he was driving, with Brown and another friend as his passengers. "Jerry flipped a beer can out the window, and this was just when they had started the new anti-littering campaign. A highway patrolman was right behind us, and soon these big red lights were flashing, and we were just shaking in our boots." According to Finnegan, "Jerry gave a phony name. He was always scared to death that it was going to become some kind of a political thing, and I think I took the rap, and I got the ticket." But, Finnegan said, Brown never paid his share of the fine.

Barbara Brown said she, too, was constantly aware that she must be careful of her behavior so she would not cause any embarrassment to her father. And Finnegan recalled another beach party at the Russian River that was raided by sheriff's deputies because of "general rowdyism" on the part of the revelers, including shouting and tossing beer cans into the river. Brown, said Finnegan, had to dive into the water while dressed in a beautiful cashmere sweater and swim to the other side "because he couldn't get caught by the cops, right, he was the son of the attorney general."

McGuinness said Brown changed his attitude and began applying himself to his studies when he entered his senior year in high school, at the time Brown decided he wanted to be a Jesuit priest. "Jerry was not a particularly good student, even though he was very intelligent," said McGuinness. "He turned his grades around in his senior year and got Bs and As, after Cs and Bs, which means you have to be dedicated because you have to go back and relearn everything. Sometimes he stayed up most of the night studying."

Father William Perkins, Brown's debate coach in high school

and his English teacher at Santa Clara University, said that as a
St. Ignatius pupil Brown was "a serious kind of person, with a
sense of humor when you pushed him. He did very thorough
research. He was much more serious than many of his contemporaries, much more thoughtful, much more altruistic."

Another member of the St. Ignatius faculty at the time, Father
Leo Rock, who taught Brown Latin in the tenth grade, said that
because of the way Brown dressed and because he never seemed
to have money for raffle tickets that were sometimes sold at the
school, "I got the impression that Jerry was from a poor family."
Although most St. Ignatius students were the sons of middle- and
upper-income families, there were some poor youngsters who
attended the school on scholarships, and Rock was especially
sensitive to their situation because he had once been a scholar-
ship student at Bellarmine High School, a Jesuit institution in
San Jose. "I remember going out of my way to avoid any
situation that would embarrass him," said Rock. "I later found
out that [being poor] was not the situation at all. His indifference
to dress was honestly come by, that was very evident. Nothing of
phoniness about it or doing it for effect, that's just the way it
was."

Like Perkins, Rock considered Brown "very thoughtful."
However, Rock said, Brown was "an indifferent student in Latin,
but I came to know him as a very intelligent kid."

Rock also observed that Brown "was around school quite a bit.
His parents did a lot of traveling. My impression was that he
spent time around school because he had companionship that he
didn't have at home. My impression of Jerry [after Rock learned
who Brown's father was] was that he was in some ways deprived,
not necessarily financially, but sort of a lonely kid."

Rock once obtained some unusual insight into Pat Brown's
character. Pat and Jerry Brown arrived at a St. Ignatius father-
and-son dinner "in a flurry of excitement," and someone handed
a plate to Pat Brown, who then sat at the table where Rock was
already seated. Rock, who still has a boyish look as he approaches
fifty, was in his mid-twenties at the time, and Pat Brown mistook
him for one of the students. According to Rock, "Pat said, 'And
whose son are you?' I said, 'My mother and father's.' He took
another look at me, and I'm sure he thought, 'This smart-assed
kid.'" Following that exchange, Pat Brown left Rock out of the
conversation until another teacher noticed that Rock was being

ignored and introduced him to Pat as a member of the faculty. Rock piped up, " 'What's more, I teach your son.' And I thought to myself, *This man is very much a politician,* because for the rest of the meal he made sure I was included in the conversation."

According to Brown's contemporaries, from his younger days he almost never put on airs because of his father's status. "I'm not sure if I would have been the same way about it if my father was a big deal," said Phil Favro, a classmate of Brown.

During his school years, Brown earned spending money by working at a variety of jobs, including delivering newspapers and polishing cars in his neighborhood with Mark McGuinness. One summer, Brown and Jack Tomlinson, who years later was an aide to Pat Brown, worked as messengers for Pacific Telephone and Telegraph Co. in San Francisco. Tomlinson said he was hired because his father worked for the telephone company, and Brown got his job because he was the son of Pat Brown. "That is the first and only instance I know of his father being involved in nepotism," chuckled Tomlinson.

During that same summer, 1954, Tomlinson sold Brown, then sixteen, his first car, an eight-year-old two-door green Pontiac, for which Tomlinson received about $150. "It was paid for by the then attorney general," Tomlinson said. "I did have a consumer complaint, however, from the purchaser. The battery went dead the first day he had it." But Tomlinson said he did business under the doctrine of *caveat emptor.* And Pat Brown, who wrote the check for the automobile, said, "I told him not to buy that car."

Brown, along with Bart Lally, also worked for part of one summer in a logging camp in Idaho. The two of them surveyed future roads for the big logging trucks. "In retrospect, it was an eye opener for me," said Lally. "Two city kids going to the logging camp. It was an entirely different society." During their six or eight weeks in the camp, Brown and Lally lived in a cabin with the other loggers and ate their meals in the camp mess hall.

Brown graduated from St. Ignatius in June 1955. He wanted to enter the seminary then, but he was only seventeen and needed parental consent, which was not given. Both of his parents said they wanted him to go to college for at least a year to make sure that devoting his life to the church was what he really wanted to do. Pat Brown recalls telling his son, "I won't let you go in now, but if you want to go in a year from now, fine and dandy."

Instead of going directly into the seminary, Brown enrolled at Santa Clara University. His year at Santa Clara was a period of marking time until he was old enough to begin studying to be a priest. About two dozen of Brown's classmates from St. Ignatius were also freshmen at Santa Clara, and the St. Ignatius group formed a fairly close-knit clique. Nevertheless, Brown decided to room with his former debate foe from Modesto, Frank Damrell.

Damrell and Brown shared a taste for classical music and a fondness for late-night hours that set them apart from many of their classmates. "Jerry was always the philosopher and absent-minded," said Damrell, who was class president. "I was really the campus political sort, and Jerry had no interest in it whatsoever. We spent a lot of time talking about religion and philosophy, and Jerry's bent was very obviously in the philosophical area, just as it is today."

Two seniors, Marc Poché and Frank Schober, shared a room on the floor where Brown and Damrell lived and acted as counselors to the freshmen. Brown and Poché have been close friends ever since, with Brown appointing Poché his top legislative assistant after he became governor and later naming him a superior court judge. Brown chose Schober, a career army officer, to head the California National Guard and once remarked that the troops operated so efficiently under Schober that he might one day decide to invade Nevada.

According to Poché, Brown "asked more questions than anybody I've ever met. He hasn't changed at all, except he's hyped it up. Well, I mean, the difference is that when you were a senior, and he was a freshman, and he'd wander into your room and ask you all these philosophical questions, you could ignore him. But when he's governor of the state, and you're on his payroll, it's rather difficult to ignore him."

When Brown was not involved in such talks or in studying, he spent much of his time figuring out how to avoid attending Reserve Officers Training Corps (ROTC) classes and 7 A.M. masses, both of which were compulsory, and in devising pranks to play on his neighbors in Kenna Hall, particularly Max Baer, Jr., the son of the famous prizefighter who would later become a Beverly Hillbilly. Damrell described Baer as "a predecessor of the

Marlon Brando type. He had a motorcycle. Jerry loved to bug Max. One day we filled his room," which was next to the quarters Brown and Damrell shared, "with soapsuds, and they just literally billowed out the door." When Baer returned and surveyed the chaos, "Right away he knew that Jerry Brown had had his hand in that one."

As for ROTC, Damrell said, "We would do anything to come down with some kind of disease at the time that you had to put your uniform on and march. Jerry was not big on that number. It was hot out there marching and going through the nomenclature of whatever the rifle was in those days, and we were both pretty bad at that."

Speaking of the early-morning wakeup to attend mass, Dave Dawson, who lived on the same floor, said, "If the dorm counselors had opened the closet doors, they would have seen all these guys in the fetal position sound asleep."

Brown had good reason for his aversion to getting out of bed early: He and Damrell would stay up until all hours of the night talking. "Our light was always the last one off," said Damrell. "The big thing was to put paper under the door [to keep the light from being seen in the hallway] and we'd just sit there and b.s. for a couple of hours. Jerry's always been a night person."

Lights were supposed to be turned out by 10 P.M., which, according to Schober, whose responsibility it was to enforce that rule, "would be dubiously constitutional in the present circumstances." But 1955–56 was a far cry from the 1960s and 1970s. Santa Clara was a male-only school when Brown attended it, "and it was a very quiet, conservative campus," said Poché. Schober and Poché said students were threatened with expulsion for such transgressions as refusing to take ROTC or innocently entertaining a woman in a dormitry room, even with the lights on and the door open. Schober recalled that "*Playboy* was considered so risqué that anyone who had it had to be written up."

A freshman drinking bout led to one of the few times that Pat Brown's son tried to throw his weight around. One of the St. Ignatius-to-Santa Clara group was arrested by San Jose police for being drunk, and Brown and Barry Cummings, another member of that bunch, went to the jail to try to arrange their friend's release. According to Cummings, Brown told the police, " 'My father's the attorney general.' The cops told him something to the effect of, 'That's great, would you like to spend the night here too?' That's the one time I heard him use his father's influence—and it didn't work." Cummings said their friend spent the night in jail and was set free the next morning. Recalling that night, when about fifteen Santa Clara freshmen set out to drink beer and raise hell, Cummings said, "Brown was never a heavy drinker. But he was a regular guy. He wasn't some holier than thou type of person."

In January, 1956, during the midsemester break, Dawson and Jerry Brown happened to be hanging around Brown's house when, according to Dawson, Pat Brown walked in and said, "What are you guys doing?" When Pat learned the two youths had time on their hands, he assigned them to fly to Phoenix "to represent me and all Democrats in the state of California" and escort Adlai Stevenson, who was making his second try for the presidency, to California. Dawson, who was eager to go along, didn't bother to let on that he was a Republican.

It was also during his year at Santa Clara that Brown participated in a formal debate at which Justice Marshall F. McComb of the state supreme court was one of the judges. More than two decades later, McComb achieved notoriety when it became public knowledge that he was senile and often fell asleep during arguments before the court. In May 1977, a panel of judges ordered that McComb, who had refused to step down, be retired because of his inability to perform his duties. McComb, then eighty-three, was the first justice to be removed from the supreme court, and his enforced retirement gave Brown one of the precious opportunities a chief executive has to make a nomination to the highest court.

The year at Santa Clara, Brown's first prolonged period away from home, caused a marked change in his personality, according to Baxter Rice, who entered the seminary two months after he and Brown graduated from St. Ignatius and did not see Brown again until he arrived in Los Gatos a year later. Rice said that when he met Brown again, "I found him much more pensive, more subdued, perhaps more internalized, more like he is today. It seemed like a dramatic difference to me."

During the summer of 1956, Brown, Damrell, and Finnegan, at Brown's suggestion, spent a month on what Damrell called "a last fling" before they reported to Sacred Heart. "We had all kinds of entrees because of Brown's dad," said Damrell, "so we cut a wide swath," staying in apartments on Beacon Hill in Boston and Park Avenue in New York, attending a party in honor of Earl Warren's daughter at Drew Pearson's house in Washington and cruising on the Potomac River on a congressman's yacht.

"We were very much aware that this was the last fling . . . and it was all going to change on August 15, 1956," declared Finnegan.

Pat Brown recalled that when his son remained firm in his wish to become a priest after a year in college, "I didn't object to it. I was reconciled. I was very proud that he wanted to be a priest. I had wanted him to maybe wait a little while. But when he went in, I got a great deal of solace out of it."

However, Bernice Brown said she thought "it was sad to have him go away from home" where she could see little of her son. "I really wanted him to finish college before he went in." She remembers her son as a "quite religious" youth who missed a surprise party some of his friends had planned for his seventeenth birthday because it fell on Holy Thursday, and he was out attending about ten different churches until late that evening. "I don't know whether you get some special dispensation or something good happens to you in heaven later on if you go to ten churches because I'm not Catholic," Mrs. Brown said. Dawson said that after he went by the Brown home to pick up Jerry Brown for the ride to Los Gatos, Mrs. Brown's reaction caused him to "always feel guilty that I was taking her kid away."

According to Damrell, "We said goodbye to our parents, and it was very tearful. It's tough for any family. One day a month on a Sunday your parents could come up to see you for two hours, and that was it."

August 15 is the date when Catholics celebrate the Feast of the Assumption, and it is the traditional day for embarking on a career as a priest. Rice said that on that date, in 1955, he had smoked so heavily during his trip from San Francisco to Los Gatos that he had a heavy cough for the next three weeks. Smoking was forbidden at Sacred Heart, as was drinking—except for an occasional glass of wine at meals—contact with the outside world, and, to a large extent, talking.

Finnegan said that on August 15, 1956, he and his comrades

"kissed our girl friends goodbye and drove off to become monks. It was like going off to war. Ignatius of Loyola [the founder of the Jesuit order] was a soldier first of all. The whole thing was set out as military. We were going to train, to become intellectual giants, to take over the news media, to convert the world. Ignatius was very manipulative. The Jesuits historically would become confessors to the kings of Europe. We would get our Ph.D.'s, then we'd have a chair at Harvard, infiltrate.

"My father actually said, 'It's a greater thing to be a priest than to be president of the United States,' so to be a Jesuit was the top goal in your life," Finnegan stated. "You'd do whatever they told you to do" in order to achieve that aim.

Donald Burns, who spent two years in a seminary before he met Brown at Yale Law School and became his friend and later a member of his cabinet, said he entered the seminary because of "a feeling of malaise. I just didn't really know where I was going, and that seemed like an idealistic thing. It held out a challenge for me."

According to Finnegan, both he and Brown decided to go into the seminary as a reaction against their parents, as well as for more positive reasons. "I will never say we did not go in for the most idealistic reasons, but in looking back and examining why, at age eighteen, right out of high school, we went off to a monastery in Los Gatos, I now understand what the motive was. Jerry's was mixed, but definitely he wanted to get out of a bum family situation. It was not a very happy family," with Brown's father away much of the time and his mother "a very hard woman. I would say that neither Jerry nor I came from happy homes." Indicative of Brown's relationship with his family during that period is that for four years, after he left the seminary in 1960, he would spend Christmas at Finnegan's home.

Brown dismisses the explanations of Finnegan and Burns as "strange reasons to desire to be a Jesuit," which he says do not apply to his own case. "I know Peter's views on these things," Brown comments, and yawns. From the vantage point of late 1977, more than two decades after he went into the seminary, Brown says that his decision to study for the priesthood was a result of "the Jesuit ideal, the spiritual life. The theme is that there is the world, and then there is the spirit, and you opt for one or you opt for the other. To desire to save the world to save yourself is in effect to recognize that it [the world] is in need of saving. The spirit is everlasting, and the world is transitory, and since I was interested in getting to the more fundamental realities, that seemed like the obvious path."

Finnegan also remembers that during the spring of 1956, when Brown and Damrell came to San Francisco to tell him of their decision to become priests, he was so moved that he broke into tears because "we were going off to do the great thing." Mark McGuinness says that "maybe Jerry's going into the seminary was a rejection of his father's life in politics. But he also had a dream." Said Damrell: "I suppose it seemed like kind of a heroic thing to do. To most boys raised as Catholics, the priesthood is the ultimate in life. Jerry was a Catholic and fairly devout, certainly by today's standards. He obviously admired the Jesuits."

The way of life at Sacred Heart was so unlike that of the outside world that it is probably impossible for a person who has not been in a seminary to understand it. Finnegan cited the case of a West Point graduate who was a student at the seminary during the same time as he and Brown. The former cadet found adjusting to the seminary more difficult than getting used to the army, "because at the military academy they never tried to get inside your brain."

Damrell gave this description of life inside the seminary: The new seminarians were outfitted with the clothes they would wear most of the time, black cotton pants and black jackets that were "ridiculous, like busboy jackets. You really looked like you were right out of some prison." The seminary "was a pretty austere place in those days. You could only speak in Latin in the cloister, and you just couldn't carry on a conversation. In the evening, around 9 o'clock, there was the *magnum silensium,* they called it, the great silence.

"You lived in a cubicle with a straw mattress. There was no running water [in the room]. You had to go down with a pot and a pan to get your water in the morning."

The novices arose at 5 A.M. each day. They had fifteen minutes to dress, then they spent an hour in their cubicles—six to a room—meditating on a lesson the master of novices had given them the night before. Morning meditation lasted for an hour, and the ringing of a bell divided the hour into three portions, during which the novices would alternate kneeling, standing, and sitting. "I suppose the idea was to get you into a regimen so you were under some kind of control," said Damrell.

After meditation, the novices would go to mass, then to breakfast. There were cooks, but the novices did much of the kitchen work and also cleaned other areas of the seminary. Their day would be spent in part studying, including a daily Latin class, and in part at physical labor. "The day was broken up, so there was always something coming up or just finishing up," said Damrell. Even the daily exercise periods when the novices participated in sports were strictly run, with one student placed in charge, usually "some guy who was shy or bashful, who needed self-confidence. It wasn't a guy who was a natural leader."

On Sundays, following breakfast, there would be *defectus,* when the novices would separate into groups of three and make constructive criticism of one another: " 'It seems to me, Brother Jones, that you could be neater in your appearance.' The big thing in the Jesuit order was the rules. You lived by the rules."

Two or three months after they entered the seminary, the novices began studying the rules that Ignatius had laid down for his followers. It was "a change your life thing," said Damrell. "That has a profound impact on a young man, no question about it, who wants to lead the Jesuit life. That's really the heart and soul of the whole thing. After that, you really became disciplined in your whole attitude."

When one of the novices did something that was forbidden, which could mean anything from an expletive during a baseball game to failure to avert one's eyes from another person's eyes, "You'd tell the novice master, and then that night at dinner you would kneel down in front of the entire community and ask for forgiveness" in front of about 250 people. "It was a crushing thing for the guy that had to get up there and admit his fault."

Finnegan recalled, "I was down on the floor a lot, basically for intellectual pride," which consisted of refusing to accept all that he was taught without question.

Once or twice a month the novices would bind themselves from arm to leg with a chain for an hour at a time. They would also take a rope and beat themselves on the rear end. Bill Burman, who was a priest at Sacred Heart while Brown was a student, explained that the purpose was "mortification. We have to learn to control bodily desires and deny the body by actually inflicting pain on it."

Fifteen years after Brown left the seminary, early in his term as governor, he told a group of priests who visited Sacramento, "If you want to know what my administration will be like, look at St. Ignatius' eleventh and twelfth rules." The two rules Brown referred to dictate that a Jesuit must seek mortification, practice self-denial, abhor worldly needs and desires, and accept whatever Christ embraced. Almost three years later, when Brown was reminded of that remark, he at first said it was "offhand" and "half in jest. What else do you talk to Jesuits about than the rules of St. Ignatius?" Then he added, "I do find the rules significant," and said he still studies both the edicts and their author.

About all the seminarians had to look forward to were the two-week vacations each summer when they would live at a villa in the redwoods and the month-long grape harvest each fall. Sacred Heart had its own vineyard and winery, and the students picked the grapes. "That was kind of a treat," said Damrell. "It would get you out of that damn building during grape harvest. Jerry certainly learned how to pick grapes, I'll tell you that. They used to take us out on a big truck like a cattle truck, and you could speak, also. That was a big thing." The residents of Sacred Heart also had the satisfaction of drinking the wine they had helped produce.

There were no newspapers, radios, or televisions at the seminary. "You really lost touch with the outside world," said Damrell. "I have great gaps in terms of music and movies and sports events and political things that I read about afterward. The only way you'd know what was going on was from your parents' visits. In fact, Jerry's father ran for governor while we were in there." Rice said he did not hear of Elvis Presley until a year after Presley became an idol.

The monthly visits meant as much to family members as they did to the seminarians. "His mother and I, no matter where we were or what we were doing on that visiting Sunday, would go down there and spend two hours with him," Pat Brown said.

Damrell remembers the three and a half years at Sacred Heart as being "almost idyllic, so remote. In many respects you were freed of things, your responsibilities were so narrow and limited." The members of Brown's family who were permitted to visit him during those years found him to be in a state that bordered on bliss.

Brown's eldest sister, Barbara, recalls how happy he seemed to be when she visited him at the seminary, and to Brown's sister Cynthia, "He seemed zeroed in on things," in contrast to his "restless" youth. Joe Kelly, who married Cynthia in 1957, a year after Brown went to Sacred Heart, said Brown was "very happy down there, like a fellow who had found his way of life." Brown was allowed to attend his sister's wedding, one of the rare occasions when he was able to go into the outside world, and Cynthia was "really moved" by Brown's presence at the ceremony, according to Kelly. The seminarians were not given the privilege of owning personal property, and Bernice Brown said that once when Cynthia gave Brown an elaborate shoeshine kit as a gift, she was somewhat taken aback by her brother's reaction: "That'll be fine. The brothers will enjoy that."

During his two years as a novice, Brown impressed Father James Healy, the master of novices, as "just what we would look for in a candidate for the priesthood. He had all the qualifications," such as "steadiness, intellect, courage, and adaptability to people. I think he would have done very, very well" as a priest.

Healy's assistant, Father Joseph Meehan, who, as supervisor of the novices' daily activities, had much closer contact with them than did Healy, saw Brown as "average." Meehan said that among the twenty or twenty-five students in his group, "Jerry Brown was very ordinary. There were those who were brighter than he was, better workers than he was, better athletes than he was. Jerry was an ordinary fellow, with average intelligence and average acceptance. He had good qualities, like not being impetuous, being thoughtful, cooperative, interested. There was never any kind of attitude problem with him," which distinguished Brown from Finnegan in Meehan's memory. Meehan saw nothing to indicate that Brown would not have made a good priest. "If there was a point of failure to Jerry Brown, it was that he closely associated with former acquaintances," instead of having equally close friendships with his other classmates.

In many ways, Jerry Brown the governor reminds Meehan of Jerry Brown the theology student. "He's a plodding fellow, not quick on the draw. He conveyed to me that he was never in a big hurry, which is a good quality for a priest. So many things just can't be answered on the spot, and [patience] usually is indica-

tive that you have control of your feelings." The years at Sacred
Heart "set a direction for him, a goal to be achieved, a service to
be given." When Brown tells people they must sacrifice and that
everyone must struggle together, "those are strong religious
ideas," said Meehan.

After two years, the students took their permanent vows to the
Jesuit order and graduated from the novitiate to the juniorate,
where they had much more freedom in comparison to the
novitiate, if not to the outside world. Damrell said that when the
group that included Brown, himself, and Finnegan became
juniors, "All of a sudden you realize that the novitiate is in so
many respects so juvenile. I suppose we were looked upon to
some extent like black sheep in the sense that we were probably
much more questioning as to a lot of things about the church,"
including such issues as "the use of Latin, celibacy, the rules of
the order, the infallibility of the pope, devotion to Mary, you
name it. In those days, that was really something to get into that
kind of stuff. That's before any of this stuff changed."
Finnegan said that he and Brown used to have clandestine
meetings in the garden or take hikes and "talk about how fucked
up the whole operation was. Do we really believe this stuff?"
Bill Burman, who is ten years older than Brown, taught the
novices Latin. During summer vacation at the villa in the woods,
just before Brown's class entered the junior year, Burman had
several long philosophical discussions with him and some of the
others. Soon after Brown moved to the juniorate, in the fall, he
came to Burman's room to talk more, and "that was the start of
our rather close relationship," said Burman.
"I could see that he wanted someone to kind of unburden his
mind with, someone who wouldn't criticize. I would just listen. I
didn't think it my place to express disapproval. The orthodox
approach would have been to convince him to stay [at Sacred
Heart], but I wasn't going to counsel him one way or the other. I
wanted him to reach his own decision."
Burman was thinking about leaving the Jesuit Order at the
time himself, so "I was prepared to be more liberal than other
members of the staff." Eventually, he told Brown his own
feelings. "I was very conscious of the danger to me. It was an
unorthodox way of thinking."
After noticing how tense Finnegan was, Burman suggested to

Brown that he bring him along, too, and then Damrell was included in the meetings, and soon "the three of them were beating a path to my door." In addition to letting the three express their feelings to him, Burman provided them with books by Russian authors from the priests' library to which the students did not have access. He also loaned them his own copies of books by Rollo May, which Finnegan described as "like a breath of fresh air, I couldn't believe it."

Damrell credits Burman with helping to "get my head on straight," and Finnegan believes that but for Burman's counsel, he, Brown, and Damrell might have spent another three or four years in the seminary before mustering the courage to leave. Brown calls Burman "a good influence, a confessor. He was helpful to talk things out. He is a good person."

Although Finnegan, Brown, and Damrell had agreed to leave together, Finnegan grew impatient waiting for the other two and quit at Christmas, 1959. "I really think Jerry needed to have someone go first. It was a big deal, quitting, and we were all very scared. It was very easy going into the Jesuits but a hell of a lot harder coming out. Those were the days when the church hadn't blown apart, and we were very idealistic.

"We were zealots," continued Finnegan. "We were true believers. We were going to ascend the pulpit and preach to our fellow men, and the reason I think we left is because we couldn't ascend that pulpit and preach something we didn't really believe in.

"There was absolutely no freedom," Finnegan added. "It was like a goddamn Communist prison. We were encouraged to rat on each other. It's amazing that some of us are not crazier than we are. It's a hell of an experience, an experience that very few people could go through." Finnegan underwent psychoanalysis twice a week for two years after he left.

At the time Finnegan quit, Brown called his father, who had been governor for almost a year, and said, "I want to see you. Leave mother at home." According to Pat Brown, his son did not want to discuss leaving with Bernice Brown because he was not sure she would understand since she is not Catholic. Pat Brown, who had originally been against his son's decision to enter the seminary, now was opposed to his quitting. "I said, 'You've given three and a half years of your life to it, why don't you wait another year?'

"He'd taken permanent vows," Pat Brown explained, "and I thought breaking out in the middle of the year was a mistake. But when a person gets to be twenty years of age, you know, even a father doesn't tell a son what to do."

From his vantage point of almost eighteen years after deciding that the priesthood was not for him, Brown says, "I felt that I had come as far as I could go in the Jesuit order and that I just couldn't fit into the program. The commitment, the vows, the way of life didn't capture my imagination. It seemed unreal. It seemed removed from life."

He now views his time in the seminary as "part of the path. One goes through a journey in life. So at one point it was the Jesuits, at another point it's secretary of state, at another point it's governor, four years from now it may be something else, ten years from now, if I'm still alive, it may be something else, who knows? I think if you don't look at it in arbitrary terms, everything has the potential for enlightenment."

One thing Brown retains from his time as a seminarian is the belief that there is "a traditional wisdom. Whether it's the Jesuit order or Buddhism or [E. F.] Schumacher [an author whose philosophy has had a profound effect on Brown] or anything else, it's all the same thing. Which is what all the philosophers have said, I don't think it can be put in words." He does cite the words *"Age quod agis"* (do whatever you are doing), with which St. Ignatius instructed his followers in the sixteenth century. And Brown notes that the same words appear in *A Beginner's Mind,* a collection of lectures by the late Suzuki-roshi, who, in 1959, founded the San Francisco Zen Center, which Brown occasionally visits. "There you have Ignatius Loyola and Suzuki-roshi giving basically the same view," declares Brown. Asked if it is not likely that Suzuki-roshi, who lived 400 years after St. Ignatius, read some of the Ignatian teachings and incorporated them into his own, Brown replies, "I doubt it. I doubt it. That is my point. That there is a common wisdom, a perennial wisdom. We're just using different words. People talk about mental health. Three hundred years ago, they talked about sin and sanctity, holiness. Social activism or corporal works of mercy— just different words relating the same underlying phenomenon of human compassion."

Brown stayed in the seminary for a month after his talk with his father, then left in time to enroll at the University of California at Berkeley for the 1960 spring semester.

"It's hard to make a change like that," said Burman, "and I think he was delaying it as long as he could." Furthermore, Burman said, a person who quit might have "lingering guilt feelings. I had decided several years before I left that I definitely wanted to leave, but it took me a long time to get around to doing it."

Burman left the priesthood two years after Brown quit the seminary. The next year, Burman married a former nun, and the couple now has two children. He became a professor of philosophy at Los Angeles Valley College, a part of the Los Angeles Community College System, of which Brown was elected a trustee in his first bid for public office in 1969.

Burman emphasized the strain of the decision to leave. He said he knew one priest who went away but was so ashamed of what he had done that he left his clothes on the beach to make it appear that he had gone into the ocean and committed suicide, "and they actually had a funeral" before he was discovered alive.

In Brown's case, Burman said, "I thought he made the right decision. I felt that all along. But I never told him that." Brown and Burman were so close that at one point Brown suggested they go to law school and practice law together, but Burman thought he was too old for that.

When Brown departed from the cloister, he wanted to be a psychiatrist or psychologist. "He wanted to help people and thought he could help them better in some other capacity" than being a priest, but the idea of havng to attend medical school didn't appeal to him, said Cynthia Kelly.

William Perkins, who has kept in fairly close touch with Brown over the years, predicts that when Brown leaves politics, "he may continue to want to just help humanity, which I think is a core issue in his life," much like being a priest on a lay basis. "We can't just say, 'Well, he's a typical politician, he's simply looking after himself.' If Jerry were kicked out of the governor's job tomorrow, I think he would still try to benefit humanity in some way. And I'm sure that's closely related to the kind of life we lead. I don't feel he's been corrupted, or his idealism has been corroded by what he's living in, and I really admire him for that."

Brown agrees with his sister and Perkins that his "underlying quest hasn't changed. I try to understand the right path to live. I don't think these things change that much. Understanding how to live and what one should do with his life, that's a continuous question. The Jesuit order was one path, and now I'm on another, but I don't think they're all that different." He says his desire to be a priest, then to be a counselor, and finally to be a politician is all part of his attempt at "understanding the human mystery and equation."

There is also a negative side to a Jesuit education, which can give someone a sense of infallibility, according to James Straukamp, fifty, a former priest who taught Brown at St. Ignatius High School in the early 1950s when Brown was a student there. Straukamp later became a professor at Sacramento State University, and Brown stayed with him for about six weeks after being elected secretary of state while he sought an apartment of his own.

Straukamp says, "It's not that he remembers details of Jesuit training and Jesuit life, but there is a process, an attitude, an underlying approach to problem solving and people relationships that remains. Your will and mind are in control all the time, and therefore there's a danger in being too heady and not having enough heart. Oh, you're going to feel emotion, but I think there is a mechanism that controls the external expression."

Straukamp related that when he was in the seminary the novice master gave an example of the perfect Jesuit: "He's teaching class, and the principal comes in and says, 'Your mother just died,' and he [the perfect Jesuit] says, 'Fine, thank you,' and closes the door and then continues teaching the class. Now that's the perfect Jesuit, at least in the training that we got and that Jerry got.

"The Jesuit training can be such that you can be thoughtless of people's feelings. It's not that you don't care if you're cold and heartless. You don't think about it." A Jesuit can care for, even anticipate, other people's needs, "but somehow you can still make it very impersonal."

Straukamp added that the training provides "a self confidence which could be a dangerous thing because you get the tools of a broad education, and you start feeling a little overconfident, that you've got all the answers . . . to all the world's ills. St. Ignatius

High School had this very special spirit, you know, 'We're number one,' and [that] there was no equal to them in the city of San Francisco. [And that] they were better even though they could be dumb, and they could be lazy, which a lot of them were. Well, the students pick that up from the teachers themselves, who feel there's something special about being a Jesuit. St. Ignatius students are noted for that particular cockiness, and Jerry, I think, has that, too. It's a sort of flippant offhandedness."

Straukamp has had a love-hate relationship with the church. He lives in a small but comfortable house in Sacramento, and in the spring of 1977, just before he finally renounced his vows of poverty and ceased being a priest, he bought a Mercedes-Benz.

Bill Burman's years as a Jesuit student and priest convinced him that "blind obedience is their ideal. So you believe simply because the superiors tell you to, not because your own mind is convinced. As I got older, that seemed less acceptable."

Barry Cummings said he had personal problems for many years because he felt he had fallen short of what was expected of him. Speaking of his education, he said, "I almost think it's harmful in some ways. It was for me." Cummings, an insurance agent, said, "For a long time there, I felt I should be making some money, living in a bigger house, all the things that aren't that important. It's something the Jesuits instill in you, a sense of superiority" that can be hard to live up to. "Now I'm happy, and that's all that counts."

Assemblyman John Vasconcellos, (D, San Jose), who also received a Jesuit education, found that his and Brown's similar backgrounds created "both a rapport and an awkwardness." Vasconcellos classifies himself and Brown as "pretty stiff and distant Catholic intellectuals" who had trouble working together after Brown first became governor even though Vasconcellos had been Pat Brown's travel secretary and had accompanied him on visits to the seminary to see Jerry. Vasconcellos describes his own Jesuit education as "terribly cerebral, intellectual, unemotional, and narrow." He has been participating in encounter groups for the past ten years.

One carryover from Brown's education that he frequently cites, says his top aide in the governor's office, Gray Davis, is the Jesuit rule that an individual should not hold the same job for more than seven years. States Brown: "I think it's good to not stay in one position too long. I see the value of moving on. You develop a whole structure and context, and at some point it can become counterproductive. An institution shouldn't depend on one personality. The idea of changing, that you put one person in charge and then after a while you let him do a more mundane job and bring someone else up, that's classical in the Jesuits. It's a good idea."

It is at least theoretically possible that Brown could be elected president in 1980, serve two full terms, and leave office in early 1989, when he will be fifty, with many potentially productive years ahead of him and little hope of matching the stature of the job he would have recently completed. As Marc Poché says, "Where do you find psychological solace" after you've had a job like governor or president and "you're not going on retirement age like Ronald Reagan at least was, but rather you're really at the peak of all your physical and intellectual powers? What do you do for an encore just in terms of keeping your own psyche together?"

So the Jesuit rule against job longevity could well come in handy for Brown. "It's good to have a theory to reconcile yourself to what is inevitable," states Brown. He feels there should be more dignity to jobs that are now considered relatively unimportant. "It would be a good society if we exchanged jobs and roles without so much ego. People would be a lot happier. But the whole structure conspires against it. I think we lose a lot of creativity that way."

CHAPTER TWO

FROM NOVICE TO NOVICE POLITICIAN, 1960–70

One night in early February, 1960, Jerry Brown called Mark McGuinness in San Francisco, said he was leaving the seminary, and asked his boyhood friend to pick him up at El Retiro, a Jesuit retreat in Los Altos where students from the Los Gatos seminary were taken when they decided to drop out of the course that led to the priesthood. The departing seminarians were given little advance notice of when they would be free to leave El Retiro, and Brown's release occurred at a time when his family was out of town.

Brown spent his first night outside the confines of the Jesuit order alone at his own house in San Francisco. The next day, McGuinness took him across the bay to Berkeley, where he enrolled as a second-semester junior majoring in classics. During those two trips, Brown told McGuinness that "he was through with that part of his life" and that he had changed his mind about wanting to become a priest.

En route from San Francisco to Berkeley, McGuinness stopped in the garage of St. Mary's Hospital in San Francisco to get gas. His mother, Anne McGuinness, who worked as a volunteer at the hospital once a week, came down to the garage and was surprised to find Brown in the car. "I didn't know that [Brown had left the seminary] until I felt these arms around me that weren't familiar to me, and it was Jerry, I just said, 'Jerry, hello, dear, how are you, it's wonderful to see you.' I was afraid to say anything more. He looked almost sick. I think he had been under a tremendous strain deciding to leave the seminary."

McGuinness left Brown at his new residence, International House, where several hundred American and foreign students lived together and where he would room with Frank Damrell, who had also entered the university. Before driving away, McGuinness said to Brown, "Jerry, how did you get a place at International House and enrolled so quickly?" According to McGuinness, Brown's reply was, "Are you kidding, my father owns the university."

Marc Poché, a student at the Boalt School of Law at the university, got the opposite impression of Brown at dinner that night. Brown told Poché that he had been two hours late for an appointment with a counselor and that nevertheless she was very gracious to him. "It didn't dawn on him that one reason for the graciousness was the fact that his father just happened to be governor of the state and ran the university," recalled Poché. "I think he was oblivious to the sort of power that his father had at that stage of the game." Poché's other recollection of Brown that night is that "he seemed a little subdued."

During his year and a half at Berkeley, Brown met three people who became his lasting friends: Rose Bird and Ken Reich, who also lived at International House, and Carl Werthman, who lived off campus. Brown would later make history by appointing Bird the first female cabinet member and the first woman to serve on the supreme court in California. She remembers him as "a very quiet, rather serious person, quite reserved. A lot of us were very interested in politics, and he didn't seem interested at all. I don't think he's the typical kind of person who gladhanded or who was off and running for a lot of things that you associate with someone who might go into politics."

Reich, who would later cover Brown as a political reporter for the *Los Angeles Times,* said, "If you had asked any of us who was going to be the politician, it would have been Frank Damrell."

During the last week of the 1960 presidential election, John F. Kennedy spent part of a day campaigning in the Bay Area. Brown persuaded his father to let him ride in Kennedy's car, and Reich drove Brown to a navy base near San Jose where Kennedy landed. Brown then accompanied Kennedy to rallies in Oakland and in San Francisco's Union Square. According to Reich, Kennedy was "dog tired. He was a physical wreck at the time. And Jerry complained rather vociferously to me that he had talked the whole time and asked Kennedy a great many questions but that Kennedy had not proved very responsive. How unimpressed he was."

Werthman, who has conducted public-opinion surveys for Brown in most of Brown's races, is now a professor at the Center for Public Affairs at the University of Southern California, where his boss is Houston Flournoy, Brown's opponent in the 1974 election for governor. At Berkeley, Werthman and Brown worked in YMCA-sponsored support groups for farm workers before Cesar Chavez became president of the United Farm Workers. Werthman and Brown took Cal students to work in the fields for weekends, raised money, and did research on farm labor law. "I think that's where he came across the farm labor situation," said Werthman. "There was a mood of exploration."

As far as Damrell is concerned, Berkeley was "another world" from the sheltered life in the seminary at Los Gatos, and he and Brown tried to make up for lost time socially. The two graduated from the university in 1961, and Damrell got married before they entered Yale Law School that fall.

Early in the first year that Brown and Damrell were at Yale, they were in a class together when the professor asked if anyone knew the translation of a Latin term. A student sitting next to Damrell gave the answer, and Damrell later asked him where he had learned Latin. In a Jesuit seminary in Louisiana was the reply. After the class, Damrell introduced Brown to the fellow ex-seminarian, Don Burns, a brilliant scholar who would later serve as a cabinet member in the Brown administration.

On one occasion, while they were at Yale, Burns and Brown went out on a double date. Burns later recalled that Brown's date "started out with some kind of a thing about how all politicians are crooks, and it really went on for about a half hour. At one point she asked him, 'What does your father do?' And he said, 'Well, he's a lawyer.' 'Is he in private practice?' 'No, he works for the government.' And that was it. So the next day I got a call from the other girl, and she said, 'We just found out that his father's governor of California,' and she was just so crestfallen. And she asked, 'What should we do?' and I said, 'Come on, forget it, it didn't bother him at all.' "

The next year, Brown's next-door neighbor was Tony Kline, a newcomer who would also prove to be an exceptional student and would later advise Governor Brown on key issues. Kline said he knew Brown for almost six months "before he bothered to tell me that his father was then the governor of the state. If his name had been Rockefeller, I would have figured it out for myself."

Brown introduced Kline to the writings of Rollo May, who was not nearly as well known then as he is now. Kline is Jewish, and neither Brown, Burns, nor Damrell fit his stereotype of what a former seminarian should be like: "somebody whose connection to dogma is stronger than my own." In fact, Kline still finds it fascinating that Brown and his close friend, Dan Greer, an Orthodox Jew who operated a kosher kitchen at Yale, were opponents in a moot court case in which "the Orthodox Jew was taking the position ordinarily connected to Catholics and the Catholic was taking the side ordinarily connected to Jews." The mock trail was based on an actual case involving two students who were expelled from the Catholic St. John's University on Long Island for getting married in a civil ceremony. Brown argued on behalf of the couple, and Greer represented the university authorities.

To Kline, Brown was then "in many ways the kind of a person he is now. He was very inquisitive, very querulous, very interested in ideas, and even then unwilling to automatically accept a conventional assumption."

While Brown was at Yale, he traveled to the South to observe civil rights activities. After he had been in Mississippi for several days, his father received a phone call from Governor Ross Barnett, whom Pat Brown knew from governors' conferences the two had attended. Pat Brown later recalled that Barnett said, " 'Your son's down here and he's going to get himself into trouble. He's in with a very bad crowd.' I remember I was panicky. I'll never forget, I told his mother, 'That was Governor

Barnett of Mississippi. Jerry's in jail down there.' She says, 'What?' I said, 'No, he just called me and told me Jerry had better get out of Mississippi.' I don't think she's ever been more mad at me."

Shortly afterward, Jerry Brown called his parents. He had already left Mississippi. "I remember being very concerned," said Bernice Brown as she thought of the period between the calls from Barnett and her son. She recalled what passed through her mind at the time: "They're not playing games down there. They play for keeps. There's going to be trouble."

During Brown's senior year at Yale, Stephen Reinhardt, a Los Angeles attorney who has long been a power in California Democratic circles, filed a suit that attempted to keep Pierre Salinger, who had been President Kennedy's press secretary, from running for the U.S. Senate seat in California, on the grounds that Salinger was not a resident of the state. Pat Brown, who was then governor and who opposed Salinger's candidacy, suggested to Reinhardt that his son could help with the research on the case. According to Reinhardt, "Jerry did a pretty good job with a few nights' research in the library" at Yale. But Salinger won the case and went on to defeat Alan Cranston in the primary before losing to the Republican candidate, former actor George Murphy, in the general election.

After graduation from Yale Law School in 1964, Brown served for almost a year as a law clerk to Justice Mathew Tobriner, whom Pat Brown had appointed to the California Supreme Court. Brown was selected for the clerkship on the basis of friendship, according to Tobriner, and is the only one of the more than two dozen law clerks Tobriner has had during his fifteen years on the bench who failed the California bar examination. Both Brown and Damrell, who was working in the State Department of Justice, failed the bar exam on their first try in the summer of 1964, then passed it six months later. Justice Tobriner believes that Brown didn't really apply himself the first time. After the results were released, Brown spent several weeks isolated in an out of the way room at the Governor's Mansion in Sacramento preparing for his second try.

"He was a good, competent law clerk, but not brilliant," said Tobriner, contrasting Brown with Kline, whose clerkship for Justice Raymond Peters coincided with part of Brown's and who shared an apartment in Berkeley with Brown at that time.

While Brown was a student at Berkeley, he had often come to talk to Tobriner, who found him to be "very interested in the philosophical implications of cases. That's why I felt he'd be better at Yale, because they look at law more from a social standpoint than Harvard" and other leading law schools.

As a clerk to Tobriner, Brown "was not necessarily the prisoner of precedents. He was perfectly willing to improvise. He had a wide-ranging attitude toward the law and sometimes was impatient with it, even radical. Jerry's got a good mind. He was not a top student. But Jerry was a fellow who would work awfully hard.

"He was fairly awkward at meeting people. He was somewhat of a loner. That's his nature. Jerry is not a gregarious person as such, not like his father. He is a thinker, kind of a dreamer at times, and he was a heavy reader. He wasn't at ease at a social gathering, at least with older people like myself."

After Brown finished his clerkship for Tobriner, he moved to Los Angeles. Both Tobriner and Paul Halvonik, a young lawyer who car pooled from Berkeley to San Francisco with Brown, Kline, and Damrell, felt he had made the decision to relocate because he had already determined to enter politics and saw the Los Angeles area as offering more political opportunity. According to Brown, "I wouldn't say politics was totally absent from my mind," but he says he was more concerned with job possibilities at the time of his move. "The Bay Area, as I understood it at that point, seemed to be more static. It just seemed that Southern California was a more growing, exciting atmosphere, and I was primarily focused on the job, on being a lawyer, on learning about the law and progressing in it." However, Brown said, "I was aware" of the enhanced political prospects in the Southland. A political career "obviously was a possibility. It always has been," because of his father.

Tobriner suggested that Brown join a firm that specialized in labor law "because I thought he kind of had a burning interest in the underdog," and Stephen Reinhardt, whose law firm handles many labor cases, offered Brown a job. To Reinhardt's relief, Brown turned down the offer. Reinhardt and his partners "weren't particularly unhappy that he didn't take it" because they anticipated that he would soon enter politics. Said Tobriner: "He must have been thinking of politics even then. So he wanted to go with a respected law firm."

The firm Brown picked was Tuttle and Taylor. Ray Fisher, who joined the practice about the same time as Brown and is still a member, describes it as "a very high class business firm." The number of lawyers associated with Tuttle and Taylor has grown from sixteen at the time Brown and Fisher entered it to about forty today, through a very selective hiring process that usually requires the new attorneys to have been outstanding scholars in law school or to have worked as clerks for judges.

Fisher observed that Brown "tended to work a lot by himself because he was interested in the smaller litigation cases," such as breach of contract and criminal charges, instead of the major corporation or antitrust matters that were the firm's bread and butter. Brown "was kind of off doing a lot of his own things," and although the jobs he worked on did not bring in much money, nobody minded because, Fisher said, Tuttle and Taylor has traditionally been "a collection of academics. It's not a firm that goes and hustles a lot of business. This firm is highly individualistic, a nonregimented firm."

Brown's life style was probably more readily tolerated at Tuttle and Taylor than it would have been at some of the other prestigious firms in downtown Los Angeles, Century City, and Beverly Hills. Fisher noted that Brown drove "an old ratty Chevy. He kind of had a whole bunch of junk in his car and lived in a ratty apartment. He's never been one for elegant living. When he left the firm, he owed me a lot of money for lunches he didn't have money to pay for."

Ken Reich lived a block from Brown's apartment, which he described as being in a "very ramshackle building" just off Sunset Boulevard near Griffith Park. "Piles of junk" covered the floors, and the overall ambience reminded Reich of a room in a college dormitory. Reich said he "used to urge him to let me send over my maid to clean the place up once a week, but Jerry would never spend the money to do it or never was interested in doing it."

In November 1966, just as Brown was getting started with Tuttle and Taylor, Pat Brown was defeated in his bid for a third term as governor by Ronald Reagan, whom Jerry Brown regarded as an intellectual lightweight. According to political scientist Richard Maullin, "He's always said that he decided to run for governor when his father lost for governor." Maullin met Brown when they both happened to be in Colombia in 1966 and, along with Tom Quinn, was one of his two closest political associates from 1969 until he was elected governor.

Brown tends to play down theories such as Maullin's. While he concedes that "just being in a family with a father as governor makes that a possibility, a thinkable thought, a thought that was always there," he quickly adds, "but it was one of many others. My mind doesn't work that way. Normally, I think of many possibilities and often take steps that are consistent with a variety of alternatives or outcomes." Furthermore, says Brown, "I don't think much about the past. I'm just not at that point in my life where I've started to reminisce yet. Most of my thinking is very directed to the future."

During the late 1960s, Brown was active in the antiwar movement in Los Angeles, and in 1968 he helped form a peace slate to back Eugene McCarthy against President Johnson for the Democratic nomination. As a leader of the McCarthy campaign in California, Brown worked closely with Howard Berman, a leader of the state's Young Democrats, who saw him as "relatively new in terms of Democratic party activities in Southern California, but he had a great name for strengthening the credibility of that cause."

The friendship with Berman that was formed that year would come in handy for Brown later because Berman was elected to the state assembly in 1972 and was named majority floor leader in 1974. Most Sacramento observers believe that any success Brown has had in dealing with the legislature results from the efforts of Berman and Assembly Speaker Leo McCarthy.

Brown went to the 1968 Democratic convention in Chicago as an alternate delegate for Eugene McCarthy but left before the proceedings were over. However, the experience of working for McCarthy had a lasting effect on him. His sister Cynthia says that "sometimes when you get into things with someone other than your father, it can strongly influence you. I think they [McCarthy and Jerry Brown] had a lot in common."

Brown agrees that in terms of his political development "that was an important campaign." Speaking of McCarthy, he comments, "He's a person whose thoughts I respect. His concept that the process of government should be orderly, that institutions should be respected, that the cult of the individual politician or personality should be limited, avoided where possible, the concept of job sharing"—all of these ideas Brown sees as valuable. "Often it is very easy to get caught up in the emotion of the moment and personalize the chief executive's job. It's good to some extent to limit that, where possible. The press and the structure of the media tend to personalize everything, and I think that has dangerous consequences. It undermines the traditions of our government. A cabinet officer will say something and they [the media] will say, 'The Carter administration today said,' or 'The Brown administration today said.' " Brown credits McCarthy for making him aware of such ideas, and their friendship, which began in 1968, continues in spite of the changes in their respective positions.

When Brown was not involved in politics, "he sat around Tuttle and Taylor just sort of twiddling his thumbs," according to Ken Reich. "I didn't think Jerry ever really liked the law," said Pat Brown, and Ray Fisher thought that Brown "was bored by the practice of law here. He likes action, he likes immediacy, he likes issues. That's one of the things he liked about small cases."

Looking back over his four years as an attorney, Brown comments, "I enjoyed practicing law, but there were parts of it I didn't like. There's a certain abstract quality about it with respect to questions that I didn't find that interesting. I didn't find the problem-solving that interesting or that exciting or that challenging or something." The practice of law he said, "struck me as narrow and confining. The procedure certainly seems to take precedence over the substance. I can look back on cases now that went on for years and that really should have been just arbitrated instead of this very cumbersome procedure of discovery and correspondence back and forth and depositions and trials and appeals. If a solid arbitrator could have been presented with the competing arguments, a judgment could have been made in a matter of weeks instead of a matter of years. That's something that the entire legal system is going to have to confront, and I'm going to help 'em confront it."

At the end of Brown's first year as a political activist, 1968—a year during which an incumbent president decided not to seek reelection, two popular leaders were gunned down, the Vietnam War escalated, riots took place in many U.S. cities, and Richard

Nixon was elected president—Brown walked into the office of Joseph Cerrell, a Los Angeles political consultant and publicist who had played an important role in Pat Brown's three campaigns for governor and had been a leader of the state Democratic party for almost a decade.

Brown said he had decided to run for the newly created Los Angeles Junior College Board. Cerrell later recalled that Brown asked him, "What do you think I need to do?" Cerrell replied, "If you just sit there in that chair and never get up, you'll get elected. Now what's your real purpose?" He said, "I want to win. I want to win big."

Brown also contacted Bill Burman, who had been his confidant in the seminary and who had joined the faculty at one of the schools in the Junior College District in 1966. Brown invited Burman and his wife to dinner and told them of his plans to run for the college board. He also mentioned that the incumbent secretary of state was likely to retire soon and that he might seek that office. But "you could sort of see that he wasn't going for that [secretary of state] as his ultimate goal," said Burman.

Among those who were taken by surprise when Brown decided to run for office were his parents and Marc Poché and Frank Damrell, who had been two of his closest friends during much of the previous thirteen years. "He hadn't shown any particular inclination toward politics," said Bernice Brown, but she added that because he was "the only son . . . of course Pat was dying for him" to become a lawyer and enter politics. "That was the first time that I'd seen any indication that he was even interested in politics," recalled Poché, who was practicing law in San Jose. Damrell, who had been president of the freshman class when he and Brown were at Santa Clara and was president of the student body at Yale Law School, said, "I am sure if you took a poll of the freshman class at Santa Clara or the graduating class from Yale that not too many would have thought Jerry would have gone into elective office." Brown was "somewhat of an introvert, and he was not a political animal for a long period of time, before and after the seminary," Damrell said. It was not until Brown moved to Los Angeles "that he exhibited these political tendencies, commitments, and involvements in the political life that he never really displayed before."

A total of 133 candidates ran for the seven seats on the college board, with the 14 who received the most votes in a preliminary election on April 1, 1969, qualifying for the May 27 runoff. Brown finished far ahead of the rest of the field in each election, receiving 40 percent more votes than runner-up Mike Antonovich, a future assemblyman, in April, and beating Antonovich, who again came in second, by 61,000 votes in May. In fact, in the second election, Brown, with 466,000 votes, got 19,000 more votes than incumbent mayor Sam Yorty, who defeated future mayor Tom Bradley.

Although municipal elections in California are nonpartisan, many of the college-board candidates ran on slates. But Brown, who was identified as one of the liberal contenders, ran more as an independent than as a member of a slate. "He was a loner then, just as quite frankly he is a loner now," said Cerrell. "He ran as Edmund G. Brown, Jr. If his name was Edmund G. Green, I wouldn't have wanted to bet on his running in the top fourteen."

Sharing Cerrell's views are Justice Tobriner, who said Brown "was elected on his name, I'm sure," and Fisher, who attributed Brown's "phenomenal success" to his "name ID."

Brown and the two other leaders in the second election, Antonovich and Frederic Wyatt, were elected to four-year terms, and the next four finishers won two-year terms, but Brown had little interest in spending his career on the junior college board. Fisher was struck by how "very brash" Brown and his two most trusted political advisers, Tom Quinn and Richard Maullin, were when they immediately started discussing "what he should be doing on the board as a future candidate for other offices," such as governor or U.S. senator.

Brown's year and a half on the junior college board was almost a continuous dress rehearsal for the way he would conduct himself as governor: liberal on social issues, conservative on fiscal matters. He cast the lone vote against the use of district tax revenues to fund student newspapers and was one of two board members who voted against the construction of individual offices for the seven members of the board. Nor did Brown limit his aversion to spending tax dollars to big ticket items. He voted against the expenditure of twenty dollars a day for Kenneth Washington, the only black member of the board, to attend a four-day conference of black elected officials and against reimbursing Antonovich the sixty dollars cost of attending an educators' conference at Stanford.

On social issues, Brown, Washington, and Wyatt generally constituted the liberal minority. The attitude of the other four board members, according to Wyatt, was: "We've got the votes, and there it is, and jam it down your throat." Brown voted to recognize Martin Luther King's birthday; to lower flags on the district's eight campuses for two days in memory of four Kent State University students who were slain by national guardsmen in May 1970; against a requirement that district employees be fingerprinted; and in favor of allowing school facilities to be used for meetings or rallies by the Huey Newton-Eldridge Cleaver Defense Committee, Students for a Democratic Society (SDS), and a Chicano activist group. Brown's side was outvoted in each instance.

The *cause celebre* of Brown's term on the college board was the case of Deena Metzger, an English teacher whom the conservative board majority voted to dismiss after she read in class a poem called "Jehovah's Child." Board member Robert Cline, like Antonovich a Republican who was later elected to the state assembly, recalled the poem as dealing with "abnormal sexual relations with God, Christ, and animals." Brown consistently voted against the ouster of Ms. Metzger and was on the losing side against the contingent led by Cline and Antonovich. The case was appealed through all three levels of the state court system before the state supreme court ordered Metzger reinstated with back pay.

In the opinion of Cline, while Brown was on the junior college board, he had "the support of those who were detractors of the system." Many liberals saw Brown as "a young patron saint. I saw him as an opportunistic politician, knowing where the people were and getting out in front and leading them."

Antonovich remembers Brown as supporting "those creating the unrest" and as tending to be "in the pocket of the AFT [the American Federation of Teachers]." Antonovich added, "Now he's portrayed as the hard worker, long hours. Then he put in minutes, not hours. When he was on the college board, he would come late and leave early. He would just come, take his shot, and leave." A review of the minutes of the weekly board meetings during Brown's year and a half as a board member substantiates what Antonovich said. Brown usually arrived late and then would leave the meeting and return several times during each board session.

"Reflecting back," said Antonovich, "I would assume his

concern was to get to Sacramento. I don't think his heart was in serving on the college board. I think that [Brown's role as a board member] was all contrived to project his name in the paper and then to be elected secretary of state."

Cline claims that he and Brown, each with an eye on higher office, contrived to get their names in the news media. "We discussed it point blank," according to Cline. On issues like the firing of Deena Metzger, if "it was going to be controversial, we might as well be getting the coverage. We would essentially argue it for the benefit of the press," while avoiding personal attacks on each other.

Ray Fisher, Brown's friend and former law associate, views the media blitz like Cline, although in a more charitable light. Brown "kind of moves right in and looks for the way an office can be used. He used the community college board to surface a number of issues."

Never far from Brown's side, starting with his election to the college board, was the media master, Tom Quinn. Quinn "was there constantly," Cline said. "They were essentially programming Brown to get the greatest amounts of publicity." Antonovich perceived Quinn as "very adroitly placing newsworthy items with Jerry's name before the public every week."

The success of Quinn's strategies was to be proved within the year.

CHAPTER THREE

THE TOM AND JERRY SHOW, 1970–1974

It is no accident that A. Thomas Quinn understands how to deal with the news media. While Quinn was growing up in Los Angeles, his father, Joe Quinn, at one time a United Press International news executive, joined with former mayor Fletcher Bowron to found City News Service, a wire that provided coverage of Los Angeles news for various media outlets. Tom Quinn spent a year with ABC News after he graduated from Northwestern in 1965 and then joined the staff of City News Service. A year later, he and his three brothers organized Radio News West, which offers audio feeds of news events to radio stations. Quinn served as president of Radio News West from 1967 until 1970, when he went to work full time for Jerry Brown. He still owns a substantial interest in the audio service.

The boyish-looking Quinn, who resembles actor Ryan O'Neal, first met Brown in 1969, when he was twenty-five and Brown, thirty-one. Soon after Brown was elected to the junior college board, Quinn began helping him plan for future efforts. When Quinn said he had never been inside a campaign office, Brown, according to Quinn, responded with "something like, that's fine, he'd been in lots of them. Whatever benefit one gets from that, he'd picked up. He wanted someone fresh who hadn't spent their life hanging around campaign headquarters."

Brown says that even before he ran for the college board, "I was aware of the secretary of state's office." The idea of running for the position was one "that came into my mind" while he was practicing law in Los Angeles, although "momentarily I considered [running for] Congress" in 1970.

On March 2, 1970, in a scenario that would recur many times in the future, Brown announced his candidacy with a press release written by Quinn and edited by Brown, at a press conference that was staged by Quinn in accord with Brown's specifications. Brown promised to "vigorously enforce campaign disclosure laws now on the books. These laws require candidates to report the precise source of all contributions. Yet most reports are so vague they're actually more funny than informative." Brown cited examples of candidates' identifying their sources of funds as "all others," "the victory committee," and "various associations and orgs." He added: "I believe it is essential for the taxpayers to know who's paying for the campaigns of our elected officials, and I will refuse to certify the election of any candidate who fails to fully and honestly report every campaign contribution."

Just before the formal announcement, Peter Finnegan received a call in San Francisco from Quinn, asking him "to come down to Los Angeles to go out to Jerry's pad to get Jerry moved out of this place because it was a shithole. It was a fucking dump. There were a bunch of hippies there, people blowing pot, and he's about to run for secretary of state." Finnegan was familiar with Brown's apartment. "I stayed at his dump once. I couldn't believe it." During his previous visit, Finnegan had borrowed Brown's car, "and he had a flat, and I had to buy two new tires for his car." After Finnegan helped move Brown to new quarters, "'we went out and bought Jerry some suits. That was the start. That was the new Jerry."

Secretary of state had never been an office that attracted much attention, and for the Democrats who voted in the 1970 primary the name Edmund G. Brown on the ballot, even with a Jr. after it, was enough to pull almost 70 percent of the vote in a three-way race for the nomination.

The campaign in the general election was also uneventful, although Brown got somewhat nervous near voting day. According to U.S. Senator Alan Cranston, who was elected in 1968 after his unsuccessful try in 1964, someone knocked on the door of Pat and Bernice Brown's home late at night a few days before the election, and Mrs. Brown, mindful that some of the Manson murders had occurred not too far away, warned Pat not to answer for fear their caller might be a robber or murderer. Nevertheless, Cranston related, Pat opened the door to find his son, who said, "Pop, I need more money for television," and the elder Brown's comment to Cranston about the incident was, "It would have been better if it had been a bandit."

In spite of his fears, Jerry Brown won by 300,000 votes and 5 percentage points at the same time Ronald Reagan was overwhelmingly reelected. The only other Democrat to win statewide office that year was another son of a famous father, Congressman John Tunney, who ousted George Murphy from his seat in the Senate by 600,000 votes and nearly 10 percentage points.

The duties of secretary of state include managing the state archives; keeping all state records; issuing commissions to notaries public; overseeing state elections, which means checking to see that ballot propositions have enough signatures to qualify, keeping records of campaign expenses, and certifying and publishing election results; and issuing charters to corporations that do business within the state. Seven years after Brown was elected secretary of state and three years since he left that office to become governor, he still points out with pride that "the idea that the secretary of state could question a campaign report was never asserted until I made that announcement. That thought had not entered anybody's brain. I'm the keeper of the records [as secretary of state]. If the records are not in order, I could refuse to file them. And that refusing to file became the legal hook on which I based the campaign disclosure effort."

On January 26, 1971, three weeks after he took office, Brown demonstrated his concept of the role of secretary of state by filing a $250,000 lawsuit against foes of a 1970 ballot measure that would have allowed the use of gas tax funds for development of rapid transit. The charge by Brown: making illegal secret donations. Brown stated that "for many years some of the largest and most influential corporations" had failed to comply with campaign spending laws, but "beginning today that will no longer be true. I have filed suit—perhaps the first suit ever—to force compliance with the state election code. Laws aimed at guaranteeing open and honest elections must be enforced because the public has a right to know all the facts."

Within three days, Gulf Oil admitted it had given $20,000 secretly, and Standard Oil of California acknowledged an anonymous donation of $45,000 in addition to the $30,000 contribution against the ballot measure that had been listed publicly.

Eight months later, on September 16, Brown warned 134 candidates who had run for various offices in 1970 that he would prosecute them for failing to disclose the sources of their campaign funds unless they fulfilled the provisions of the law by October 15. Brown also advised the former office seekers that if found guilty, they would face terms of from six months in county jail to five years in state prison. Among those on Brown's list were George Murphy; Norton Simon, the business executive who had challenged Murphy in the June 1970 GOP primary; and Robert Scheer, whose path crossed with Brown's again in 1976 when *Playboy* featured his separate interviews of Brown and Jimmy Carter (the one in which candidate Carter admitted he secretly lusted after women other than his wife). Scheer had run as the Peace and Freedom Party candidate for the U.S. Senate seat in 1970, drawing 57,000 votes, compared to 3.5 million for Tunney, 2.9 million for Murphy, and 61,000 for the American Independent Party nominee.

Brown's announcement set off an uproar. A few hours later, he felt forced to add, "Norton Simon is a close friend of my family. He was a schoolmate of my father's, and my father appointed him to the Board of Regents of the University of California. I obviously am unhappy that his name appears on the list of candidates who did not file timely campaign contribution reports. However, it is clearly my duty to act against my friends when they violate the law, as well as against those people I do not know. To do otherwise would be a mockery of justice and a violation of my oath of office."

None of the threatened prosecutions ever resulted in jail

terms. Most of the candidates met Brown's deadline, although he later filed suit and asked for an injunction ordering nine miscreants to file their reports. Some of the edge was taken from Brown's sword when he had to admit that one of the people on his list, John E. Leadbetter, who had run for secretary of state in the Republican primary, had filed his report on time but that it had been lost in the state archives. Nevertheless, Brown got good mileage from the original admonition to the 134 candidates, only 33 shopping months before Democrats had to choose their 1974 gubernatorial nominee.

Another publicity plum fell into Brown's lap in August 1972, after Deputy Secretary of State Quinn and other members of the staff discovered that both the pro and con arguments intended for distribution to the state's voters on a measure that would be on the November 1972 ballot had been typed on the same typewriter. Propositon 8 was intended to grant significant property tax exemptions to businesses that curbed pollution. Brown's press release charged that two executives of Union Oil Company and an employee of the State Senate's Revenue and Taxation Committee had met in a committee room and drafted both statements. "This means that the argument against the measure was really written by persons who want the measure adopted," said Brown. "This is a shocking fraud on the public. It is clear that Union saw a chance to help pass a measure which could give the firm a massive tax break and then secretly conspired to write a phony and intentionally weak argument against the measure. The goal obviously was to deceive the voters." Brown announced that he would therefore invoke a "never before used section of the election code" and select a ballot argument against the measure that had been written by two legislators who vigorously opposed it. The experience of examining type face on documents would come in handy later in the Brown-Quinn regime in the secretary of state's office, and the publicity against Proposition 8 helped send it to defeat by a margin of almost three to one.

The drive against big spenders in the private sector who were seen by Brown and his staff as inimical to the public interest continued in March 1973 when Brown revealed that employees of the secretary of state's office had been denied access to supposedly public records by the legislature's lobbyist control committee. On April 10, 1973, the effort continued when Brown and representatives of Common Cause and People's Lobby announced plans to gather signatures in favor of placing a Fair Political Practices initiative on the ballot in June 1974.

The measure, which Brown called the "most fundamental and far-reaching reform of our California governmental system in more than sixty years," provided that campaign reports be strictly audited, that key public officials disclose their assets and income and not act in cases in which they had conflicts of interest, and that state agencies make their public records available to the press and public; outlawed secret slush funds, gifts, or political donations to candidates from lobbyists; banned secret meetings of legislative committees; and placed limits on campaign spending.

Daniel Lowenstein, a magna cum laude graduate of Harvard Law School and former poverty lawyer who did the bulk of drafting Proposition 9 as a member of Brown's staff, and whom Governor Brown later named head of the Fair Political Practices Commission that was created under the initiative, explained the "shotgun marriage" that brought the three groups together:

"Common Cause had the name but wasn't moving fast. People's Lobby had people to circulate petitions, and Brown's staff had the technical expertise to write the law and also lended respectability."

The delicate coalition almost fell apart just before the April 10 announcement, according to Lowenstein, because at the last minute Brown decided he wanted the proposition to include a campaign spending limit, which Common Cause opposed. Brown's support of the drafting had "peaks and valleys," Lowenstein said, and the secretary of state appeared to lose interest as the process of hammering out the wording dragged on. "That was part of what created the problem. I mean, if he had given a better signal on the limits on spending at an earlier stage, that could have been handled very smoothly. In fact, he actually, or we for him, were in a very strong bargaining position because there was a lot of friction" between the two public-interest groups, but each one trusted Brown and his staff. "If he had focused his attention on that aspect of it earlier, we could have saved a lot of trouble later on.

"I don't mean to be criticizing him. On the other hand, I suppose I should say that I was mad as hell when he sort of turned around on that at the last minute." Lowenstein said he considered resigning over what he considered Brown's breach of faith, but he decided to stay on, and Common Cause agreed to the spending limit in order to help secure passage for the parts of the law its members favored.

Actually, the impetus for the spending limitations came from Quinn, who presented the proposal to Brown. "I felt strongly about that point," Quinn said. "The actual dollar limitations were numbers I came up with after going through various campaign reports, determining what I thought it would cost to run an effective campaign."

Quinn had little trouble selling the idea of a spending limit to Brown, who compares a political campaign to "a boxing match or a football game" where "there is a finite amount of time during which the contest takes place. Figure out what the fair time limit is and say that's enough." Brown says he has observed "a lot of excessive spending" in election efforts. "A lot of it was just wasted, there are ripoffs, there was a squandering of money to no end. And if each side has a reasonable amount, and they're both limited, I don't think the public loses any information. I don't think the candidates are put at a disadvantage.

"See, I think a lot of the spending is just defensive. It's just, 'You spend, I spend,' and it has no meaning. All it is is giving money to television stations and public relations firms and television [commercial] makers." Also, Brown said, "Anything that would free up more of your time for other campaign activities than just sitting around raising money or speaking on the telephone [to solicit funds] I viewed as a good thing."

The initiative qualified for the ballot as Proposition 9 in the June 9, 1974, primary and passed at the same time Brown won the Democratic nomination for governor.

One effect of Brown's push for the modifications that were finally incorporated into Proposition 9 was that "he wasn't too popular" with some members of the legislature, according to State Senator George Zenovich (D, Fresno). Brown's proposals, most notably the one that prevented a lobbyist from spending more than ten dollars a month on an individual legislator, which was included in Proposition 9, seemed to question the integrity of the legislators, "which sort of offended a lot of people," Zenovich said.

However, one of the foremost lobbyists in Sacramento at the time, Richard "Bud" Carpenter, who was executive director and general counsel of the League of California Cities and who had publicly chastised Brown for his attacks on lobbying and lobby-ists when Brown was campaigning for secretary of state, praised Brown for getting Proposition 9 passed. The initiative, Carpenter states, created "a more professional approach between lobbyists and legislators. You get away from the very close personal relationships which we developed. There isn't any question in my mind but that you had an advantage over people who simply came to Sacramento for the first time." At the start of his administration, Brown named Carpenter to the Fair Political Practices Commission, headed by Lowenstein, and Carpenter served for more than two years before he resigned to return to lobbying.

A call from a reporter at the *St. Louis Post-Dispatch* put the secretary of state's office into the Watergate business late in 1973. The call concerned Frank DeMarco, Herbert Kalmbach's law partner, who had notarized the document by which Presi-dent Nixon had given away his vice-presidential papers in return for an income-tax deduction of half a million dollars.

Quinn and Press Secretary Doug Faigin, who had worked for Quinn at Radio News West before he joined Brown's staff, paid their first visit to DeMarco in December 1973. At the time, DeMarco impressed Faigin as "a very nice, very cordial" person, "just the right image for an honest, self-effacing lawyer who had been caught up with some very odd people, had not known what was going on, had done his thing just perfectly, and had been caught in some clerical errors that were just not of any real significance, and was as horrified by them as anyone else would be. He really exhibited a resentment of these White House people dragging him down into this thing." At one point, while Quinn stepped out of DeMarco's office, DeMarco recounted to Faigin how John Ehrlichman had treated him, a prominent attorney, like an errand boy and bitterly described how Ehrlichman had once complimented him in such a way that "it was like, 'Good boy, Rover, good boy.' "

To Quinn, DeMarco's story about the Nixon gift seemed

"strange but not necessarily untrue." In spite of that, Quinn and Faigin began exchanging information with other agencies that were investigating Nixon, including the Internal Revenue Service and the Senate Watergate Committee, headed by Sam Ervin. Things started to fall into place in January 1974 when Quinn noticed that some of the Nixon documents that had been prepared by the Kalmbach-DeMarco law firm appeared to have been typed on different machines.

Quinn knew that shortly after the April 21, 1969, date that was on the Nixon gift documents when DeMarco notarized them, DeMarco had moved his offices from Century City to the Arco Plaza tower in downtown Los Angeles. He also knew from experience that when businesses moved, office equipment was commonly updated, and new typewriters were often purchased.

Further investigation by Quinn and Faigin disclosed that the DeMarco firm had used IBM Executive typewriters while the offices were in Century City but had switched to IBM Selectrics in the Arco Plaza offices.

"It seemed pretty clear," said Quinn, "looking at the typeface [of the Nixon gift deed] that it was typed on a Selectric. And they didn't have a Selectric at the old office. I was now firmly convinced that there was at least a strong likelihood that this thing was a phony.

"I called him [DeMarco] and bluffed him," Quinn said. He told DeMarco it appeared that the deed had been backdated. At first, DeMarco denied Quinn's allegations, but after Quinn declared, "Frank, that's the way it is," DeMarco admitted that the deed had not been signed until April 10, 1970, several months after the repeal of the law under which Nixon had made the donation of his papers.

The DeMarco investigation bore fruit at the perfect time: midway through the campaign for the Democratic nomination for governor. Furthermore, with public interest in Watergate at a fever pitch and President Nixon's credibility becoming increasingly strained, Brown was picking up votes for himself and Proposition 9 by advocating honesty in campaign financing. In fact, Proposition 9 was becoming the critical issue in the gubernatorial race, with the state AFL-CIO deciding not to back Brown or Congressman Jerome Waldie because of their support

of the initiative but instead to endorse San Francisco Mayor
Joseph Alioto and Assembly Speaker Bob Moretti, who had
refused to come out for the measure.

On March 7, 1974, less than three months before the primary,
Brown, as the state officer in charge of overseeing notaries public,
filed formal charges against DeMarco, seeking to revoke the
lawyer's notary license on the grounds that he had backdated the
Nixon deed. Brown also revealed that two days earlier he had
written President Nixon and requested that he waive the
attorney-client privilege so that DeMarco could answer more
questions about their dealings. There is no record of a response
from the White House. Subsequently, Brown issued a list of
people who might be called as witnesses in the DeMarco hearing.
Among the proposed witnesses were President and Mrs. Nixon
and John Ehrlichman.

Two weeks after Brown was nominated, on June 17, 1974, he
announced that DeMarco had resigned his commission rather
than proceed with the hearing, which was to have started that
day.

Vic Biondi, who was a reporter for NBC when Brown was
secretary of state and is now press secretary to Superintendent of
Public Instruction Wilson Riles, scoffs at the DeMarco episode as
a tempest over "a lousy fourteen-dollar notary public" license.
But, he added, "by now we had been conditioned" by the adroit
moves of Brown and Quinn "that when Junior said something
we had better go." Houston Flournoy, Brown's opponent in the
race for governor in 1974, said that from his standpoint Brown
"was suing everybody all the time" when he was secretary of
state. "He was like Drew Pearson. If you swing enough times,
you're going to hit a home run now and then."

During the secretary of state years, Brown and Quinn managed
regularly to hold press conferences or issue press releases in
which Brown offered something for almost everyone, including:

Young people. "I believe the current calm on our campuses is a
direct result of allowing 18-year-olds to vote" (February 24,
1971). "The 18-year-old vote will create a peaceful revolution, a
revolution at the ballot box. And within this decade that

revolution will change the course of American politics" (April 5, 1971).

Consumers. Brown orders all 220,000 corporations licensed to do business in California to list names and addresses of key officers or face loss of their charters: "Consumers who have been victimized by unscrupulous corporations all seem to have the same complaint, that they usually can't discover the identities of top corporate executives" (March 16, 1971); charges that private insurance companies administering federal Medicare programs in California have wasted more than $100 million in public funds on duplicate payments to hospitals and doctors, trips for wives of company executives, and unneeded equipment (January 19, 1972); urges ban on advertising by public utilities, which spent $73 million on advertising in 1971, even though they are monopolies and face no competition (April 25, 1972).

Nixon critics. Urges the public to join with Congressman Pete McCloskey (R, Calif.), a Nixon foe, in a "massive national debate" to bring about the impeachment of Nixon and Vice President Spiro T. Agnew as a means of ending the Vietnam War (April 3, 1971); says the televised speech in which Nixon denied guilt in Watergate but refused to answer specific questions was "a grave disappointment" that left "a cloud of suspicion" over the president (August 15, 1973); refers to Nixon as a "reverse Robin Hood" (numerous occasions); asks California congressional delegation to start impeachment proceedings because of Nixon's refusal to release the White House tapes and because of the firing of Watergate Special Prosecutor Archibald Cox (October 21, 1973).

Women. Announces his support of a bill in state legislature that allows women to write Miss, Mrs., Ms., or nothing before their names when they register to vote (February 1, 1972); criticizes Governor Reagan for filling but one of the top 156 jobs in state government with a woman (June 9, 1973).

Jews. Voices his "personal outrage" over a recent Standard Oil of California letter to stockholders that advocated support for "the aspirations of the Arab people"; says that as a result of the letter he will not buy any Standard products (August 6, 1973).

United Farm Workers. Praises Cesar Chavez for "leading a courageous effort" and for doing "more for agricultural workers than anyone else has been able to accomplish in the last fifty years" (August 18, 1973).

Chicanos. Points out that none of the top sixty-one jobs in the Reagan administration was held by person with Spanish surname (November 18, 1973).

Poor people. Says nationwide gas rationing is needed in order to avoid turning the energy crisis into a "yoke of injustice" for low-income people who can't afford to pay more for gas (December 17, 1973).

The press. Calls the American Telephone and Telegraph Company policy of providing government agencies with records of phone calls made by reporters "dangerous to democracy," says it could create "a puppet press with its strings pulled by government. We cannot tolerate such a Gestapo tactic, which places the press under secret surveillance by the government it is supposed to report freely on" (December 24, 1973).

Only Brown's proposal that corporations list the names and addresses of their top executives had anything to do with his duties as secretary of state.

John Jervis, who was a television reporter when Brown was secretary of state and is now the staff director of the State Senate Democratic Caucus, says that on occasions when he went to interview Brown in the secretary of state's office, "It occurred to me that he wasn't doing very much. I mean his desk was spotless, and Tom Quinn was there orchestrating the publicity drive obviously with the intent to become governor, which Quinn did very effectively, of course."

Midway through the Quinn-Brown media blitz A. Alan Post, the state's nonpartisan legislative analyst, issued a study that citicized the secretary of state's office for charging excessive fees; not having enough employees, and as a result having to pay too much overtime; having a work backload that caused hardships to people required to deal with the office; and having an employee turnover rate of more than three percent a month, which "is generally held by those in state government to be high and indicative of an undesirable condition."

According to Faigin, most members of the Sacramento establishment and the Capitol press corps, which includes bureaus of the two wire services as well as the major newspapers and broadcast outlets around the state, "refused to believe that Pat Brown's kid could have any substance or significance. And anything good coming out of that office had to be explained some way other than through any ability that Jerry Brown could have." Faigin said he was often told "how great a staff Jerry Brown had. I would always point out that we did not do one single thing that Jerry Brown had not authorized . . . and in fact that did not have his absolute print on it. Jerry was always, always, the leader of the discussion. Most often he would initiate whatever we were doing. He was running that office, no doubt about it."

Quinn has no question, "none at all," that Brown is his own man. "Jerry Brown makes his own decisions and sees that they are carried through. There's no behind the scenes power.

"Sure, when you work for someone you give advice," Quinn continued. "Hopefully, that advice helps the person. I don't think a great tennis player teaches someone to play tennis well who doesn't have some innate skill. I don't think we invented anything. There was a lot of activity in that office, which had languished for many, many years. I think also that Jerry was sort of an interesting figure to the press" because his family background "perhaps amplified the attention that the activities might otherwise have received."

In November 1977, three and a half years after passage of Proposition 9, the political reform act was declared unconstitutional by a lower-court judge in Los Angeles. The ruling was on technical grounds, and Lowenstein and the Fair Political Practices Commission are appealing the decision to higher courts.

Meanwhile, the act remains on the books, and the effect of Brown's tenure as secretary of state continues to be visible at Sacramento dining spots where politicians were wined and dined at lobbyist expense before the passage of Proposition 9.

Frank Fat is an immigrant whose Chinese and American

restaurant has been the favorite spot of influential legislators and influence seekers for more than thirty years. Here is the effect Propositon 9 has had on his business, as reported by the *San Francisco Chronicle* on April 30, 1977:

> "Not like used to be," he reminisced. "They don't come with lobbyists so often. No dinner parties like used to be."
>
> In the old days, lobbyists would rent the upstairs room to throw lavish banquets for legislators. Any new legislator would be introduced to Frank Fat by a lobbyist as his initiation to Sacramento soul life.
>
> Now, new legislators slip into Frank Fat's unannounced and unnoticed by the proprietors. Often, but not always, the legislators pay their own, more modest, tabs, even if they are dining with lobbyists.

And anyone who receives a meal, a drink, or a gift from a lobbyist does so with the knowledge that his name, along with the date, location, and amount, will be filed as a public record with the Fair Political Practices Commission.

CHAPTER FOUR

THE CAMPAIGN FOR GOVERNOR, 1974

"When he talked about running for governor, it seemed like a preposterous idea." —CYNTHIA BROWN KELLY

Jerry Brown had been thinking about running for governor for years. According to Tom Quinn, who had known Brown since 1969, "I think he clearly wanted to be governor as long as I've known him, and he made no secret about that. There's a difference between deciding to run for governor and maybe wanting to be governor. We certainly were thinking a lot about the governor's race and talking about it as early as 1971. I think the determining factor was whether he thought he had a good chance of winning or not."

While Brown was secretary of state he met frequently with John Tunney, who had been elected to the U.S. Senate in 1970, to discuss, in Tunney's words, "mainly his desire to be governor." Brown was interested in what Tunney thought of his running, as well as in Tunney's opinion as to what image he should project if he did decide to take the plunge. At first, Tunney thought it would be "natural" for Brown to follow in his father's footsteps and run for attorney general next, and that for the thirty-six-year-old Brown to attempt to jump from secretary of state to governor would be tough. But that was before Watergate caused President Nixon to resign in disgrace, and, Tunney said, "My initial advice, as it turned out, was based on completely inadequate information." Tunney says he told Brown that if he did run for governor, he should present himself as a young, energetic, dedicated, totally clean politician who wanted to change the conditions of the past that had led to such disasters as Vietnam and Watergate. Brown's response was that that was exactly what he had been doing as secretary of state. Tunney said he thought Brown was on the right track and should continue.

Brown's old friend Marc Poché shared Cynthia Kelly's more skeptical view. Like Pat Brown, Poché was originally a Republican, but he became a Democrat when his then law partner in San Jose, John Vasconcellos, ran for and was elected to the state assembly in 1966. Poché later sought unsuccessfully to win a seat in the legislature and was active in Democratic politics until September 1977, when Brown named him a judge. When Brown mentioned to Poché that he was considering entering the race for governor in 1974, "I thought it was a crazy idea that he should run for governor at that time," said Poché. "My theory was that if he would wait a little while, they would hand it to him. He was articulate and had the right name." But Poché saw the 1974 race for the Democratic nomination as "an uphill battle" for Brown, given the other potential candidates, notably Mayor Joseph Alioto of San Francisco; Bob Moretti, the powerful speaker of the assembly; and George Moscone, a popular and effective state senator from San Francisco.

"The traditional way politicians operate," Poché said, "is to wait for a free run, and you can't blame 'em. Not many people want to risk the job they have for another job." As far as Poché was concerned, secretary of state was "an absolute cushy job" that paid a good salary, and if Brown served two terms, it would result in his being eligible for a generous pension as soon as he left office.

Brown's reply, according to Poché, was " 'Look, life is short. Staying as secretary of state is just ripping off the taxpayers. You don't do anything. There are a lot of things to do in life. If I were governor, I could do some good things. If I can't be governor, that's fine.' I remember being impressed," said Poché.

Although Brown had been running unofficially for governor for most of his term as secretary of state, he did not formally announce his candidacy until January 28, 1974. In his statement, he identified himself as a former leader of the antiwar movement, promised a "new spirit of activism and hope," but also warned that government cannot "do miracles." Brown said his main concerns as governor would be upgrading the state's educational system, promoting environmental protection and development of energy, looking after the state's economic health, and working for political reform. In language similar to that of Jimmy Carter in 1976, Brown said his first major task would be to reorganize the executive branch. "At the present time, for example, more than two dozen separate agencies, bureaus, and departments share responsibility in the area of environmental protection and energy planning," where there should be one overall agency instead, said Brown. In a reference to then Governor Ronald Reagan, Brown declared, "Under my administration, irresponsible attacks on the University of California will come to an end." Brown also pointed out that in 1966—Pat Brown's final year as governor—the state's job placement agency found 665,000 jobs, but under Reagan that number had dwindled to 408,000 in 1973. "This trend must be reversed, and along with it the state must encourage growth of nonpolluting industry," Brown stated.

Carl Werthman's public-opinion surveys on Brown's behalf revealed that the voters perceived Brown as "young and kicking the ass of the establishment," according to Werthman. Brown's main task in the primary, according to Stephen Reinhardt, was to attempt to prevent labor from endorsing one of his foes, especially Alioto.

The job of denying labor support to Alioto—the most likely object of labor's affection since Moscone had dropped out of the race early on—fell to Herman "Blackie" Leavitt, a friend of Reinhardt. The dark-haired, heavy-browed Leavitt, then fifty-three, had come up the hard way and was not afraid of a little political infighting. He was raised in a home for Jewish orphans in Chicago and supported himself as a youth by working on a pickle truck during the day, then donning a tuxedo and selling opera glasses at the Chicago Civic Opera House at night. He moved to Los Angeles in the early 1940s and, classified 4F during World War II because of a bad arm, went to work as a bartender at a lounge on Wilshire Boulevard. He began climbing the ladder of organized labor in 1954 as business representative of Bartenders Union Local 284 and in 1973 was elected chief executive officer of the Hotel, Restaurant Employees and Bartenders Local 11 in Los Angeles, as well as vice president at large and administrative assistant to the general president of the culinary workers' 500,000-member international union.

In early 1974, at a time when, according to Leavitt, Alioto "had the labor movement sewed up," the labor leader received a caller in his office: Secretary of State Edmund G. Brown, Jr., who "looked like a young school kid. I was shocked at first." Brown wanted to know how to win labor backing. "He said, 'All I'm looking for is some labor support.' All he was looking for was *some*. You know, he had none."

Brown's persistence and Reinhardt's support succeeded in winning Leavitt into the Brown camp. "The next thing I knew," said Leavitt, "he was in the other office" in Leavitt's suite. "And he was here day in and day out trying to get labor support. After being with me day and night for five or six weeks, I said, 'Do me a favor, Jerry. I'm not getting any work done. Find yourself another place.' "

Because Brown was behind Proposition 9, Jack Henning, chairman of the state AFL-CIO, "just wanted to drink his blood," according to Leavitt. (Henning and Brown later became friendly, and in June 1977, Brown named Henning to the University of California Board of Regents.) Leavitt was able to persuade the AFL-CIO's Committee on Public Education (COPE) to vote for an open endorsement in the Democratic primary instead of supporting Alioto, the most likely beneficiary of COPE's clout. Thanks to Leavitt, the culinary workers also decided not to make an endorsement and gave the Brown campaign $25,000, the same amount the union had previously given to its favorite, Alioto. Several local chapters of the union also donated large sums to the Brown campaign at Leavitt's behest. As a token of his gratitude, Brown invited Leavitt, Leavitt's fiancée and his sister and brother-in-law to dinner. "As usual, he didn't have any money with him," said Leavitt. "So I paid the check." But Leavitt still appreciated the gesture on Brown's part: "That was the first time he seemed to know the words 'thank you.' "

At about the same time, Leavitt had another office visitor, Gray Davis, a young attorney who was running for state treasurer in the Democratic primary against Jesse Unruh, who had previously been assembly speaker and was the Democratic nominee for governor against Ronald Reagan in 1970. Brown and Davis, two youthful antiestablishment candidates, had become friendly during the campaign. Leavitt had to tell Davis that he didn't have time to help him and that he thought Davis was in over his head against Unruh, but all the attention made Leavitt feel important, and he enjoyed it. "At this stage, every word I utter is gospel. It was a big ego thing for me. There was no amount of money that could have paid for it."

In early spring, with matters apparently safe on the California labor front, Leavitt flew with his fiancée to Israel to meet his future in-laws. He checked in at the Tel Aviv Hilton, "just beat to death" after a sixteen-hour flight, and almost immediately the telephone rang. On the other end was Reinhardt. "Blackie," said Reinhardt, "you've got to get back here." As soon as Leavitt had left, Alioto supporters had begun pressuring COPE to reconsider its decision. Then, said Leavitt, Brown got on the phone and "makes a desperate plea to me, so I said, 'I'll be on the next plane home.' " Leaving his fiancée in Israel, Leavitt flew to San Francisco, where the COPE board was meeting. Brown, Reinhardt, and campaign manager Quinn drove him from the airport to the session and explained that they wanted COPE to endorse all the candidates except Brown, which would deny Alioto the sole endorsement and would also make Brown "look like the knight in shining armor standing up to the labor unions." Leavitt was able to talk the board into doing just that, without telling the members that it was exactly what Brown wanted.

After that, according to Leavitt, "there was a turn in Brown's personality. He was a very, very difficult candidate to handle from that time on. He wouldn't listen to anyone. He never said thank you to this day for my trip back from Israel.

"When he wins the primary, he is totally impossible," Leavitt added. He said that Brown then invited Davis, who had lost in the primary to Unruh but had made an impressive showing, to join the campaign. From then on, said Leavitt, Richard Maullin, the deputy campaign manager, was treated as just "another piece of garbage," and "I was a stranger" to Brown and his inner circle. "The only able guy in the campaign was Tom Quinn."

Three years later, Leavitt reflected on the 1974 campaign as "an enjoyable experience. We took a guy in a zero position and made him governor. The Hotel and Restaurant Union. That's we. That's who did it for him. Don't forget, all of our people were pledged to Alioto, and we had to turn them around. That was a major task. Most of the people in the labor movement didn't want to do a thing for him."

Don Burns, who spent the eve of the primary with Brown, says Brown took it for granted he would win and believed he had sewn up the primary several months earlier when the other leading candidates, Alioto and Moretti, conceded the Proposition 9 issue to him. Burns said Brown could not understand how, especially in the year Watergate was reaching a conclusion, his opponents could leave an issue like that to him. Actually, Alioto and Moretti had little choice. To support a proposal that Brown had helped draft might have been even more harmful to their campaigns than their refusal to back it. On Election Day, Brown drubbed Alioto and Moretti, who each received about half as many votes as he did. The two other major candidates, William Matson Roth, a shipping heir and member of the University of California Board of Regents, and Congressman Jerome Waldie, finished far back. And Brown emerged further victorious with the passage of Proposition 9, which won by a margin of seventy to thirty.

Assemblyman Willie Brown, who endorsed his close friend, Moretti, in the primary, is one of many people to attribute Brown's successes to "the residual love that people had developed for Pat Brown since Reagan had defeated him. All of that inured to the benefit of the young Jerry Brown, and the young Jerry Brown was as quick as a whip. For the period of time in which he'd been the secretary of state, he was best known for his ability to file lawsuits and hold press conferences. And beyond that he really didn't have much of a track record."

Moretti commented, "In retrospect, I think that was probably the only possible outcome, for a lot of reasons, not the least of which is the fact that Jerry had the name Edmund G. Brown, Jr. I think the fact that he chose as his issue that year political reform was either exceptionally wise or tremendously fortunate because that's when Watergate broke, so that anybody who was for quote good government or political reform or what have you had to be on the side of the angels. Nobody knew that Watergate was coming when my campaign started, but as it ended up, it was *the* issue that counted that year."

Furthermore, said Moretti, the kidnapping of Patricia Hearst one week after Brown's formal announcement of his candidacy was another advantage for the leader, Brown, "because she was getting *all* the news attention. And it was very hard to squeeze into the media. Jerry had the initial jump, and he just stayed out in front the whole time. In view of what came down in the course of that campaign, I don't think anybody ever really had a chance of beating him."

In the spring of 1975, almost a year after the primary race, a furor occurred when newspapers around the state reported that Brown's staff had compiled "dossiers" on Alioto and Moretti, allegedly to be used if either or both of them tried to smear him during the race by implying that he was a homosexual. The stories were based on remarks made by Quinn during a symposium on the election in San Francisco in March 1975. In a story on April 4, 1975, the *Los Angeles Times* quoted author Richard Reeves, who attended the seminar, as saying that the files contained "politically embarrassing" information about Alioto and Moretti. The same story quoted Quinn as saying that the information about Alioto dealt with some of his business interests, while the file on Moretti focused on his campaign contributions. Reeves himself subsequently wrote about the dossiers in an article about Brown in the *New York Times Magazine* on August 24, 1975.

Quinn denies that there was any aspect of blackmail about the files. "They were all public documents," he said, and added that there was nothing underhanded about them "unless you want to consider the public statements or public record of somebody sinister. I can't imagine a campaign where you wouldn't want to know what your opponents talked about."

The Alioto and Moretti folders are still among the files in the governor's office, and they bear out what Quinn says. In them are speeches by the two candidates, press releases, and newspaper clippings, the same material that most candidates gather about

their opponents. Much of the data in the file about donations to
the Moretti campaign was made public, anyway. Both the *Los
Angeles Times* and the *Sacramento Bee* said that the Brown staff
gave a copy of the information to Ed Koupal, director of People's
Lobby, and that Koupal distributed copies even though Quinn
had asked that he return the material without disclosing it to the
public.

Exactly who was running the Brown campaign for governor
was made clear to Don Muir, a veteran professional fund raiser
for Democratic candidates. In 1974, Muir was on the staff of
George Moscone, the senate majority leader, when he was
approached by Brown's top aides. Even though Moscone had
dropped out of the race for governor, the senator objected to
letting Muir work for any of the candidates in the primary.
Therefore, it was agreed that the fund raiser would join the
Brown camp afterward.

"This is a very strange incident," the tall, thin, dark-haired
Muir remarked. "I was asked by Maullin and Quinn to go to work
for Brown in the general election to be his fund raiser, and
through a series of bizarre incidents that didn't happen."

What did happen, according to Muir, was that right after the
primary Brown asked him to a meeting at the Clift Hotel in San
Francisco. The salary Muir had agreed on with Quinn and
Maullin amounted to $5,000 per month for the five months
between the primary and the general election, or a total of
$25,000. In advance of the meeting at the Clift, Muir told Brown,
"The five thousand dollars a month for five months, I'll take
care of that in one shot." At the Clift, Muir introduced Brown to
a donor, who presented him with $25,000 for his campaign fund.
Then, Muir later recalled, "Jerry said, 'I want to talk with you.'
And I said, 'Fine.' I thought we were going to talk about
campaign strategy regarding finance, and he said to me, 'I'm
upset at this price of five thousand dollars a month.' " Muir
explained to Brown that he had reached agreement with Quinn
and Maullin. "And he said, 'Well, I'm not going to pay that.
Nobody should be making that kind of commitment. I make my
decisions.' " Brown also told Muir that paying him twice as
much as Quinn was earning would cause dissension within the
campaign even though it was Quinn who had made the offer in
the first place.

"He wasn't allowing anybody, and I think that's true today, to make any decisions for him," said Muir. "Quinn and Maullin had acted unilaterally, unbeknownst to me at that time, and had made a commitment, and I assumed that they were speaking for Brown, which was a logical assumption." In the interim, Muir had quit his job with Moscone. A few days later, he and Brown talked again, and each refused to give in, so Muir left the Brown campaign, and Moscone rehired him. In their final conversation about the job, Brown said he hoped Muir had no hard feelings, and Muir answered, " 'No, but I don't want to be left out hanging, and you guys were the ones that called me, not me calling you.' And he said, 'Well, I make the decisions. Nobody else makes them for me.' "

Muir now concedes that Brown was right because he had no real need for a professional fund raiser. Even though Proposition 9 would not take effect until January 1, 1975, Brown and his Republican opponent, Houston Flournoy, had agreed to be bound by its terms, which meant that Brown would need to raise only about $1 million for the general election, a relatively easy sum to produce in a state the size of California. Furthermore, Brown was far ahead in the polls immediately after the primary, when the negotiations with Muir took place. Brown's version of the Muir incident is that it was a simple "salary dispute. There were times that people in the campaign, their ideas on salary would often differ from mine. I've never been one to want to spend that much."

Muir also observed that the 1974 Brown campaign was unique because no traditional political activists were involved. "I don't know if that adversely affected Brown. I think it adversely affects democracy. The fewer people who participate in campaigns, I think, the more unhealthy to our process. Brown understood, though, very early that in a state of twenty-two million people, media was the key."

Another experienced Democratic activist, Jack Tomlinson, a San Francisco attorney who had been travel secretary to Pat Brown in 1974 and who was part of Jerry Brown's campaign for governor, made a similar observation. Soon after the primary, Tomlinson met with Quinn, Maullin, and the candidate. When Tomlinson mentioned a voter-registration effort for the general election, Brown's response was " 'I'm not so sure we need a voter-registration drive,' which, coming from a Democratic candidate, is blasphemy," said Tomlinson. He also said that

Peter Finnegan, a leader of Brown's campaign in Northern California during the primary, was dropped from influence "because he was a thorn to the collective boob-tube genii."

A California poll taken right after the primary showed Brown with a lead of forty-seven to thirty-nine over Flournoy, who did not have nearly as much name recognition around the state as the son of the former governor. Flournoy, who, at forty-five, was nine years older than Brown, was a former professor of government who had served six years in the Assembly and had been state controller, an elective post that carried little power, since 1967. In August, several weeks before the traditional Labor Day launching of the general-election campaign, Brown's margin in the California poll had increased to fifty to thirty-six. His position was similar to that of a football team with a 21 to 0 lead in the first quarter, according to Democratic leader Charles Manatt, and the strategy was to "play it fairly moderately." Stephen Reinhardt agrees that Brown ran "a very cautious, conservative campaign which was designed not to lose the lead. You take small risks, not big ones. Jerry was an unknown quantity, and there was no telling how people would react, so he played it low key."

S. Jon Kreedman, a Beverly Hills banker who was Brown's statewide chairman in 1974, said that with any candidate except an incumbent, the voters are "not too sure of what's there. Jerry had the lead, and why fight it, why make the one big mistake?" He added that it is common for candidates "to not say too much when they're in the lead."

Except for the inner circle, most people think Brown made a conscious effort to avoid discussing specific issues in the race against Flournoy. Assemblyman John Vasconcellos, who had endorsed Moretti in the primary, says he did not endorse Brown until four days before the general election "because I thought his campaign was just sheer bullshit, and then I finally realized he would probably appoint better people than Hugh Flournoy would." According to Carl Werthman, "For good political reasons, he wanted to be fuzzy, he didn't want to come down on any controversial issue. He had this whole issues staff, but he never used any of it." Jim Lorenz, who was a member of the research staff, said Brown knew he was ahead, and "he wanted to show a limited amount of stuff. It was more style than substance in the campaign. Jerry and Tom both felt that substance could be death to a politician," and, according to Lorenz, both Brown and Quinn often cited the 1972 George McGovern campaign as proof of what could happen to a politician who used too many specifics. Lorenz said the main purpose of the research office was to keep Brown from being embarrassed by Flournoy during the six televised debates between the two.

"It appeared that he was shadowboxing," said Tunney. Muir felt that Brown's campaign "did not indicate what thrust he would take once he was governor of California."

Not unexpectedly, Houston Flournoy was not very impressed by Brown's tactics: "Our goal in the campaign was based on the strategy that the more people got to know about him and the more they got to know about me, the better it was for me. I felt that he was doing everything possible to avoid having any real issues. . . . When he got elected, I didn't have the first idea of what he would do on anything because he viewed the campaign, in my judgment, in the same way he views his posture today: He was going to do anything that was necessary to get elected. It didn't necessarily have anything to do with what he was going to do after he got elected. The campaign was one thing. Being governor was totally different." Flournoy says that Brown raised "phony issues" when he did choose to deal in specifics, such as halting construction of the Governor's Mansion, "which he ultimately did not do because he could not do it. And anybody who knew anything about it knew he couldn't." The mansion was seen within the Brown campaign as a good issue to use against a Republican because it was one of Ronald Reagan's pet projects.

Flournoy said he would have preferred to run against his close friend Moretti "because I like Bobby, I respect him, I know where he's coming from. I wouldn't have been as concerned as I was about what was going to happen to the state of California if he were governor versus if I were governor."

Most of the people who worked closely with Brown during the election, including Quinn, Davis, and business executive Leo Wyler, who was finance chairman, deny that there was a conscious effort to avoid issues. Said Quinn, "We were desperate—that's probably overstating it. We were anxious throughout the campaign to find good issues and develop them." According to Quinn, the only issues that he, Brown, and the other insiders were not eager to deal with were the legalization of possessing small amounts of marijuana, which Brown favored, and the death penalty, which Brown has always opposed. Wyler said that "in 1974, he addressed himself at least in part to some specific issues and things that had to be done." Although Wyler refused to support Brown's 1976 presidential bid because he thought Brown avoided the important issues, he takes a favorable view of Brown's statements during the governor's race. "The whole tone was one of being an activist governor," Wyler said.

Llew Werner, who was a campaign press aide, thinks the press was to blame for any failure to completely air the issues. He said reporters were determined to emphasize the angle of a progressive young Democrat against a traditional Republican, and as a result, the press did not pay much attention to what the two candidates were saying. "The most fascinating thing about the campaign of 1974 was that Jerry Brown, if anybody was listening, would not have surprised anyone as governor. But for some reason they didn't listen."

Brown, too, says the media did not pay attention to the content of his speeches. "I think basically the choice was clear between the two candidates. Flournoy was emphasizing his experience, and I was emphasizing activism, more change. . . . And that really was the issue in the gubernatorial campaign. Activism, change, introduction of new ideas, moving an idea from the margin to the center of decision making. Moving it from the public interest magazines or *CoEvolution Quarterly* to the conventional wisdom." Brown maintains that he attempted to raise and discuss issues in 1974 and that he listened to "anyone who had ideas that I thought were helpful. I try to derive information from as many sources as I can," including people he meets, reporters, and others. As a matter of fact, Brown observes in retrospect, "Maybe I might even say that Flournoy was one of my close advisers because I learned from what he was doing."

Brown considers the most important ideas he propounded in 1974 to have been his pledge to hold the line on taxes, a tough approach to fighting crime, the introduction of new people and ideas to state government, and an activist attitude toward the role of the chief executive regardless of what might be happening in the legislature. And as far as he is concerned, "The campaign was a relatively simple one. The main activity was a logistical one, namely, to raise and spend money and to move the campaign from one part of the state to the other and try to hopefully keep on top, and that was all there was to it."

One observer who understood Brown's philosophy was Mary Bergan, a lobbyist for the American Federation of Teachers, who had been assigned to work as a labor representative in the Brown campaign. She said that Brown repeatedly called for reduced class sizes in schools even though "he had no idea what the cost of that was. I mean, I know the cost of that, and I laid it on him one day." She told Brown that to decrease classes by two pupils in the first four grades alone would cost $30 million a year statewide. "I could see him get nervous right away," she said with a laugh. "He blanched. So I knew that when it came to money . . . he was not going to be the big liberal that people had expected, at least those people who equate liberalism with big spending or big programs."

As the campaign progressed, Brown favorably impressed both Jon Kreedman and Ray Fisher. Kreedman, chairman of the board of American City Bank, had thought "it was rather early in his career to undertake that seat" when Brown first mentioned running for governor to him, but "as the campaign went on, I gained more respect for Jerry as a campaigner." Kreedman accompanied Brown to many meetings with businessmen, contributed about $75,000 to the campaign, and raised another $250,000. Fisher, who had practiced law with Brown at Tuttle and Taylor, also traveled with Brown and said that in meetings with business groups—"Houston Flournoy's natural constituency"—Brown "would engage in this incredible display of knowledge about issues. I think we neutralized a number of them" and demonstrated "that it wouldn't be a disaster if he became governor." Brown achieved "just incredible growth" during the campaign, according to Fisher. "I watched him mature."

Like Leavitt, Maullin, who was still participating in the strategy sessions, noticed that "there was a great tendency toward the end of the campaign for Jerry to want to take off on his own and go in his own orbit. You know, he was going to be governor, he was the candidate, and after all, it was what *he* thought that really counted. At the same time, the campaign, which had begun in January as a feeble enterprise, you know, by September it was an institution. And I perceived Jerry wanting to break loose from the direction of his institution, do whatever the hell *he* wanted to do. Well, this led to some fairly severe contests of will between the candidate and the managers. As you can see, when he became governor, Jerry has somewhere in his head a whole agenda of little things that he wants to do to leave his personal mark on anything. And I think he began to feel, as he was getting close to the general election, that he wanted to express himself. And you know, there's a natural conservatism in any institution. We would be saying, 'Look, it's better to be on time and do these four things than to do your trip.' And his reaction was, 'It's better for me to do my trip than just to be an efficient campaigner.' "

One source of disagreement between Maullin and Brown was the value of polls, which Maullin swears by and "Jerry always thought was a lot of crap. We'd find Jerry to be extremely interested whenever we had a poll, but then as soon as he had digested the information, he would just poopoo the idea of the poll's benefit." One reason for Brown's attitude, said Gray Davis, was that Maullin's polls told Brown he was losing his lead but failed to explain the reason.

As November 5 came closer, Brown started manifesting his independence by presenting himself as the head of the Democratic ticket. "The last couple of weeks," Wyler said, "he thought that he could pass some of his ostensible popularity on to other candidates. He started posing as the leader of the ticket, and many of the statements that came about that time, I think, brought about the dropoff in popularity. I think the people resented his urging the other candidates." Maullin believes that Brown became "shrill and insistent" at the end of the campaign "and maybe threatening to some people who were afraid that he might be too radical or too wild or too young." From Quinn's standpoint, "At the tail end of the campaign, he was nervous and tense. I think most candidates get that way." Frank Mesplé, Pat Brown's former aide, observed that the public perceived Brown as being overconfident and resented it. He believes the Brown campaign thought 1974 was going to be a Democratic sweep and started coasting toward the end. "Well, the sweep was there, but he was the lower end of the sweep."

One independent step that Brown took, against the advice of his top campaign aides, was to stop his television advertising for a week. "I intentionally reduced my TV just to save money. I couldn't see the point. I thought the ideas were being communicated, and the TV commercials had been broadcast enough. I didn't really think it would have an impact." At Kreedman's insistence, when the polls showed that Flournoy was making dramatic gains, another $250,000 was allocated for advertisements right before the election.

Maullin, Davis, Kreedman, and Werthman, among others, attribute the Flournoy surge as the race neared the wire more to the effectiveness of Flournoy's campaign than to any potentially decisive mistakes that were made by the Brown forces. Werthman said Flournoy put on a media blitz in the final three weeks that enabled him to narrow the gap. "I saw it falling apart. I called him [Brown] right away. I can't even remember the names of the programs I was watching. It was just Flournoy, Flournoy, Flournoy" advertisements. "Jerry's votes were always soft. Some people couldn't distinguish him from his father. I would say the media was handled very badly in the campaign." Betty Werthman was keeping track of the political commercials on television, "And I never saw Brown" as Election Day neared.

On November 5, Brown outlasted Flournoy, but by only 180,000 votes, or 2.9 percentage points, in the closest gubernatorial election the state had seen in more than fifty years. Brown's slim victory was in sharp contrast to sweeps by Democrats both in California and nationwide. In California, Democrats took all the statewide offices except for attorney general, which was won by the incumbent, Evelle Younger. Democratic Senator Alan Cranston was reelected by a landslide margin of nearly 1.5 million votes and 25 percentage points. The only Democrat who won by a smaller margin than Brown was his running mate, Mervyn Dymally, a veteran legislator who was elected lieutenant governor by 175,000 votes. (California voters can split their ballots for governor and lieutenant governor.)

Around the country, Democrats received 58 percent of the total Congressional vote; won 43 new seats in the House of Representatives in addition to the 248 they already held; increased membership in the Senate from 58 to 61; added 5 governorships to the 31 Democratic governors before the vote; and gained control of an additional 8 state legislatures, to bring the party's total to 36.

In the last few days before the election, Flournoy gained an estimated 1 percent of the vote per day, which *Time* called a "startling rate," while *Newsweek* termed Brown's close win an unimpressive showing over "lackluster opposition."

Despite the narrow victory, Brown's mother feared that being elected governor might go to his head. According to Cranston, who walked on stage with Jerry, Pat, and Bernice Brown at the election-night victory party, as the group approached the podium, Bernice admonished her son, "Humility, Jerry, humility."

Flournoy ascribes Brown's election success to the resignation of Richard Nixon less than three months earlier and to Gerald Ford's pardon of his predecessor within two months of Election Day. "The timing of the pardon was very disadvantageous," said Flournoy. "It really stopped all momentum for a couple of weeks. And we could have used those weeks."

Flournoy said that but for Nixon's resignation, the pardon, and the ex-president's presence at San Clemente as a reminder to Californians, he would have been able to raise more money and begin his television commercials the first week in October instead of a week later. "At the rate we were closing, I think it's fair to assume we might have switched that extra ninety thousand votes" with one additional week of advertisements, said Flournoy. "We'll never know." Scoffs Brown, "Another week of TV, what does another week of TV mean?"

Two Democrats who agree with Flournoy's assessment are Joe Cerrell and John Tunney. "Jerry Brown should just thank God, whether he wants to do it in the Zen fashion or the Catholic fashion, that Jerry Ford pardoned Richard Nixon and that there was Watergate," stated Cerrell. Said Tunney, "I think that's what won for him."

Other observers hold Brown and his staff responsible for his near defeat. "That election was so close that it has to call into question the techniques of the campaign," said Jack Tomlinson. "There was nothing wrong with the candidate. He figured out precisely the right tone, which is that government can only do so much. With that program, if you can call it that, any issue becomes a delightful target." Both Reinhardt and Moretti believe that Brown purposely chose style over substance and that the decision hurt him. The election was "so close that I'm not sure that's such a good strategy," Reinhardt commented, while Moretti said Brown's methods "almost caught up with him in the general" election.

Brown disputes suggestions that he lost a huge lead; he asserted that he never had one and that the polls that showed he did were faulty. "I was much better known than Flournoy, so when the early polls were taken, people just didn't have any awareness of who he was. As the election drew closer, and as he was able to communicate his views and character to the people, the election became closer, much closer. The early polls don't mean very much. That's why I don't think polls are very important."

As to Watergate and the Nixon pardon, Brown holds their effect to be "very hypothetical. I try to have an honest, clear understanding of what facts are, what is speculation, what is an unknown. Certainly the dynamics of an election are not susceptible to precise quantification. It represents the collective and diverse judgments of millions of people, and what motivated them, even if known, could not be stated because there are too many people, and it would involve just as many pieces of paper as there are people. So I don't think you can isolate an event and say the Cuban missile crisis threw Nixon off stride and allowed my father to win the election in 1962. It contributed, but if it wasn't that, it might have been something else. There's any series of events that catapult people forward. I'm not denying there's an impact. I'm just saying the context is sufficiently complex that I would not identify as a cause a single event."

Another factor in Brown's victory may have been public disenchantment because of political scandals, which helped keep the state's voters away from the ballot boxes on election day. In any case, as secretary of state (and governor-elect) Edmund G. Brown, Jr., pointed out in the official summary of the results, "The biggest vote of all last November was a vote of no confidence. More than half of the people who could have voted refused, apparently believing that what takes place in government has so little impact on their lives that they need not pass judgment on it."

According to Brown's figures, there were 14.2 million Californians who could have registered to vote for the November 1974 election. The number of registered voters was 9.9 million, or 64 percent of those who could have registered, and voter turnout was 6.4 million, or 45 percent of the people who were elegible to register and vote. Under this method, the voter-turnout rates in the previous two gubernatorial elections were fifty-four in 1970 and fifty-nine in 1966.

From 1969 until Brown was elected governor, Tom Quinn was his top aide: during the campaign for secretary of state, the years in that office, and the race for governor. Jon Kreedman described Quinn and Richard Maullin as "the driving force. I don't know where that campaign [for governor] would have gone without those two. There is nobody better with the press than Tom."

The 1974 election, however, brought to a close the period when Quinn would be Brown's closest deputy and adviser. Just how Quinn's part came to be diminished is a matter of dispute. Leo Wyler says Brown shunted aside Quinn and Maullin, Quinn in particular, in order to establish his own identity. Brown was "trying to get away from the tutelage of Maullin and Quinn. Basically, he wanted to assert himself. Quinn and Maullin pretty much ran him, and he had trouble asserting himself" when Wyler first met Brown while he was secretary of state. "I think that was something that he let happen until he felt strong enough to establish his own identity."

Several weeks after the election, according to Wyler, he and Warren Christopher, an old friend of Brown who is now a deputy U.S. secretary of state, met with Brown to attempt to persuade him not to go through with his stated intention not to hire Quinn and Maullin in his administration. "It was basically a psycho-analytic meeting" is the way Wyler describes the five-hour session. Wyler said he and Christopher explained to Brown "how we had to find a place" in the administration for Quinn and Maullin, whom Wyler characterized as "the two people who had helped him most," and "the main architects of Jerry's career." During the meeting, Brown was told pointedly that "he would look ungrateful, that it would be a tremendous political mistake just to cut them off." Ultimately, Brown appointed Quinn his special assistant for environmental programs and chairman of the state's Air Resources Board. Maullin was named chairman of the new Energy Resources Conservation and Development Commission, of which Moretti was also named a member.

Quinn has an entirely different version of how and in what

role he came to be a member of the new administration. "I know that's not true," Quinn declared in reference to Wyler's statement that he had to intervene in order to see that Brown hired him and Maullin. "I don't know that he didn't talk to Jerry on my behalf," said Quinn, but "I had actually planned not to come to work in government, and I told Jerry that. He prevailed upon me to change that decision. I was just emotionally torn. I'd had it. I just wanted to get away from government and politics." Quinn also said that he had no desire to be chief of staff in the governor's office because of "the continual demands on your time, the lack of any individual life, the inability to do things on your own or to have some individual sense of accomplishment," and that he informed Brown of these feelings.

Brown agrees that it is "not true" that he did not intend to include Quinn and Maullin in his administration. He does say, however, that he did not consider Quinn for the job of chief of staff because "I thought it would be good for Tom to get into a more substantive role where he could have his own identity and constituency and be able to work in an area that was significant, that was significant to me, and it's turned out that way." The same is true of Maullin, according to Brown.

Quinn's status after the election was seen by the *Sacramento Bee* as a demotion. "Although he was Brown's campaign manager, Quinn found himself in the doghouse even before the campaign was over. After the inauguration, he got a major appointment but was kept out of the inner circle," the *Bee* reported on August 10, 1975.

Quinn was not much involved in Brown's bid for president in 1976 because he disagreed with Brown's decision to enter the race that year. At Brown's insistence, though, Quinn reluctantly agreed to join Jimmy Carter's California campaign for the last few weeks before the November election. "I didn't want to get involved in the Carter campaign," Quinn said. "Jerry really wanted me to, so I did. I think they just wanted me there as a sort of symbolic gesture of Jerry Brown's commitment to the cause, which is one of the reasons I really didn't want to do it."

After Carter was elected president, in spite of his narrow loss in California, Quinn expressed interest in being appointed head of the federal Environmental Protection Agency (EPA). According to one source, Quinn was willing to sever his ties to Brown in order to obtain the post, and he assured Carter people, who were hostile toward Brown, that he would not be Brown's spy in Washington if he were given the job. Quinn takes issue with that: "If I were working for Jimmy Carter, I'd be loyal, but I would remain friends with Jerry Brown. I have a great deal of respect for Jerry. And I don't think I'd put myself in a position where I'd want to choose up sides, do something to damage Jerry."

Quinn doubts that his relationship with Brown was an advantage when he was under consideration for the EPA job, which ultimately he did not get. "I just don't think there was any way that Carter was going to pick anybody who was close to Brown for an important role."

Quinn also said he believes Carter wanted someone for EPA who would be more acceptable to the business community. Business leaders in California have been displeased with many of Quinn's actions as head of the Air Resources Board, notably his lack of enthusiasm for a proposed $500-million oil terminal at Long Beach. In July 1977, two members of Congress from Long Beach went so far as to urge Brown to remove Quinn from control of the planned structure.

Quinn says he might run for office in the future, but that if he does, the only jobs that would interest him are governor, mayor of Los Angeles, and perhaps a seat in the U.S. Senate. If Quinn ever does seek office, he might make a formidable candidate. Politics in this era, at least in California, is television; Quinn understands the medium and how to use it. And the favorable impression Quinn has made on people such as Leavitt and Wyler, who calls Quinn "a very spectacular young man," can be translated into money in the campaign bank account come election time.

To take Quinn's place as his chief assistant, Brown picked Gray Davis, who was then thirty-two, two years older than Quinn. Midway through the two-month period between the election and the inauguration, Brown asked Davis what job he would like to have, and Davis said he would like to head the Department of Consumer Affairs. Brown's reaction, according to Davis, was: "I don't think that would be a challenge. You could do that. I think you ought to try executive secretary."

Davis had first met Brown at a labor luncheon in the San Fernando Valley in the fall of 1973, when Davis was running against Jesse Unruh for state treasurer, Brown for governor, in the primaries. Brown arrived driving himself in a gray sedan, which continued to run "for at least a minute after he turned it off, and it smoked," said Davis. "That was not the image I had of the front runner for governor." Although the group Brown and Davis were addressing was openly pro-Alioto, Brown managed to win several standing ovations and to impress Davis by his self-confidence in an unfriendly situation.

The paths of the two men crossed periodically during the next few months on the campaign trail. "I think there was a mutual empathy," said Davis, who was then an aide to Los Angeles Mayor Tom Bradley. "Both of us were called too young, too ambitious, too inexperienced. You tend to resort to the same defense mechanisms. Your handshake is a little firmer, your walk a little more brisk. And I think we sensed that about one another."

And so within a few months of meeting Brown, Davis emerged as his closest aide as he entered the challenging new office of governor.

CHAPTER FIVE

FORGING A
FARM LABOR PEACE

In his inaugural address on January 6, 1975, Jerry Brown, who had become familiar with the hard work of picking grapes while he was a seminarian, told his audience, which included the members of the legislature:

"This year I hope you'll give the governor another chance to sign an appropriate bill, including farm workers within the protection of unemployment insurance. I also believe it is time to extend the rule of law to the agriculture sector and establish the right of secret ballot elections for farm workers. The law I support will impose rights and responsibilities on both farm workers and farmer alike, and I expect that an appropriate bill that serves all the people will not fully satisfy any of the parties to the dispute, but that's no reason not to pass it."

Five months later, on June 5, 1975, Brown signed into law a bill that guaranteed the state's 250,000 agricultural workers the right to decide in secret elections whether or not they wanted to be represented by a union, and, if so, which union. The Agricultural Labor Relations Act (ALRA) that was put together by Brown and his aides was the first of its kind in the nation and has been hailed by Brown's friends and foes alike as the major achievement of his term as governor.

Brown himself is not sure the Farm Labor bill has been his greatest success as governor. "I don't think it's possible to know what is the greatest accomplishment or what that term means," he says, "because what's the measure—the effect on the happiness of human beings, the changes in the ways society operates, the number of people or families that are positively affected, the amount of discussion and thought that a particular initiative engenders? I'm reluctant to identify one particular measure as being numerically or quantitatively the greatest, whatever that might mean.

"All that can be said about the farm law is that it was a problem that had festered for a long time, that I acted quickly, that the parties were brought together, that it has had an impact in the fields, that it's given workers rights they hadn't had before, and that it will have an impact on the lives of a group of people who had been left out of the mainstream."

Aside from Brown, the bill's chief architect within the governor's office was Secretary of Agriculture and Services Rose Elizabeth Bird, whose interest in farm laborers dated back to her girlhood on Long Island when she wrote her high-school thesis on migrant workers in New York State. Bird; Paul Halvonik, assistant to the governor for legislative affairs; and the governor's director of administration, LeRoy Chatfield, a former leader of the United Farm Workers (UFW), talked to the various sides in the farm labor dispute—such as the UFW, the Teamsters, who were battling the UFW for recognition by the field laborers, and the growers—and found out exactly what each group wanted.

Once they had that information, the negotiators sat down with Brown; Assemblyman Howard Berman, a former labor lawyer who would sponsor the ALRA in the lower house of the legislature; and Stephen Reinhardt, the Los Angeles labor lawyer who had been called to Sacramento by Brown to assist with the drafting of the legislation. The leader of the group throughout the process was Brown, who "participated fully in (resolution) of difficult and technical labor problems, and he did it as ably as the experts," according to Reinhardt.

Then Brown initiated his own form of shuttle diplomacy, moving among the various parties who were in separate rooms in the Capitol and hammering out a compromise on each part of the complex bill. Berman, whose office wall is adorned with a copy of the final version, inscribed "Howard—an historic step forward in democracy" and signed by Brown, said that "the basic focus" was to bring the warring groups together "and then to present them with a negotiated package and basically take away the major lobbying forces that would work against that kind of a proposal were it not a negotiated package." Brown "was brilliant," he added. He doesn't feel the ALRA could have been drafted and enacted without Brown's work. Reinhardt said that representatives of the factions who worked with Brown during the marathon negotiations which often lasted most of the night, were "somewhat dazzled by his performance because they had some regrets afterward" about what they had conceded.

All parties got the best they thought they could, said Chatfield. "The only condition that they had was that nothing could be changed. In other words if they agreed to it, not a comma, not a word, nothing" could be amended. "Because that's one of the problems with legislation. People sign on to it, and then it starts making its way through the process, and this amendment gets put on, this one gets taken out, and then, you see, they're stuck. I'll bet you it's one of the first times in history in this state that any bill has gone through the legislature—from introduction it went through eight committees over a two-month period—and nothing was changed."

Chatfield said that from the UFW standpoint, "I honestly thought it was something they could live with and be successful in organizing the farm workers. By no stretch of the imagination did they get what they wanted." The provision for secret ballot elections "was the guts of the thing, and who could tell in advance how people are going to vote? You just don't know. An agreement was hammered out that everyone felt they could live with and profit from, be they growers, farm workers, Teamsters, whatever."

Said Bird, "I think it brought about a lot of resentment within the legislature because it was not in any way, shape, or form their product. The governor may have in some ways had to pay heavily for that fact. They had tried for years and years to bring about some kind of resolution and never had been able to do it.

So I think after the bill went through, and he reaped so much praise for it, there was some envy there."

"I don't think Rose Bird was an asset of his," said State Senator George Zenovich (D, Fresno), a leader of the farm bloc in the legislature. Zenovich, a tall, husky, dark man of Slavic descent who was a professional musician before he became a lawyer and then was elected to the legislature in 1962, said Bird "left a lot of people sort of turned off. She was very persistent in her on beliefs with respect to whatever she felt. I can still remember her precise words to me when we were going through the farm labor thing, that any change during the legislative process would kill the bill. I mean, in fifteen years around here, I've never heard that from anyone."

Yet, Zenovich admitted with grudging admiration, the fact that "they managed to get that bill out of these two houses without any change at all" was "a fantastic coup" for Brown. "It was really a work of art the way he handled that whole thing" even though it was "a total preemption of the legislative process."

Zenovich is of the opinion that the growers yielded more than the labor groups, particularly the UFW, for whom the secret-elections clause was the *sine qua non*. The farmers were in a vulnerable position at the time because they were feeling the effects of the nationwide boycott on buying nonunion farm products that Cesar Chavez had called on behalf of the UFW, Zenovich said. "The union housewife back East is much more sophisticated. She does look for a label. If there's no label, no union bug, on it, she won't buy. It doesn't matter whether it's a Teamster or UFW label."

Assemblyman Willie Brown (D, San Francisco) considers Governor Brown's method of creating the ALRA a "corruption" of "what the legislative process shall be. He put the farm labor bill together before it was introduced and announced that there would be no amendments to it except those which he approved. Now if *that* isn't messing with the legislative process, I don't know what is. Ordinarily, the executive would just submit his program and leave it to the legislature's will without any further interference to do as they deem appropriate.

"That agreement should never have been hammered out outside of the legislature. That's constitutionally what we're supposed to be doing, in open public hearings." He went on, raising his voice, "You know, suppose you and I got together and did a private number. We'd probably be prosecuted. Yet Jerry Brown did that in open plain view of everybody and told everybody he was doing it."

Rose Bird's response to such criticism is: "The legislative process is a very difficult one in which to get warring groups together because they have to, in an open forum, take positions that they don't necessarily really believe in, but they have to articulate them for their followers. So a legislative committee is not the best forum in which to try to bring about a compromise."

Describing what happened after the package was put together, Berman said: "It was not that difficult a job to get it through the legislature." Getting all the parties to reach agreement set a national precedent that generated a tremendous ground swell of support, so that "an opposing legislator would be run over by that kind of momentum."

In announcing that the ALRA would be introduced in the legislature on April 10, Governor Brown had voiced the hope that the bill "will commend itself to the people of this state, perhaps even of this country" and said he had talked about the proposed legislation with AFL-CIO head George Meany.

When he signed the ALRA June 5, Brown hailed the new law as one that "provides the framework so that people who have to stoop over and do the labor have the same bargaining rights and the same dignity as management and those who own the farms."

In late July, when Brown appointed the five members to the Agricultural Labor Relations Board (ALRB) that was created by the bill to oversee farm worker elections, the fragile coalition that had made possible passage of the bill started to fall apart. Growers, who expected Brown to name members who would be impartial, felt betrayed when three of the appointees turned out to be ex-UFW leader Chatfield; Joe C. Ortega, an activist Chicano lawyer; and Catholic Bishop Roger Mahony of Fresno, who had been secretary of a church committee on farm labor and was known as a friend of the UFW. Mahony was named chairman of the new board.

Senator Zenovich had offered to give Brown advice when the list of potential nominees to the board had been narrowed down to fifteen or twenty. However, Brown never consulted with Zenovich, "and when I found out it was Mahony, I couldn't believe it."

Said Houston Flournoy, "It was just abject bad faith or sheer insensitivity" on Brown's part to expect the farmers to accept the appointments of Chatfield, Mahony and Ortega. Furthermore, said Flournoy, the appointments caused the ALRB to be "blown out of the water right after he signed" the law. Flournoy gave Brown credit that "it was a feat of no small magnitude to get any kind of Agricultural Labor Relations bill passed at all," but he considers it Brown's only significant achievement during his term as governor.

Another critical view was expressed by former Republican State Senator Howard Way, who had been a farmer before his election to the senate in 1962 and, like Zenovich, was a leading spokesman for the agribusiness community. Way retired from the Senate at the end of 1976 and was named by Brown as head of the Adult Authority, which oversees the release of inmates from state prisons. Gratitude for the new job, which pays $31,500 a year, did not stop Way from recalling that Brown had "assured us he would appoint an impartial board, and then he loaded that board up with people who just could not be objective."

Brown felt the board "was balanced." He said he thought that the parties to the farm labor dispute would perceive Chatfield and Ortega as representing the interests of the farm workers; Richard Johnsen, Jr., executive vice president of the California Agriculture Council, and Joseph R. Grodin, a labor law professor, as being representatives of the farmers; and Mahony as being the impartial swing vote. "I didn't see that Bishop Mahony was as much of a polarizing force as he [turned out to be]. I didn't know him that well. His image in the farming community was more pro-UFW than I understood.

"I wanted to make sure that the board worked," Brown added, "and I felt it was important to have a board that all sides would have some confidence in, but particularly the Farm Workers. It's one of those situations that it is very difficult to reach a point of equilibrium."

The farm labor act went into effect on August 28, 1975, and the original $1.3 million that was appropriated to fund it was used up three months later. The State Department of Finance loaned the board another $1.2 million to allow it to continue in operation, but representatives of the farm bloc in the legislature, unhappy with Brown's appointments and with some of the board's rulings, managed to stop any additional funding for the board, which ran out of money and was forced to cease operation on February 6, 1976. Additional outlays for the ALRB required a two-thirds majority in each house of the legislature, and Brown's proposal that another $2.5 million be spent to fund it for the rest of the 1975–76 fiscal year received a majority vote in each house but not the two-thirds that was needed.

Of the 359 elections that were conducted by the ALRB during its first five months in existence, the UFW won 195, the Teamsters 120, other unions 19, and no union got a majority vote in 25 of the elections.

Cesar Chavez called the shutdown of the board "a day of infamy for the farm worker." Soon after the loss of funding put the board out of business, a ruling by the state supreme court that was favorable to the unions attempting to organize farm workers did little to improve the growers' attitude. The court upheld an ALRB edict that union representatives should be allowed access to growers' property to talk to the workers for an hour before work, an hour at lunchtime, and an hour after work. That holding by the California Supreme Court was allowed to stand when the U.S. Supreme Court declined to take jurisdiction over the case in October 1976.

Without funding, the ALRB languished, and three of the five board members resigned, including Chatfield, who joined Brown's presidential campaign and later returned to the governor's staff. The board remained in limbo, while Brown spent most of his time on the campaign trail outside the state. An editorial in the *Los Angeles Times* on April 21, 1976, called on him "to resolve the conflict in California's largest industry. It would require nothing more of him than prompt action to fill the three vacancies that now exist on the five-member board" with people "whom all parties perceived to be at least neutral."

On June 20, 1976, after the board had been inactive for almost five months and while the legislature had the 1976–77 state budget under final consideration, Brown acted to end the crisis by naming three new board members, including as Chairman Gerald A. Brown of Austin, Texas (no relation to Governor Brown), a former member of the National Labor Relations Board. The legislature responded by including $6.8 million in the budget to fund the board during 1976–77.

Meanwhile, the UFW had gathered more than twice the

number of signatures required to place an initiative similar to the Agricultural Labor Relations Act on the November 1976 ballot. The initiative, known as Proposition 14, quickly became the most controversial issue before the voters. Passage of Proposition 14 would mean that the law could not be changed except by another vote of the people and that "a handful of legislators representing special interests could never again" use "political blackmail" to "demand amendments as a condition of funding," Chatfield wrote in an article in the *Los Angeles Times* on October 24, 1976. Chatfield, who was on leave from Brown's office to work for passage of Proposition 14, added:

> For over three months, Governor Brown sought a special appropriation to allow the board to resume its work. When it became clear that his efforts were futile, supporters of farm workers' rights gathered more than 700,000 signatures of California voters to place the initiative on the November ballot. Only then did a few rural legislators who had steadily opposed funding vote to give the ALRB money for the 1976–77 fiscal year. Without the threat of Proposition 14, the ALRB would still be out of business.

Chatfield's written statements were similar to those made by Brown in voicing his support for Proposition 14 at a September 3, 1976, press conference:

"It was only after the qualification of Proposition 14 that the money became available for financing the farm labor law." Furthermore, Brown declared, "Proposition 14 is the rule of law that will permit a quasijudicial body, the farm labor board, to render justice outside the politics and the blackmail of the budget process, which will only undermine its credibility and authority."

And in an interview with the *Sacramento Union* published two weeks later Brown said:

> Right now every time they [the ALRB] turn around it becomes a matter of political, and legislative debate. If the PUC [Public Utilities Commission] makes a rate increase you don't take away their money for it. If the Supreme Court makes a decision you don't like, you don't try to second guess it

by taking away their money. And I think that's what happened in this case.

Brown's endorsement of Proposition 14 was made in the face of contrary advice from such people as Richard Maullin, one of his key political strategists during the secretary of state years; Speaker of the Assembly Leo McCarthy, Brown's number-one ally in the legislature; and Senator George Zenovich, who understood the feelings of people in the state's farm belt. McCarthy said he also warned Brown that their close working relationship would be jeopardized if Proposition 14 cost Democrats any seats in the legislature. Fortunately for Brown, the initiative did not hurt in state legislative races; in fact, Democrats made their best showing in history in the assembly, winning fifty-seven of the eighty seats.

Most liberal politicians praised Brown's stance, although both Democrats and Republicans from farm areas were critical. According to a story in the *Sacramento Bee* on September 4, 1976, Assemblyman John Thurman (D, Modesto), chairman of the Assembly Agriculture Committee, called Brown "damn flaky" and "very, very dishonest" for backing Proposition 14. "Thurman, a dairy farmer who previously welcomed Brown's assistance on the campaign trail, said that if the governor comes to his area this fall, 'when he's in Stanislaus [County], I'll be in Merced, and when he's in Merced, I'll be in Stanislaus.' "

In spite of endorsements from Brown, Jimmy Carter, and Senators Alan Cranston and John Tunney, Proposition 14 went down to an overwhelming defeat, with 4.8 million no votes (62 percent) to 2.9 million for (38 percent). Many observers blame the Proposition 14 backlash for Carter's loss of California by 140,000 votes to President Ford, as well as for Tunney's defeat by former San Francisco State University President S. I. Hayakawa by 250,000 votes.

Zenovich said he had polls taken after the Democratic Convention that showed Carter could beat either Ford or Reagan in the Fresno area by three to one, but that after Carter endorsed Proposition 14, those poll results were reversed.

To Tunney, in 1977 a lawyer in private practice in Los Angeles, there was "no question" but that he would have won had it not been for Proposition 14. "It was a losing issue for me either way," he said. "I would have preferred not to take a position."

Tunney said he told Brown and Carter he would not endorse Proposition 14 unless both of them did. He added that he did not try to dissuade them from endorsing it, but that once they decided to back the proposition, he felt he had to do so as well or risk losing many Democratic votes.

Nevertheless, Tunney expressed no ill will toward Brown, whom he regards as responsible for persuading both him and Carter to support Proposition 14. "People of your own party may have different fish to fry than you have," said Tunney. "I've always felt that Jerry had good reason to do what he did. I can't possibly blame Brown for what happened to me."

But Tunney cannot get rid of the opinion that Proposition 14 "was a state issue. It had absolutely nothing to do with the federal government. It was a completely meaningless issue, and yet it defeated Carter, and it defeated me in this state."

Sharing similar sentiments is Senator James Mills (D, San Diego), the President Pro Tempore or highest-ranking member of the State Senate. Mills, who has been in touch with some of President Carter's top aides, said, "I think there's concern in the Carter camp that Jerry Brown talked President Carter into supporting the farm-labor initiative when he shouldn't have done it.

"I think it clearly cost him California. The interesting thing was that I supported the proposition and the Speaker [McCarthy] opposed it, and we were both of the opinion that the presidential nominee should have nothing to do with it."

But Cranston remarked, "It was a calculated decision by both [Carter and Tunney]. They both knew what they were doing when they did it." He doubts if the endorsement caused either Carter or Tunney to lose in California because the votes they lost among conservatives were offset by votes the two candidates picked up from liberal activists who had reservations about them.

Said McCarthy: "I couldn't support that kind of initiative in *any* area of the law. That's absurd on its face. The members of the legislature are elected by the people of the state. They have public committee hearings where the public can participate, and to require a public initiative in the future to amend a complex labor law was a very stupid kind of suggestion. I thought it was an insult to the legislature . . . and to the entire process, which I happen to believe in very deeply." Furthermore, McCarthy

declared, there was no need for "radical surgery" unless the
ALRB had a history of several years of failure. McCarthy had
been instrumental in the drive to get the Agricultural Labor
Relations Act through the legislature in 1975 and in the fight to
win funding for the ALRB in the spring of 1976.

Brown said that he did not want Chavez to place Proposition
14 on the ballot. "My preference would be not to have had it on
the ballot, yes. Because I didn't think it was necessary. That was
an unnecessary polarization."

In Brown's opinion, "The funding [for the ALRB starting with
the 1976–77 fiscal year] came only as a result of the initiative,"
but having accomplished that much, Chavez should not have
proceeded farther. But Brown said he understands why Chavez
"felt that he had to go through with it to maintain the credibility
of his own commitment. If you're not willing to stand up for
something and make a strong case, then the next time people will
be tempted to push you instead of pull back."

In spite of his own reservations, Brown decided not only to
endorse Proposition 14 publicly, but to campaign for it after he
heard Chavez's arguments. By way of explanation, Brown later
said, "I felt in view of my past efforts on behalf of the farm labor
law there was no legitimate position of neutrality or tepidity that
I could accept. So I went out with full force." Back during his
days at Berkeley, Brown had slept on the floor of a church in
Stockton and then gone out with the workers to pick strawberries
the next morning, before Chavez joined the movement. He had
also marched to the Mexican border with Chavez and the UFW
to illustrate the plight of field workers.

As for any relation between Proposition 14's overwhelming
defeat and its impact on the Carter and Tunney campaigns,
Brown said that as a general rule, "I don't like to say what caused
what. I don't think any human mind can know that." He added,
"If an election is close, you can attribute the loss of a state to
anything." Brown said that in talks with Carter, "I communicated to him the significance of fourteen, told him he should
think about it long and hard. We talked about it, but I generally
hesitate to tell a person what he should do if it's his career and
his campaign that's on the line."

In regard to the initiative's effect on his own career, Brown
commented, "I'm reasonably optimistic about the future. I think
fourteen has had a diverse impact on my relationship with the

people of California," and that the impact is not necessarily either negative or positive. But, Brown said, "I learned from that [the Proposition 14 experience]. I learned of the limits of my ability to persuade when an issue goes against the grain of the majority of the people."

At least one columnist thought Brown's career suffered as a result of his support for Proposition 14. Gil Bailey of the *San Jose Mercury* wrote on December 2, 1976, under the headline, "Jerry's in Trouble," that many California politicians "feel he [Brown] has lost a lot of clout because of the defeat of Proposition 14, which he strongly supported. 'Jerry Brown lost the election and Leo McCarthy won it,' " said one unidentified campaign worker.

Chatfield thinks Proposition 14 was doomed once the growers were able to define the issue in terms of trespassing on private property. The growers' advertisements against the initiative stressed that union organizers would be allowed to enter the farmers' land to talk to the workers if the measure passed. Brown agrees that "the importance of private property in the minds of people in the state" hurt Proposition 14's chances for passage. "I think private property is an important value, and linked very closely to it is privacy. And the two are in effect legally and intellectually protected zones where the individual can flourish and maintain his or her own identity. And that's a value that is important. It is not lightly tampered with."

Gray Davis, Brown's top aide, said he and Brown "were hopeful that we could resolve the problem through the legislative process. We certainly did not encourage any of the parties to go to the initiative process." But, he added, once Chavez was committed to putting the referendum on the ballot, "Nobody pushed him [Brown] harder to support Proposition fourteen than I did. I claim responsibility for that 24-point loss. I felt we had an obligation to see it through."

Davis is extremely critical of the legislators who held up funding for the ALRB after creation of the board had been debated during lengthy hearings in each house of the legislature. "Their remedy had passed, in essence. I felt they were fighting in an inappropriate forum. It's almost unheard of around here to relitigate a question."

The ALRB continues to function, and in April 1977, the UFW and the Teamsters Union reached an accord that gives the UFW jurisdiction over all field wokers in thirteen western states. By 1979, the two unions will try to reach agreement on the organizing of farm workers in the rest of the country.

In addition, the California legislature approved a law that extended unemployment insurance to farm laborers in September 1975, eight months after Brown had called for such legislation in his inaugural address. Similar bills had been passed four times in the previous five years but were vetoed by Ronald Reagan.

Brown's advocacy of the farm workers' cause may well have repercussions in his future campaigns. Within a year after the defeat of Proposition 14, growers had collected more than a half million dollars to help finance the campaign of Assemblyman Ken Maddy of Fresno, a candidate for the Republican gubernatorial nomination opposite Brown in 1978. Furthermore, if Brown seeks the presidency again, his pro-UFW position will be a handicap in such states as Florida and Texas, places in which Brown's candidacy might not be so favorably received in any event. Many farm workers do not stay in one location long enough to become registered voters, and of course the field laborers do not have nearly as much money to give to political campaigns as the farmers do. In future elections, the farm workers' clout will be far smaller than that of the growers and their allies, who can be expected to oppose Brown with their ballots and their dollars.

CHAPTER SIX

THE PERSONAL
JERRY BROWN

"Jerry guards his personal life like other people guard their fortunes," said Marc Poché in explaining why Brown pays the rent on his apartment rather than living in the Governor's Mansion or using part of the $15,000 a year the state allocates to lease a residence for its chief executive. Poché said that by paying the rent—$250 a month when Brown became governor and since raised to $275 a month by the landlord, the state of California—out of his pocket, the governor feels he denies the public the right to intrude in his home.

Brown's efforts to retain his privacy are successful only insofar as his celebrity status permits. He is more accessible to the public than are most other people in comparable positions because he travels on scheduled airlines—tourist class at that—and because, being a bachelor who does not like to cook, he eats most of his meals in restaurants. Strangers can, and frequently do, come up to him and chat. One advantage of his favorite eatery, Lucy's El

Adobe, a Mexican restaurant in Los Angeles, is that it is across the street from Paramount Studios, and many of the patrons are fellow celebrities who respect Brown's privacy to the same extent they value their own.

Not long after Brown was elected governor, his friends Carl and Betty Werthman suggested that he go away for a solitary vacation. Recognizing the tradeoff inherent in becoming a public figure, he replied: "I'll never be able to do that again. That's all over." On the eve of his inauguration as governor, Brown watched Senator Alan Cranston stroll near the Capitol, and according to Cranston, "He said, 'Damn it, if Alan can just wander around like that, I can, too.'" But Father William Perkins says the lot of a politician is "such a horrible life. And he [Brown] knows it. We've talked about that."

Jacques Barzaghi, who may be Brown's closest friend since he became governor, observed with his French accent, "If I think about Jerry Brown and only think about his personal life, I would say, 'Okay, you know what it is, you did it for four years, why don't you go on vacation.' Now if I think about me and my wife and my kids and the people who depend on somehow, somewhere, good or bad politicians, I mean, there is no doubt in my mind, I say, 'Jerry Brown, I am sorry for your personal life, but stick to it.' The way that man work, I don't see any time for personal life. I think the word servant of the people is almost too pompous, but yes, that's what it is."

Although Brown puts in huge chunks of time at his job—twelve- and fourteen-hour days, six and seven days a week—the pace is not unpleasant for him because he enjoys what he is doing. He says that although he occasionally swims in the ocean or goes into the mountains for relaxation, "I spend a lot of time just doing what I'm doing. It's fairly diverse. There's opportunity to keep interested."

Brown's apartment is one of two on the top floor of a fifty-year-old building at 1400 N Street, a walk equal to about three blocks through a park to his office in the Capitol. There is no public access to Brown's floor, and the apartment next to his, which is kept vacant for security reasons, is at his disposal.

Very few people have seen the inside of Brown's apartment. Among those who have never been in it is his sister, Barbara, who has lived in Sacramento for many years, including the whole time Brown has been in office. "What he does is his thing, and what I do is my thing," declares Barbara Brown Casey, adding that because of the difference in their ages, she and her brother have never been close. On being informed that a Japanese restaurant near the Capitol where she is considering eating is one of Jerry Brown's favorite dining spots, his sister expresses doubt that he would recognize her if they were to encounter each other.

Scarcely a feature story is written about Brown that fails to mention what a nationally syndicated Newspaper Enterprise Association article on April 16, 1976, referred to as his "small, spare apartment." It is true that he declined to live in the $1.5 million Governor's Mansion, which was commissioned by Ronald Reagan but was not completed until Jerry Brown took office and has never been inhabited. However, Brown's apartment is anything but modest. It contains about 1,500 square feet, with two bedrooms, two baths, a large living room with a fireplace, and a formal dining room. Although it is of little concern to Brown, his apartment also has a kitchen; he stated on the nationally televised Phil Donahue show on May 3, 1977, that "I have a very low utility bill. I have not cooked anything since I moved in."

The building at 1400 N is one of Sacramento's finest residences, a sturdily built structure with walls eighteen inches thick that allow the tenants to live there without air conditioning in spite of the area's sweltering summers. To set an example for development of solar energy, Brown persuaded the state in late 1977 to install a system that uses the sun to heat the building's water. Over the years, 1400 N has been the home of some of Sacramento's leading citizens, and a wealthy business executive had to be displaced to make room for Brown when he selected his living quarters. Among his eight neighbors in the building are a member of the assembly, legislative aides, and at least one lobbyist.

Brown's well-publicized low rent simply reflects the fact that 1400 N Street is located in Sacramento and not in San Francisco, Los Angeles, or Manhattan, where his apartment would cost several times what it does. The California state capital is a pleasant city of 250,000, but the only thing that distinguishes it from Fresno, Stockton, Bakersfield, and dozens of other small cities in the Central Valley is the presence of the government offices. To see housing costs in Sacramento in flat dollar terms is like applying the same standard in Albany, N.Y., or any other state capital that is not a large city.

What does set Brown's Sacramento residence apart is its location and furnishings; 1400 N Street is by far the most luxurious building in an area of mostly rundown or rehabilitated housing for people of diverse social, economic, and ethnic backgrounds. Most of the professionals who live in Brown's neighborhood do so for the same reason he does: to have an easy walk to the Capitol and the surrounding state office buildings. Brown's apartment house is the only structure left on an entire square block that was acquired by the state in 1966 as the possible site for a new Governor's Mansion. The remainder of the block is now used as a parking lot for state employees.

A few blocks from 14th and N Streets, at 16th and H, is the old Governor's Mansion, which has been vacant for the last decade and is now a state historical landmark. Pat Brown was the last governor to live there full time; Ronald Reagan lived in the old mansion briefly at the start of his term in 1967. Midway between where Pat Brown and his family once lived and 1400 N Street, within about three blocks of Jerry Brown's apartment, prostitutes walk the street, openly soliciting business. A short distance in the other direction, at 1725 P Street, is the house in which Charles Manson follower Lynette (Squeaky) Fromme shared an attic apartment with Sandra Good until September 5, 1975, when Fromme tried to assassinate President Ford as he walked through Capitol Park between Brown's apartment and the Capitol. Ironically, Ford was in Sacramento that day only because Brown, in a typical break with tradition, had refused to give the customary governor's welcome to an annual meeting of state business leaders. The corporate executives, stung when Brown turned down their invitation, had responded by asking Ford to appear in his place.

Inside, Brown's apartment contains what his former press aide, David Jensen, described as "pretty average" furniture, which has been used before in other state-owned apartments. The cooking and eating utensils, which turned out to be unnecessary, had previously been used by Reagan.

The most notorious feature of Brown's apartment is his bed, which consists of a mattress on a box spring that rests on the floor without a bed frame. Frequent references in the news media to Brown's sleeping arrangements finally drove him to comment at a press conference on September 26, 1975, "I don't know how you describe it, but the mattress is on a box [spring], and the box is on the floor. . . . I am not much of a furniture analyst, but it's appropriate . . . it's appropriate for the need, I'll tell you that. I get enough sleep at night." Perhaps even more widely publicized was the bed's effect on Queenell Cournelious, a state-employed maid who hurt her back while bending over to tidy it up. Cournelious remarked at the time that she had been making governors' beds for eight years, and she had never had any trouble preparing Governor Reagan's bed, which stood on a frame with legs.

Brown owns a comfortable home in Laurel Canyon in the Hollywood Hills, although he spends very little time there. With the exception of that home and a house at Malibu Beach that he rented briefly while he was running for secretary of state, Brown's apartment in Sacramento is probably the most luxurious residence that he has occupied since he graduated from high school and went off to Santa Clara University. The furnishings, though, are much more in keeping with the standards Brown has maintained since he left the family home in San Francisco. As Brown told William F. Buckley during an October 11, 1975, appearance on "Firing Line," "I try to live the way I've always lived, which is in some sense impossible in the job I have. But a simpler view of life is coming upon us. I have no doubt about that. The accumulation of possessions and material indulgence is impossible over time because of the ecological limits imposed on this planet."

"The way I've always lived" has been with little regard for material needs. "Jerry wasn't the tidiest roommate," said Frank Damrell, who shared a dormitory room with him at Santa Clara. "Jerry has very minimal needs today, and he did then, in terms of creature comforts." From Santa Clara, Brown went on to the seminary and then to Berkeley, where James Straukamp visited him and found him "living in these awful digs. This Berkeley situation, it was really a hovel, and here's Jerry living very happily, where he could have had a lot more. But it didn't bother him."

After Berkeley, there was a dormitory at Yale for three years and then back to the San Francisco area for his clerkship with Justice Tobriner. At first, Brown lived in Sausalito, and accord-

ing to his friend Paul Halvonik, "All he had in his apartment was
a bed on the floor. That was it, that was his furnishing." After
Tony Kline arrived, he and Brown shared an apartment in
Berkeley in an old Victorian house, since demolished, for which
the rent was forty-five dollars a month each. Damrell, who also
lived in Berkeley at the time, said, "Tony was a very meticulous
guy. God, he was always bitching and moaning that Jerry was
never keeping things organized." Baxter Rice spent two weeks in
Berkeley at that time and stayed in Brown's apartment, "if you
want to call it that. It was a jerry-rigged room. I wouldn't even
call it austere. I would have to call it unattended." Then Brown
moved to Los Angeles, to the apartment that Peter Finnegan
called a "shithole" in the building that Ken Reich described as
"very ramshackle." After Brown was elected secretary of state he
accepted an offer to stay in Straukamp's apartment in Sacramento for a short period until he could find a place of his own.
The brief stay turned out to be two months. "What it comes
down to," said Straukamp, "is that he's just not interested in
going out and finding an apartment and outfitting it."

In reference to the Berkeley apartment where he visited
Brown, Rice said there was "no sense of sloppiness. No sense of
anything other than it was a place to sleep, and that was about it.
Jerry has never, never struck me, from the youngest time that I
can remember him until now, as one who really had any kind of
attachment to any kinds of material things. It is an obliviousness.
If it's a chair, you sit on it. If it's a car, you drive it. It's not
whether it's a Chevy or whether it's a Rolls. If it gets you from
point A to point B, and it serves its purpose, and it doesn't
aggravate you—he's not going to sit on a bed of nails—but if it
serves its purpose, that's fine."

In fact, Brown has not owned a car since he became secretary
of state, and those automobiles he did possess were Chevrolets
and similar vehicles. "He doesn't like luxury in any shape or
form. I don't know why," says his mother.

Brown remarked, "I feel I had a reasonably fortunate background. But my parents have led relatively simple lives. I don't
think I come from a family of big spenders. We didn't go out to
dinner a lot, and we didn't buy a lot of things. Items seemed to be
carefully measured. That's just the way I was brought up."
Brown added that his parents started with very little. "My father
was poor. So was my mother. They watched their nickels, that's

true. My mother took the streetcar to Berkeley" when she was in college. "My father took the streetcar to work."

Pat Brown has been a successful lawyer, and he and his wife have adjusted their style of living. The house where Jerry Brown grew up in San Francisco, where his sister Cynthia and her family now live, is in a neighborhood of $200,000 homes. And Pat and Bernice Brown reside in a large house in the Benedict Canyon section above Beverly Hills with a swimming pool and a spectacular view down into Century City.

Says Jerry Brown, "I have a reasonably nice home [the one in Laurel Canyon], and I get a pretty decent salary [although not nearly as much as he could be making as an attorney]. I'm not complaining. So I'm fairly well taken care of, but I do think that the income disparities and the excessive consumption should be tempered. That's an important idea that has to be communicated." He says he tries to set an example by the way he lives.

The most conspicuous part of Brown's modest life style is his refusal to live in the new Governor's Mansion, a 12,000-square-foot structure with eight bedrooms and eight baths. The mansion is located on seven acres overlooking the American River, fifteen miles east of the Capitol. According to Brown, he saves the state about $400,000 a year in furnishings, maintenance, security, and other expenses by not living in the mansion, which, as Brown put it at a press conference on January 21, 1975, "will save enough money to build a new mansion if the next governor would care to have two of them instead of just the one we have now." On another occasion, during an interview with the *Sacramento Union* on September 19, 1976, Brown quipped, "My father suggested that it ought to be a home for retired governors. He and Reagan could alternate. Six months each year." But in general Brown has referred disparagingly to the new mansion as a "Taj Mahal" that is a waste of the taxpayers' money and would require a waste of his time in commuting back and forth. As Tony Kline says, "He's always been uncomfortable amidst great opulence, and what the hell is he going to do with a twenty-five-room mansion?"

When a bill that would have permitted the mansion to be used for other purposes was defeated in a senate committee in June 1975, Brown declared, "At a time when public funds are very scarce, it's a shame that we can't put the mansion to some productive use. If nothing else, it will symbolize for generations to come the excesses of the old politics." More than two years later came an agreement that allowed the mansion to be used for seminars and training sessions for state employees as of early 1978.

Brown also attracted much media attention when he selected his residence and headquarters at the 1976 Democratic National Convention in New York: the seedy old McAlpin Hotel, which was shut down when the convention was over.

Brown's lack of concern for creature comforts extends from his living quarters and mode of transportation to his dress and diet. Frank Schober, who teamed with Marc Poché to oversee the freshmen on Brown's floor in the dormitory at Santa Clara and is now head of the California National Guard, said Poché told him that when Brown was running for secretary of state, Poché advised the candidate "to get a better suit of clothes." Poché called Brown "the worst-dressed politician in California." During that campaign, Mark McGuinness recalls he once drove Brown from Cynthia Kelly's home in San Francisco to the airport; Brown was carrying the essentials, a toothbrush and a change of underwear, in a paper bag. According to McGuinness, "Jerry was something else." Several years earlier "he was in my wedding. I had to get him a white shirt. Got him a shoeshine the day of the wedding. I used to ask him, 'Jerry, why the hell don't you shine your shoes?' And his attitude was, anyone who had time to shine their shoes wasn't doing the important things in life." Later, when Brown was running for governor, McGuinness had occasion to ask him, "Who the hell's dressing you? You look pretty good." And Baxter Rice, whose acquaintance with Brown goes back about as far as McGuinness's, notes that Brown in recent years has become a veritable fashion plate and wonders "whether someone coaches him."

Soon after Brown was elected secretary of state, he contacted poverty lawyer Dan Lowenstein about working for him. The two had never met, and it was agreed that someone would pick Lowenstein up at a newsstand and take him to Brown. "So I went there," the tall, thin Lowenstein recollected, "and I was waiting, and this little kid in blue jeans comes up to me, and he says, 'Are you Dan Lowenstein?' And I said, 'Yes.' I was just about to say, 'Are you going to take me to Jerry Brown?' or something like that, when he said, 'I'm Jerry Brown.'" Lowenstein also said that one of his friends met Brown at a party early in Brown's term as secretary of state and later remarked to Lowenstein, "Your boss certainly isn't very impressive."

Another time, when Brown was campaigning for governor, Peter Finnegan picked him up at San Francisco Airport to drive him to a campaign event in San Jose. Brown's aura in Finnegan's cramped sports car moved Finnegan to remark, " 'Christ, you've got b.o. like crazy, man.' And he says, 'Yeah, I've had this same shirt on for three days, and I almost missed the plane.' " At Brown's suggestion, he and Finnegan, along with their police escort, pulled into a shopping center, where the candidate bought "some poof juice" and a comb. Then, Finnegan said, "he comes out, and he gets in my car, and he takes his shirt off, psst, psst, psst, psst, psst, psst, and he had to borrow my tie. Then he looks over and sees two little honeys sitting in the car next to us" who were watching the whole performance. Brown asked Finnegan for some campaign buttons, and "he gets out, he has to undo his pants, kind of turns around so the girls can't see, puts his shirt in, buttons up, fixes his tie, and says, 'Here [handing campaign buttons to his audience], my name is Jerry Brown. I'm running for governor. I'd like you to vote for me.' " Finnegan also said that after Brown became governor and was living at 1400 N Street, Finnegan read "some blurb about he's cut back his shower in his apartment . . . So I said to him, 'Jesus Christ, you've always had a problem with b.o. Is it really a fact you're taking a shower only every other day?' And he kind of laughed." At this point in the conversation, Finnegan paused and commented, "I'm not very respectful."

Brown eats when food is handy; when there is none in reach, he goes for long periods without eating. Early in 1976, his dietary habits, which included fasting for up to forty-eight hours in attempts to lose weight and then living for days at a time on hamburgers, French fries, and greasy tacos, came to the attention of Dr. Jerome Lackner, the state health director. Lackner tried to direct Brown to more nutritional food. Although Lackner is still "concerned about the way people eat over there [in the governor's office]," he adds, "I think we've affected his diet some. I'm concerned that a guy who works as hard as he does" should eat proper food.

Brown now thrives on Japanese and Chinese food, an improvement over his former dietary mainstays. When he is in Los

Angeles, Lucy Casado, who with her husband, Frank, owns El Adobe, takes a motherly interest in his welfare. In addition to "always telling him that he has to rest," she looks after his diet. Brown makes himself at home at her restaurant, often going into the kitchen and helping himself. The "Jerry Brown special," chicken with Spanish rice, appeared on the menu one day after Brown piled the ingredients on his plate and suggested jokingly that the dish be named after him.

Although the Casados enjoy Brown's raids on their kitchen as proof he feels at ease with them, Finnegan says his mother "never liked him because he used to walk into the goddamned house, wouldn't even say hello, go right to the refrigerator, and just make himself a sandwich. My mother always thought he lacked certain social graces."

People who work with Brown report that leaving food around while he is present is akin to throwing it out; the "donor" will never see it again. According to Schober, Poché was dieting at one point while he was on Brown's staff, and he left two apples on his desk while he went to a legislative hearing, "and he was very hungry, and he was thinking about eating these two apples as soon as he got back. He opened the door, the governor was seated at his desk and eating apple number two." Schober calls that "a typical Jerry Brown food story; if there's any food around, the governor will glom onto it."

Descriptions of Brown's spending habits are as abundant as those about his eating. In some cases, the anecdotes overlap. Schober said that early in Brown's term, the governor invited him to attend a meeting of the University of California Board of Regents in Berkeley. The two of them went to lunch, and Brown "reached around, and he said, 'Gee, I don't have any money.' And I said, 'Well, I have a credit card.' " That night, Schober continued, Brown suggested they and some other people eat at a French restaurant in the Berkeley hills, and "the same thing occurred. He was fumbling for money. I pulled out the credit card again, and the waiter came back and said, 'Sorry, sir, we don't take this credit card here.' And I said, 'Governor, both of us are going to have to wash dishes.' At that point, he reached further into his pocket and pulled out a huge roll of bills and paid for everybody's meal. He had it, and I don't think he was aware of it."

Alan Rothenberg, a youthful vice president of the Bank of

America, replaced Don Burns as secretary of business and transportation in late 1976, after Burns resigned in order to return to a private law practice. To offer Rothenberg the job, the governor invited him to dinner at Frank Fat's in Sacramento. Said Rothenberg, "I knew something was up because he paid for dinner," with money that Rothenberg had recently noticed Brown borrowing from his administrative assistant, Lucie Gikovich. Also, Rothenberg said, "He was only a half hour late, which I knew meant I was really important."

Mark McGuiness remembers affectionately that his old friend is "not [fiscally] conservative. He's cheap. He's always been cheap. I know that he's not one to pick up the check and never has been." McGuinness's mother says approvingly that Brown is "tight with his own money, and I think he would be equally tight with our [the taxpayers'] money." According to another friend of Brown from his school days, Bart Lally, Brown "was always frugal. I think that's why he's done such a good job with the budget."

Is Jerry Brown gay? Few people come out and ask that directly, but it is a topic that interests many. The answer, according to every one of his friends who was willing to comment, is "definitely not." His sex life is the part of Brown's personal life that he guards most jealously. Even though there have been covert attempts to use Brown's sex life against him, and even though he is aware the same sort of thing could happen again, Brown chooses to keep his own counsel, except to deny that he is a homosexual. When the subject came up during Brown's appearance on an interview program on KNBC-TV in Los Angeles on July 23, 1977, Brown responded by asking the questioner, who is in his midthirties and divorced, "By the way, are you married?" When the reporter said he was not, which Brown knew, Brown said sharply, "I won't ask you why." Three months earlier, when television talk-show host Phil Donahue asked Brown about his love interests, the governor replied, "I think I should be able to date who I want without explaining on a television show," a remark that drew applause from many people in the audience. *New West* magazine ran a cover story in its July 18, 1977, issue entitled "Haters head West: Will Anita Bryant's crusade smear Jerry Brown?" According to an informed source, that cover was to have featured a drawing of Brown hiding in a closet. After the authors of the story threatened to withdraw it if the planned cover were used, a "toned down" replacement showed Brown being pelted with rotten eggs.

Singer Helen Reddy and her husband, Jeff Wald, are among Brown's best friends. According to Wald, Brown is "not a fag. He doesn't feel he has anything to prove. The people around him are a lot more concerned about it than he is." In fact, say people who were part of Brown's 1974 campaign, some campaign strategists considered, mostly in jest, producing a television commercial in which a beautiful Swedish blonde would have gazed into the camera and murmured, "I don't know a thing about American politics. All I know is, I'm voting for Jerry Brown because he's great in bed."

Finnegan says that when he was in the Peace Corps in Caracas in the mid-1960s Brown once showed up there because "he was hot for some chick's body." McGuinness is another who makes a point of saying that Brown is "far from queer." He recounts the time he broke his leg and was in the hospital, where he received a call from Brown. McGuinness said he asked his friend, "How's your love life?" and Brown said he had a date that night with a celebrity. "Give her my love," McGuinness told Brown, who answered, "No, I think I'll give her *my* love."

Brown's dates with such stars of the entertainment world as Liv Ullmann, Natalie Wood, Candice Bergen, and Linda Ronstadt have been widely reported. Of that group, the one he dated longest was Ronstadt, who has given concerts to raise money for his campaigns.

The people who know Brown best say the most serious romance of his life involved a woman he dated for about two years after he graduated from Yale Law School. That woman, who has since received a doctorate in plant pathology, now teaches at a large university. She has been married for three years, but she still considers Brown a friend, and even though more than ten years have passed since she and Brown broke up, her parents think highly of him, and they still see him occasionally. Brown's former lady friend, who is three years younger than he, is said to be a "brilliant" and "unassuming" woman, "the kind that goes hopping off to some other country every few minutes." The two were introduced by a friend of Brown, who once worked for the woman's father, a doctor. People close to both say they were "very fond of each other" and that Brown was "very, very unhappy" and moped around for quite a while after their relationship ended. The woman refuses to discuss her friendship with Brown other than to say that she once dated him seriously, but she does not feel it would be proper to discuss her relationship with him in greater detail. Brown declined comment. His former girl friend is typical of the women in his life: attractive, bright, and interesting.

Brown's sister Cynthia said, "A family would be new and exciting" for him after he leaves politics, and Finnegan has a similar comment: "I think maybe after he gets out of politics, he ought to find himself a woman and spend a couple of years finding out what the relationship between a man and a woman is. That's pretty fundamental. I'd like him to do that a lot sooner."

Brown points out his job and the amount of time he spends at it are "not conducive to strong relationships. That absorption, you pay a price for that. You can't be home by the fire talking about the family if you're out there hustling to be . . . the governor of California." But he says he does hope to marry and have a family someday.

Except for Brown's love life, no topic seems to provoke as much curiosity as his religion. That issue came to the forefront during his presidential campaign when a story appeared in the *New York Times* on May 16, 1976, reporting that Brown "now admits he is no longer a practicing Roman Catholic." The *Times* story prompted a member of the staff of *The Monitor,* the newspaper of the archdiocese of San Francisco, to query Brown, whose answer was, "I was born a Catholic. I was raised a Catholic. I am a Catholic." "We can only point out," *The Monitor* editorialized on May 20, 1976, "that no other candidate for the presidency has been pressed to answer questions on his religious practices. . . . Even John F. Kennedy was never asked the direct question, 'Are you a practicing Catholic?' " Nor, said *The Monitor,* were other recent presidents, such as Nixon and Ford, asked if they practiced the religion they professed. Therefore, the editorial continued, "it seems to us unfair to pin down a man just because he is in public office—and demand a profession of faith—while the rest of us remain secure in the privacy of our own deficiencies and our own sins in regard to the practicing of our faith."

Brown sometimes participates in activities of the San Francisco Zen Center, which operates an organic farm at a spectacular oceanside site just north of San Francisco and a retreat at a hot spring south of Carmel, in addition to its headquarters in the city. Although Brown visits the Zen Center's facilities, he uses them primarily as a place where his privacy is respected, where he can talk, meditate, or do whatever he pleases without being watched. In the words of former seminarian Don Burns, "Jerry's no more a Zen Buddhist than you are or anything approaching it."

The true significance of the Zen Center in relation to Brown is that through the center Brown has become acquainted with several people he has appointed to government jobs, including two cabinet members, Huey Johnson, the second secretary of resources in Brown's administration, and former Secretary of Business and Transportation Alan Rothenberg, as well as State Architect Sim Van der Ryn.

Assemblyman John Briggs, an ardent follower of Anita Bryant and an extremely long-shot candidate for the GOP nomination for governor in 1978, once supposedly claimed that Brown reviewed bills passed by the legislature while he sat upside down in the lotus position in a candlelit room with Jacques Barzaghi. The statement prompted Assemblyman Leroy Greene, a Democrat, to recommend that Briggs' comments "be printed upside down in the Assembly Journal so Brown could read them," according to a story in the *Bee* on January 13, 1976.

The latest from Brown on religion: "I'm not ready to label myself. I don't feel very comfortable with labels. Certainly the Catholic tradition would be a big part of my life."

What is it like to be Jerry Brown's friend? Peter Finnegan, who can no doubt answer that better than anyone else, considers Brown a "shitty friend" because he "does not reciprocate." Most people who know Brown well think it is much easier for him to relate to people on a group basis—he shows compassion for the farm workers, the poor, minorities—than on a one-to-one friendship. "That insensitivity," says Finnegan, "it's Jerry's Achilles heel. It's very hard for Jerry to reciprocate any kind of love."

Finnegan does not think Brown is a happy person: "I'm still not convinced that Jerry Brown truly enjoys being governor. In fact, my impression is just the opposite." According to Finnegan, "Jerry is still kind of homeless," as he was while growing up. "You gotta get off on it. You walk in, and you're the governor, right? But he talks about, there's no privacy, you can't get a good lay. I feel for Jerry in the sense that I think he's just one poor, lonely son of a bitch, and I don't think being governor solves those fundamental problems. I don't know if he can."

Finnegan said that soon after Brown was inaugurated, Finnegan suggested that he appoint Bill Burman and Baxter Rice to jobs, and Brown's reply was, " 'I can't get all my friends jobs.' I said, 'What do you mean, all your friends? All three of them?' Jerry doesn't do too much for anybody. So what you do is, you kind of psychologically gird yourself so that you don't get hurt. Like I never call Jerry. No way. 'Cause I ain't going to have the whole experience of him not calling me back." (Brown named Rice head of the Alcoholic Berverage Control Department but did not offer Burman a job.)

Finnegan believes that Brown could be elected president of the United States. "I really, truly believe that he has the talent." But, Finnegan says, "if Jerry Brown is going to be president someday, he needs to have that close group of friends around him. . . . You take Kennedy. Kennedy had people that he felt very comfortable with. Jerry has Jacques now," and other people "have been simply emotionally cut off."

Why, then, does Finnegan want to be friendly with Brown? "I don't know. I've asked myself that question. You don't always control things in life, right? I got stuck with him as a friend, don't ask me." Finnegan goes on to say, "I'm in politics, and he's in politics. There's that kind of thing where you want to hang around because you can get something out of it. So I've got a goddamn appointment out of this." Also, says Finnegan, "I like the guy." As for his appointment to the Alcoholic Beverage Control Appeals Board, Finnegan says he is grateful to Brown, although he resents the fact that when Brown told him of his selection, he added the caution, " 'And always remember, always remember, that everybody perceives you as being very close to me.' It's kind of interesting that he had to tell me that. I kind of went, 'Oh, yeah, really?' "

Finnegan also expressed the hope "that in the next few years Jerry will have some kind of an emotional awakening and be able to [satisfy] some of the real needs that I think you have as a human being. Believe me, you don't get 'em in this political crap, you just don't."

Two former priests who were once friendly with Brown, Bill Burman and James Straukamp, feel they were dropped by him, although neither one professes bitterness. Burman's feeling about his former relationships with Brown and Finnegan is "I think I was a very instrumental person in their lives. Peter is perhaps more aware of it than Jerry. But I don't think they have an obligation. What happened then happened then. Life goes on. I don't think we have to be pinned to the past. I think I got as much out of it as they did. Any idea of anybody being obligated to anybody else in this thing is out of line." Still, Burman adds, "I'm sort of at a loss" as to how to get in touch with Brown.

Straukamp says that from the time Brown moved out of his apartment in Sacramento, "I never heard from him." At that time, seven years ago, Straukamp loaned Brown a card table and some folding chairs to outfit his new home because he had no furniture. "And I never have seen those. I thought it would be kind of funny to bring him into small claims court to retrieve my possessions." Straukamp hastens to add that he is just joking. Becoming philosophical, he goes on, "I just think I was part of his life for that time. It was convenient [for Brown to stay with him], we had enjoyable conversation, and then he's moved. The way I see it, he's evolved into something else. I'm just not part of his life anymore. I just took it that he moved out of my sphere into another sphere, and I'm not uptight" about it. Straukamp is still friendly with Rice, Schober, and others who remain in touch with Brown. If anything bothers Straukamp, it is that he has invited Brown to dinner parties with some of their mutual friends and never received a reply. But, Straukamp rationalizes, "I'm just not into his life, so I can't expect him to be answering."

Father William Perkins also had trouble getting a response when he invited Brown to give the 1975 commencement address at Santa Clara. Perkins took to calling Brown's secretary and pretending to be another person, such as "Emperor Hirohito or somebody like that." Finally, after trying to reach Brown a half-dozen times without success, Perkins called one night and told Brown's secretary, " 'Eesa Popa Paul Seex. Ima call froma Vaticano ina Roma. I wanna speaka to Governor Brown.' She starts to laugh. She knew who it was. And apparently the door was open, and Jerry called out, 'What are you laughing about?' And she said, 'It's Pope Paul VI. You'd better pick up the phone.' So he picks up, and I said, 'Jerry, what the devil is the matter with you?' [Brown replied] 'What do you mean?' I said, 'You're very impolite, and you're very rude, and you're inconsiderate.' " Perkins then explained why he was calling and how much trouble he had had contacting Brown (which was at the time the governor was occupied with creation of the Farm Labor Board). Brown asked, " 'Well, how do I know anybody wants to hear me talk?' And I said, 'I'll give you a simple answer to that: the seniors said they either wanted you for the commencement or no one. Do you need any more proof?' " And so Brown agreed to give the address.

State Senator Alan Robbins (D, San Fernando Valley) found an innovative way of getting a response from Brown when traditional means of communication failed. Robbins related that he tried for almost six months after Brown's inauguration to persuade the new governor to create a Motion Picture Development Council to help lure filmmakers back to Hollywood. The issue was important to Robbins because many of his constituents were unemployed workers in the movie industry. Robbins wrote and called Brown's office repeatedly, but there was "just no success," he later recalled. "I just couldn't get the attention of the governor."

Finally, Robbins had his wife, Miriam, then a graduate student in linguistics at UCLA, write Brown on June 23, 1975:

> *Tibi scribo per linguam Latinam, quia, credo, solum si ita ago, securus ero hanc litteram te equidem attingere. Namque nulli ministri alii apud te possunt comprehendere ullam litteram scriptam per Latinam, itane est? Frustra, conatus sum impetrare ut concludas questionem pecuniae pro Motion Picture Development Council, sed etiam nihil valebat. . . . Responsum tuum petitur ad temporem locumque atque in lingua tibi commoda.*

Translated, the Robbins letter reads:

I am writing to you in Latin on the presumption that doing so is the best way to ensure that the letter reaches you personally. After all, who else on your staff can understand a letter written in Latin? I have tried in vain and with great frustration to get you to bring the funding question of the Motion Picture Development Council to a conclusion, but to no avail. . . . Your reply is solicited at a time and place of your convenience and in a language of your choice.*

"By golly, it worked," said Robbins. "The letter in Latin got through." Brown soon called Robbins, told him he thought the letter was a cute idea, and agreed to provide $36,000 from the governor's office fund to support Robbins' project for the rest of the 1975-76 fiscal year. Brown also promised to include $70,000 for the council in the 1976-77 budget. Robbins said the Motion Picture Development Council has been responsible for keeping $20 million worth of filming in California "that otherwise would have gone out of the state." He considers the inspiration to write the governor in Latin "my greatest stroke in terms of relations to the governor's office" during Brown's term.

According to Frank Damrell, "Jerry's an introvert by a lot of standards. I mean, he is not a hail fellow well met. He's not a back slapper. If he were in a room right now with forty of his closest friends, he would be engaged in a quiet conversation, whereas someone like myself would be recounting some dramatic event or funny event with ten people listening." Damrell says that although Brown "was always a pretty good speaker" and is now "about as good a platform speaker as there is in California politics, and probably you could say that about the national scene," he "is not a person who likes to engage in small talk. To that extent he's uncomfortable with the platform-speech type of situation. It doesn't lend itself to anything very meaningful. He prides himself on saying something that means something."

"Socially he's pretty gauche," says teachers' lobbyist Mary Bergan. "I just don't think he has ever really learned to deal with people very well. Plus he's been in a position where he's been a governor's son, he's been this, he's been that, where does it matter?" She recalled the time she invited Brown to a farewell party for George Moscone after Moscone had been elected mayor of San Francisco in November 1975. The night of the party, Brown called about 10:30 and asked who was there, what kind of

* Latin letter and translation by Miriam Robbins.

party it was, had it turned out as "a drunken brawl?" Bergan answered, " 'No it isn't, it's a good group.' But," she went on "by the time he got there an hour and a half later, there was hardly a sober person in the crowd because we had bought a lot of wine. That's one thing about Prop nine; legislators can pay for their own parties." Bergan said Brown finally arrived. "He just wasn't at ease," and he left after a few minutes. "He's absolutely zilch at small talk," she added. At the parties Brown does attend, "he usually will get into some pretty urgent discussion with people, or he just won't stay."

In a similar vein, Schober said that when he dines with Brown, "there's never idle conversation going on." They usually discuss the philosophy of government or related matters. "I feel that I am the governor's friend, but if he calls, he won't call to ask how my health is. He's calling about an issue." The problem with such an attitude, as Bergan points out, is that "you stop figuring out that there's a life out there that really is what you're supposed to be serving. That's a hell of a way to live." Or, as money raiser Don Muir states it, "I think there's a Sacramento syndrome that basically says that what we do and what we say here has incredible effect throughout California, when I think that most of the public, about ninety percent of them, don't give a shit in regard to specific programs."

Brown is not a grinner, not a laugher; in fact, "this governor very seldom smiles," says former State Senator Howard Way. As a result, many people perceive him as a cold fish. "Have you ever seen Jerry Brown laugh?" asks Bob Moretti. "And you never will, probably. Every once in a while, he'll cackle a little bit. I'm a people reader. I look at people who don't laugh and who don't love and who don't respect, and I say they got really deep, deep problems. I think Jerry Brown is a very lonely man, and I feel sorry for him in that respect, but I don't like what he's doing, and I'm going to keep saying so." Assemblyman John Vasconcellos cites Moretti as a person "you can have a beer with, slap on the back, put your arm around, and Jerry is not [like] that." Brown's reticence also bothers Assemblyman Lou Papan. "There is a very definite kind of withdrawal from exhibiting warmth as we understand it. Now it may be present, but it suits him and only him and may not be fully understood by others. I feel that if you exhibit contact, like put your arm around him or touch him when he's unaware, he gets a little disturbed, which I don't quite fully understand except that it indicates that he's somewhat uneasy. He doesn't have the warmth of a Mediterranean," which Papan, Moretti, and Vasconcellos are better able to relate to. According to Cynthia Kelly, even within the privacy of his family, Brown, while being a loving brother to her and uncle to her children, is not a "bouncing on the knee type."

One who has had his differences with Brown, former unemployment chief Jim Lorenz, wonders if Brown has a vindictive streak. Lorenz, who worked for Brown during the first six months of the administration and then was fired, says he has visited with several members of Brown's staff since his dismissal, but "I don't think I'll mention them because I don't want to run any risk of getting them in trouble with Jerry. He doesn't have an enemies' list," declares Lorenz, but "it might become a question of loyalty, and I wouldn't want to reduce whatever trust they've built up with him simply because they might happen to have lunch with me." Former ACLU lobbyist Ben Bycel, who crossed swords with some members of the administration, says of his onetime antagonists—although not in direct reference to Brown himself—that "they had somewhat of a propensity to make an enemies' list."

Unlike most politicians, however, Brown does not appear to engender feelings of loyalty or hatred among the people he favors or turns down. For example, he gave appointments to Moretti and Finnegan, Moretti to a job that he desperately needed and Finnegan to a post that by his admission requires little more than the ability to deposit his state paycheck in the bank. Yet both Moretti and Finnegan are harshly critical of Brown. On the other hand, Lorenz, in spite of having been fired by Brown, claims he may vote for Brown or even give money to his future campaigns. And Muir, who believes Brown reneged on a position that his top aides had offered during the 1974 campaign, is generally supportive of Brown.

In spite of Lorenz's fears about "a question of loyalty," there is no tangible evidence that Brown carries a grudge. The most important clue, as a matter of fact, is just the opposite: the job Brown gave Moretti on the State Energy Commission, even though they had been foes in the 1974 primary, although Brown's advisers distrusted the tactics Moretti might use against him, and in spite of the fact that Moretti and Brown have entirely different personalities and have never been comfortable with each other. In addition, Jon Kreedman says that although he "strongly expressed" to the governor his opinion that Brown had no right to spend $80,000 of his supporters' money to pay for a nationwide television speech in 1976 after he was already out of the running for the Democratic presidential nomination, "it did not affect our friendship."

Although Brown may seem cold to some, his friend Carl Werthman views him as being "a lot of different people," and Betty Werthman commented in reference to the remoteness many people attribute to Brown, "I have never seen that side of him." According to Dan Greer, Brown's good friend at Yale, "It's hard to get to know him, but I find him to be a very warm person, if you can believe that." Another of Brown's friends, Howard Berman, said, "I have seen him express emotion. I have seen him express gratitude. It's in a different kind of a way, and it's restrained, and I think it's much more a product of his shyness" than of being cold.

Justice Mathew Tobriner thinks his former law clerk has "developed beautifully" since he first knew him. Tobriner said that Brown "overcame" his reserve, which Tobriner said reminds him of Brown's mother and her father, the police captain. After hearing that many people regarded Brown as being cold and aloof while he was running for secretary of state, said Tobriner, "My advice to him was to empathize more. So one day he came in, and I said, 'How are you doing?' " Brown's response: "I'm empathizing." Tobriner laughed.

To Marc Poché, "The nicest thing that he's done that really touched me" occurred after Poché's father died the night Brown was elected governor. "The next morning my mother had a telegram from him. I don't know how he even knew and how he had the time during all that to do it. Later on, I thanked him. I said, 'You probably didn't even know [implying that someone else had sent the telegram on Brown's behalf].' And he said, 'What do you mean, I didn't know. I wrote the telegram.' "

Another good friend of Brown, Judy Wiseman, a Los Angeles television producer, thinks he is "a remarkably social person." But the same thing that some people dislike about Brown is what appeals to her: "I don't think he can be read emotionally. That's just him. There are some people you can just read like an open book. And he is not like that. I just happen to prefer that kind of person." Like Finnegan, who said, "It would be easier" to be friendly with Brown "if he were a garbageman," Wiseman remarked, "Obviously, being friendly with the governor is not like having a normal friend." She contrasted the present situation with the period when she met Brown while he was practicing law "and there was just a whole group of friends who would meet for dinner."

Mark McGuinness, who said that Brown has "always been a good friend," added, "I know three things about him: I know that he's dedicated, that he's intelligent, that he's a moral man. That's all I need to know about a politician. If he's got those qualities, it doesn't make any difference whose side he's on."

Because Brown is not a very social person, Jeff Wald and Helen Reddy do much of his entertaining for him. Brown's friendship with the couple dates back to 1972, when he met them at a testimonial for another politician. Wald recalls that when he and his wife first became supporters of Brown, a picture of Brown with Reddy would sometimes cause people to remark, "Who's that man with Helen Reddy?" In November 1976, Brown officiated at a ceremony in which Wald and Reddy celebrated their tenth wedding anniversary by renewing their marital vows. Brown read a service that Reddy had written. According to Wald, "He did it with humor and grace. He also enjoyed being the only bachelor there," at a gathering that included such show-business personalities as Neil Diamond, Steve Lawrence and Eydie Gorme, Totie Fields, and Rona Barrett. Perhaps it is the absence of Wald and Reddy from the Sacramento social scene that accounts for some of the gaffes people like Bergan have cited. One friend of Brown, on hearing that he was traveling to Japan on his thirty-ninth birthday in April 1977, commented: "He's probably going just to miss his birthday party. He doesn't like to be the center of attention. Last year he just ignored his cake until everyone just about dropped dead from hunger." Those who have attended the birthday parties Brown's staff has thrown for him, when he is in town, as well as the office Christmas parties, agree that they are usually a lively success—until Brown shows up.

Reddy is one of the few people who aided Brown while he was running for office and later received favors from him. She and Wald donated large sums of money and also hosted fundraising parties. In July 1977, Brown appointed her to the state Park and Recreation Commission. In the press release announcing her appointment, Brown's office sought to stress her environmental credentials by describing her and Wald as the owners of one of the few solar-heated homes at Lake Tahoe. Two years earlier, Brown had accorded Reddy the honor of including her hit record, "No Way to Treat a Lady," among the songs that were played over speakers in the park outside the Capitol. Brown's selections also included songs by Loretta Lynn, Merle Haggard, and the Sufi Choir of San Francisco, as well as recordings of Gregorian chants and Beethoven's Ninth Symphony. Nevertheless, according to Wald, "after Brown got elected, he didn't talk to me for six months. Because I was a contributor. I sublimated my ego and kept calling him until I got him and then reestablished our friendship. The best way to get nothing from him is to be a contributor."

Wald's complaint is one that is often voiced. Stephen Reinhardt, one of Brown's most capable fund raisers, says he has advised people from whom he solicits donations that "getting involved with Jerry is not something you do because you expect to ever benefit from it in any way. He has some weaknesses in the whole field of dealing with people who have been helpful to him." Reinhardt attributes Brown's attitude toward his supporters to his religious training and to instances he observed in his father's career when people who had helped Pat Brown demanded something in return.

Don Muir, whose profession is generating campaign funds, criticizes Brown's "lack of contact with specifically finance people who helped him. I'm not talking about doing them special favors, but I think there's almost a paranoia that [dictates], 'God, if this guy helped us, don't go near him, don't even talk to him!' " According to Muir, the "dominant" reason why people give large sums to politicians is "because they like to be around power." Muir suggests that "a little ego stroke once in a while" is "all that is required to raise money. Guys like to be able to pick up the phone and say, 'You know, I'm going to call the governor,' or, 'You know, I rode over last night with the governor.' " Muir added that Brown may have trouble raising money in the future because he has neglected some donors. "He has used up chits in that he went to a lot of people to raise money for the gubernatorial. He then had no contact with them. He then took a shot at the presidential. Then suddenly he was back. Now I think there's also a period in which you don't see him again until the next gubernatorial. It's a cumulative thing. Yeah, I think Brown might have some difficulty raising substantial funds in 1978. I would think not enough to cause him not to be elected, but I'd say it will be more difficult because I think guys are hurt by the fact that he has very little communications with them."

Political consultant Joe Cerrell also observes, "You don't get the ego massage" from Brown. As a result of that, Cerrell says, "I've heard the fat cats say, 'Let him go and get his money from the minorities and the women and the gays.' " And Jon Kreedman said that after the 1974 election "there was a problem with Jerry expressing his appreciation to those who supported him. You have to know Jerry. Jerry isn't the type to sit down and write someone a thank-you note."

Ray Fisher, Brown's former law associate, took a leave of absence from Tuttle and Taylor for the first nine months of Brown's administration to help Brown guide through the legislature a bill that gave public employees the right to collective bargaining. The following year, as a registered lobbyist, he helped win passage by the legislature of a law that permitted doctors—faced with skyrocketing malpractice insurance costs—to join together and insure themselves. Then Brown vetoed the bill. "That proves that he doesn't favor his friends," declared Fisher, who said the experience caused him to get "kind of upset" with Brown. The bill was subsequently introduced and passed again, and the second time around, Brown allowed it to become law without his signature.

In 1974, Frederic Wyatt, a Republican who had been Brown's ally on the Los Angeles Community College Board, went out on a limb by endorsing Brown against Houston Flournoy and taping television spots declaring his support of Brown, which won Wyatt the enmity of many Republicans. In May 1977, when Wyatt was seeking a third term on the board, he asked Brown to endorse him, but Brown turned him down because Wyatt's opponent, Wallace Albertson, the wife of actor Jack Albertson, was a liberal Democrat and a friend of Brown. Wyatt lost the election to Albertson by a mere 4,500 votes and 1.5 percentage points. Although Wyatt thinks Brown's endorsement "would have put me in without any question," he said he still regards Brown as a friend. "He had to figure his priorities," Wyatt stated.

"I understand it perfectly." But Republican Assemblyman Robert Cline, who also served on the college board with Brown and Wyatt, charged that Brown's refusal to back Wyatt in 1977 was proof that Brown "doesn't remember obligations. That's where he departs from some of his colleagues."

Brown concedes that the criticism of him by Muir, Reinhardt, and Kreedman, among others, for his neglect of people who gave money to his campaigns is "a legitimate point. We're trying to do more of that" ego stroking. Still, Brown points out, "I'm a trustee for the people. Everything I do is supposed to be to benefit the public interest. Because of the difficulty of maintaining and regaining the credibility of government, I think it is important to be very careful, and I am. But I'm appreciative of people that help. Where possible, I don't have any problem with appointing them to appropriate positions."

From the start of his term, Brown—who had said he was opposed to raising the governor's salary above its existing level of $49,000 and had criticized Reagan for causing the new mansion to be built and for flying in a state jet that cost the taxpayers substantially more money than traveling commercial would have—showed that he would bring a no-frills approach to his role as governor. On the eve of his inauguration, Brown flew from Los Angeles to Sacramento by a commercial flight aboard a Pacific Southwest Airlines 727. He decided not to hold an inaugural ball, remarking that "it's not my style." By contrast, Mervyn Dymally, the first black to be elected lieutenant governor, had two inauguration dances, one in Los Angeles and one in Sacramento. And instead of the traditional limousine, Brown picked a light-blue Plymouth Satellite as his official car. The armored Cadillac that had been used by Reagan, and before that by J. Edgar Hoover, was subsequently sold by the state.

Within two months of taking office, Brown had received, and refused, such gifts as a copy of "Peter Rabbit" in Latin; a future grave site at Forest Lawn in Los Angeles; a gold pass to Disneyland; books and works of art; a gold frisbee, and a map of California flea markets. Officials of the state Finance Department estimated that more than 150 gifts worth over $5,000 had been offered to Brown during his first 60 days in office.

Brown, noting that many of the presents came from lobbyists and other special-interest groups, said donors would receive a note from his office stating that "because of his belief that elected officials should accept no gifts, the governor has asked that all gifts to him be returned to the donors. This is in keeping with the spirit of the Political Reform Initiative [Proposition 9], which the governor supported. We appreciate your understanding." Those who sent gifts received neither a personal letter from Brown nor thanks.

Instead, Brown issued a statement in which he said, "A government job is an occasion for public service, not special privilege. . . . We are sent to Sacramento for a single purpose: to serve all the people. That . . . includes those who have no lobbyist to represent them in Sacramento as well as those who do. It includes those who can't afford to send gifts as well as those who can." Brown even used his own campaign funds to pay for returning the presents.

In similar moves, Brown has paid for at least two trips that brought benefit to the state; paid more income tax than he was liable for; resisted the distribution of his picture; and been reluctant to honor autograph requests. He also did what he could to force other high state officials to follow his lead; in August 1976, Brown vetoed a bill that would have enabled the Department of Motor Vehicles to issue regular license plates instead of special ones for cars owned or leased by the state for the use of statewide elected officers. "Those who drive cars provided by the people should not fear to have their license plates so indicate," Brown declared. The same officials who were prohibited from obtaining ordinary license plates, including the lieutenant governor, treasurer, secretary of state, controller, and superintendent of public schools, will be granted raises of up to $7,500 a year as a result of a bill signed by Brown in September 1977. However, the raises will not take effect until 1979, and the bill granting them passed the legislature only after the defeat of a previous bill that Brown had vowed to veto because it authorized salary increases of as much as $20,000.

Brown's rejection of anything that smacked of a cult of personality was documented early in his term by the San Francisco Chronicle, which on July 10, 1975, disclosed that he was the only one of fifty American governors who had not complied with a request for a photograph for a museum in Ste. Mere-Eglise, France, that was dedicated to G.I.'s who had waded ashore at Normandy in June 1944. In June 1976, Brown told an audience at the National Press Club: "I ended the cult of personality in California by ordering my picture removed from all motor vehicle offices. I hope the next president will do the same with respect to the post office." Subsequently, Jack Rosen, a Brooklyn artist, learned to his chagrin of Brown's beliefs. Rosen had drawn caricatures of all the people who addressed the 1976 Democratic convention in New York, persuaded all of his subjects except Brown to autograph his drawing, and collected the signed pictures in a book that he planned to present to President-elect Carter. In December 1976, Rosen wrote the governor's office, asking, "Please, if the governor can give it [his autograph] to others, why not for our new wonderful president?" Rosen also said he shared Brown's feelings about autographs and would never ask for another. That letter came to the attention of Brown, who wrote on it, "Cool it! Jerry." Four months later, Rosen wrote Brown and complained that he had never received his drawing back with or without an autograph. An aide checked with Brown and found out that "the governor doesn't want this [an autograph] sent out—period!" Another member of the staff was instructed to return the picture to Rosen, along with a form letter.

Brown's dislike for protocol caused him to do something that may have been unwise politically: In August 1975, he refused to send his picture for inclusion in a program for a convention in Los Angeles of the powerful Veterans of Foreign Wars (VFW). Two years later, Brown made amends with the VFW by attending the group's meeting in Sacramento, exchanging a California flag for an American flag, and telling the 1,500 members present, "It's a privilege to be here. It's taken me a while to get to your convention. About two years."

In June 1977, when President Carter made public his 1976 income tax returns and announced that although he owed no tax on income of $55,000, he would still pay $6,000 "because of my strong feeling that a person should pay some tax on his income," he did exactly what Jerry Brown had done before him. Brown has been making his personal federal and state tax returns public since he was secretary of state, and in 1974, he did not take a deduction for his charitable contributions. He explained to reporters that it would take too much time for him to recall all of his donations, and besides, "I don't want to explain to you everything I did. I don't want to have to account for every hour of my life."

Several months before Carter's voluntary gift to the government, Brown, setting an example in a different way, paid for his birthday trip to Japan even though he spent part of his time soliciting Japanese business for California. And Brown paid the entire cost of his trip, about $800, when he traveled to Colorado Springs in September 1977 to help Los Angeles secure the 1984 Olympics. Brown had pledged that "no dollar from the state of California will be used" to pay for the Olympics, in contrast to the costly Olympic ventures in places such as Montreal and Munich. However, Brown may have been maneuvered into underwriting the cost of his Colorado trip when Ken Reich of the *Los Angeles Times*, no longer Brown's friend, called Gray Davis to ask who was going to foot the cost of the trip in view of Brown's vow against spending state funds on the Olympics. It was not until after Reich's call that Brown said he and his companions, including Davis and Secretary of Business and Transportation Dick Silberman, would pay for the flight, which had to be made on a chartered plane because of the short notice given Brown by the Los Angeles delegation that was seeking the Olympics. Some members of Brown's staff have voiced complaints about being forced to pay their own way on trips that benefit either the state or Brown's political career. The offended staffers do not include either Silberman, a millionaire, or Davis, who earns $43,620 a year and believes that in general public officials are overpaid (a position that prompted George Moscone to comment, "If you think you're overpaid, you probably are. You'll never get me on tape saying I'm overpaid, I'll tell you that.")

Brown's stance in regard to the trappings of office has won approval from observers as diverse as his sister Barbara, who compliments him for having been able to avoid ribbon cutting; State Senator Alan Sieroty (D, Los Angeles), who praises Brown for showing that "the governor doesn't have to live like an emperor"; and Frank Mesplé, Pat Brown's former aide, who speaks favorably of the "decanonizing or desanctification of public officials." Or as Jeff Wald says, "You're looking at a guy [Brown] who's never had a funny hat on his head."

Brown's aversion to some of the tasks that have been a part of the traditional political process may actually win votes for him, according to political expert Nancy Pelosi. "You tell me that these people who kiss babies want to kiss babies?" she asks, adding that the voters may perceive as phonies the old glad-handing, baby-kissing type of politician. In any case, whether or not refusing to do things he does not believe in helps him, that is the way Brown is. In the words of Marc Poché, "The governor can't do things that are not genuine. He will not send telegrams to people wishing them happy birthday if he doesn't know them. He just won't do it."

CHAPTER SEVEN

FATHER AND SON

Physically, emotionally, and intellectually, Jerry Brown is his mother's child. The facial resemblance between Bernice Brown and her only son is striking. The two also share the same lean build and are quiet and reserved, in sharp contrast to the man whose name they both bear. Pat Brown is intelligent, but he is not brilliant like his son and his wife: Bernice Layne graduated from high school at fourteen, from the University of California at eighteen, and was teaching school by the time she was nineteen. As Pat Brown himself comments, "Jerry gets his intelligence from her, not from me. He's more of a Layne than he is a Brown."

The most significant characteristic Pat Brown passed on to his son was the attribute that has proved indispensable in Jerry Brown's political carrer: the name Edmund Gerald Brown. According to Pat Brown, both he and his father, Edmund Joseph Brown, were named for Edmund Burke, the eighteenth-century

Irish-born, British-trained politician and theorist. Pat Brown says
that by family legend Edmund Burke was a distant relative of his
ancestors in Ireland. In any case, Jerry Brown was not named
after Edmund Burke but after Pat Brown.

Both Edmund G. (Pat) Brown and Edmund G. (Jerry) Brown,
Jr., are well aware of how much the name Edmund G. Brown,
Jr., has meant to the current governor. Says Pat Brown: "When
he ran for the Community College Board down here, nobody
knew [who he was]. If it were Edmund Jones or something like
that, he wouldn't have led the ticket by fifty thousand votes. And
when he ran for secretary of state, they knew they were voting
for the son of the governor. Now I don't mean to diminish Jerry
at all because he's a very attractive candidate."

Jerry Brown, recalling his campaigns for the Los Angeles
Community College Board in 1969, secretary of state in 1970,
and governor in 1974, said, "Sometimes you're out shaking
hands, people look at you, and they don't know who you are." So
he would often introduce himself to strangers as Pat Brown's son.
His father's name has had a "good, positive, important, significant" effect on his own career, he said. "I used to say that if my
name was Smith, I wouldn't be running. . . . If my father had
been a carpenter, I might have been a carpenter." Jerry Brown
acknowledged publicly the importance of his name on January 4,
1971, when he was inaugurated as secretary of state and
declared, "I want to thank my mother for naming me after my
father. I grew to like that during the campaign."

Many observers cite name identification as Jerry Brown's most
valuable political asset. Political consultant Joe Cerrell offered
the opinion that Jerry Brown "would not have gone anywhere"
but for Pat Brown. "What does he have that literally a thousand
others don't have?" said Cerrell. "He had immediate entree and
access" to everybody from elected officials to labor leaders to the
voters to newspaper editors and television station managers,
according to Cerrell. He added, "It gives you that opener. At least
you can get in the front door and talk to people." As far as Cerrell
is concerned, "It's kind of hypocritical when people" like Jerry
Brown, who has on occasion tended to take more credit for his
own successes than he did on January 4, 1971, "make the point
that they made it on their own. It wasn't because he was the
number-one law student to come out of his graduating class.
Would any other community-college trustee in the state of

California have been able to be elected secretary of state?" Cerrell takes the same attitude toward the election of Brown's sister, Kathleen Brown Rice, to the Los Angeles School Board in May 1975, six months after Jerry Brown was elected governor. Questions Cerrell, if her full name were "Kathy Fried Rice, Kathy White Rice, would she be on the board of education?" He also provides the answer: "No."

Even Jerry Brown's admirers understand the value of his last name. Senator Alan Cranston says another leader of the California Democratic party once advised Jerry Brown that no matter what else he might do, "Don't change your name."

According to Cerrell, Brown gained easy access to the news media by virtue of being his father's son. Vic Biondi, who was a journalist while Jerry Brown was secretary of state, agreed: "We had a receptiveness to him because of his father. I really liked his father."

At least equally important, Jerry Brown's surname enabled him to be received favorably by people who had contributed to his father's campaigns over a period of forty years. Jerry Brown concedes that the donor lists left over from his father's final race in 1966 were "a big help" when he ran for the college board in 1969. But, he adds, "these were Democratic contributors. There's a limited number of people who give money. The pool of available contributors is five thousand to ten thousand people, and the pool of significant contributors is even smaller. Every Democratic candidate goes to the same people, with a few differences based on personal contact."

Pat Brown estimated that people who had supported him in the past contributed about $250,000 to his son's race for governor in 1974. "I don't think Jerry ever really appreciated the number of friends that I had over a long period of time," he said. During the 1974 campaign, Pat Brown toured the state campaigning for his son. By his recollection, Pat Brown turned out and turned on the crowds at the rallies he addressed that year. He attributes some of that enthusiasm to the help he got from his political associates and from the people he had appointed to state jobs, as well as to the advance person he hired, even though he was not the candidate. Pat Brown said, "I told him [his son] I was going to do it so I wouldn't be in the same place he was to compete with his crowd. He didn't object to it at all, but I don't think he ever realized the impact." It is implicit in Pat Brown's comments that Jerry Brown neither solicited his father's help nor was overjoyed to receive it.

If Jerry Brown does not fully appreciate what his father did for him, Pat Brown does. "A lot of people vote for him because of me," declares the ex-governor. Pat Brown also revealed that three years after his son defeated Houston Flournoy, one of the Republican candidate's campaign leaders told him, "They were gaining like hell until I started going around the state. He thinks it changed a hundred thousand votes," which happens to be ten thousand more votes than Jerry Brown needed to achieve his 180,000-vote winning margin. Pat Brown hastens to add that although his identity probably accounted for his son's victories in 1969 and 1970, "he would have won whether he was my son or not" in 1974. "But I think he had to have the community college board and the secretary of state under his belt" to be elected governor. Nor is it lost on Pat Brown, who harbored presidential ambitions in 1960, that although Jerry Brown's primary successes in 1976 were attributable to his record as governor and his ability on the campaign trail, his son never would have been in a position to run for president had it not been for the opportunity that came his way because he is Edmund G. Brown, Jr.

By some accounts, the closer a person had been to Pat Brown, the harder it was to vote for Jerry Brown and give money to his campaign. Frank Mesplé, Pat Brown's former legislative secretary, said, "A lot of Pat Brown's old friends are very negative toward Jerry because he's not his dad, he's not the gregarious guy who says to a hundred people, 'If it weren't for you, I wouldn't be governor. By God, I really appreciate it.' "

Another frequent participant in Democratic campaigns noted the large sums of money Pat Brown's appointees, friends, and allies donated to Jerry Brown and added, "There's nothing wrong with that. There's only something wrong with it if the son isn't appreciative. They do it for Pat at the same time, well understanding that the kid doesn't show any kind of consideration for his father." He said that the commitment of the money people to Pat is so strong that they would "swallow their pride and their revulsion at Jerry and work for him. The depth of that, I think, is unrealized by Jerry."

Even Jerry Brown's statewide campaign chairman in 1974 was a legacy. Jon Kreedman had been a top fund raiser for Pat Brown since 1958, and in 1974, "when Jerry called me it was through his father." Kreedman donated about $75,000 and raised another $250,000 for Jerry Brown's drive for governor.

Pat Brown made the ultimate sacrifice for his son's career: He dropped his own plans for a political comeback and for a shot at avenging his 1966 defeat by Ronald Reagan. Pat Brown and virtually all the people close to him viewed Reagan as the Captain Video of refrigerator salesmen, and the loss has smarted ever since. In early 1970, though, Pat Brown decided to yield the political stage to his son, who had just announced his candidacy for secretary of state. The senior Brown, in Tokyo on business, called his wife and said he had just about decided to run for governor again. Eight years later, Bernice Brown remembered that her reaction had been, "That's ridiculous! You can't have two Edmund G. Browns on the ballot at the same time." However, she added, "I don't think he was all that serious. He kids a lot."

Pat Brown later said he was not joking at all. The big-money people in Democratic politics had no use for Jesse Unruh and had guaranteed to put up at least $500,000 for Pat Brown's campaign if he would come out of political retirement. According to Pat Brown, he wanted to run and could have evened the score with Reagan. He cites private polls that showed him to be only one or two points behind the Republican governor in 1970 even though he had not announced his candidacy.

"I would have done it in two minutes," declared Pat Brown. But he yielded to his wife, who urged, "Don't interfere with Jerry's career." Unruh got the nomination almost by default and went on to be trounced by Reagan.

Both Edmund G. Browns deny any attempt to outdo each other. Jerry Brown dismisses such speculation with what amounts to a Zen "no comment," rejecting the relevance of one era to another (even though Pat Brown left the governor's office only eight years before his son took over, not exactly an era). And Pat Brown states emphatically, "I have no sense of competition with Jerry, none at all, never have had."

But do actions speak louder than words? The first time I met Pat Brown, he did not have time for the interview we had scheduled. Instead, he read aloud from Martin Schram's book, *Running for President, 1976* (Stein and Day, 1977), a passage that concerned his campaign efforts in New Jersey for his son in

1976. Schram reported that in a conversation with James P. Dugan, New Jersey Democratic chairman, Jerry Brown asked, " 'How did my father do campaigning here?' 'Great—a lot of people think he should be the candidate,' Dugan joked." Pat Brown read the lines with a flourish, then looked up and said, "Jerry can't stand to hear that."

On another occasion, Pat Brown and I were eating in a restaurant when a woman in her sixties with her hair dyed red walked up to the table and said, "Pardon the intrusion. I just wanted to say that I think the father of the present governor was a much better governor than his son." Pat Brown beamed and replied, "Thank you for saying so. He's a great governor. But I was greater. I agree with you on that." As the lady walked away, Pat Brown turned back to me and said, "I have a lot of people come up and tell me that. Particularly old people." And Pat Brown, by his own admission, enjoys telling almost any audience he addresses that "Jerry's the second best governor in the history of the state."

As to Jerry Brown's sense of competition, Blackie Leavitt, referring to the 1974 campaign, said, "The main thing he wanted to do was win bigger than his father," which was not to be. Said Peter Finnegan, "I think Jerry ran for governor to work out the neurosis with his old man. If he had gone through psychoanalysis [as Finnegan did], I doubt if he would have run for governor. So a little neurosis goes a long way. He's governor now because he never did work it out," laughed Finnegan.

Jerry Brown says of his closely scrutinized association with his father, "All human relationships have their complexities. But I wouldn't identify it as being particularly different than any other father-son relationship." Since his election as governor, Jerry Brown has sometimes made warm comments in public about his father. In June 1976, for example, five days before the California presidential primary, he told an audience in Long Beach, "I'm a student of one of the greatest political experts of all time, my father." Privately, Jerry Brown has voiced similar sentiments. Alan Cranston said that when he accompanied Jerry Brown on the flight from Los Angeles to Sacramento on the eve of Brown's inauguration in January 1975, the governor-elect was reading his predecessors' inaugural addresses, dating back to Hiram Johnson's in 1911, and "he was proud of the fact that he thought his father's was one of the better ones." And Jerry Brown is usually quick to point out that he probably never would have had the opportunity to enter politics but for his father.

However, Jerry Brown is also capable, as Finnegan describes it, of "treating his old man like a piece of shit. It hurts to watch." One incident that sticks in Finnegan's mind occurred soon after Jerry Brown had become governor. Finnegan ran into Pat Brown in a Capitol corridor and the ex-governor mentioned that he was having dinner with his son that night. Later that day, Jerry Brown invited Finnegan to dinner, and Finnegan reminded him of his previous appointment. According to Finnegan, Jerry Brown "sloughed off" his dinner engagement with his father and only at Finnegan's insistence left word in his office where they would be. About ten P.M. Pat Brown showed up at the restaurant, one of Jerry Brown's Japanese favorites. Finnegan related, "The tension is just fantastic. Pat Brown asked, 'How's it going, Jerry, how's it going? What are you into this goddamn Japanese food for? Why don't you eat right? What's the matter with you? You gotta appoint so and so to be a judge.' " Finnegan said Jerry Brown was completely turned off by his father, who then asked, " 'What's Pete's role? What's Pete's role? What's Pete's role?' And Jerry says, 'Pete is a Tootsie Roll,' So I don't think the old man shows up too much anymore."

Finnegan repeated this story in the staccato style that is very much like Pat Brown's way of talking. Like Pat Brown, Finnegan is a stocky, outgoing individual who freely expresses his emotions. It is almost as if Jerry Brown could not be the same type of person his father is, so he picked as his best friend someone who is as similar to Pat Brown as possible.

The two Browns have vastly different personalities. Pat Brown is warm, friendly, outgoing, talkative, beloved by the many who got to know him well. At least on the surface, Jerry Brown possesses none of those traits. As Joe Cerrell says, "Most people who know them both would say that it's not easy to know Jerry. It is very easy to know Pat. I'd say they come about as close to night and day as two people could." Cerrell remembers times when Pat Brown, who loved to meet people and give speeches, would be at a hotel or a convention center and would purposely wander into another meeting and say, "Gee, I must have walked into the wrong room." Invariably, according to Cerrell, the people in "the wrong room" would invite Pat Brown to say a few words to them, to the governor's great delight. Jerry Brown, by contrast, would never go out of his way to give a speech. Although he has become an exceptionally good campaigner, he has never been eager for personal contact.

Frank Mesplé says that the difference between the former and present governors Brown is that Pat Brown has much more sympathy for other people. Mesplé hypothesized that if both men were to stumble upon a drunk lying in the gutter, "I think Jerry would step over him, and his dad would sit there and kind of commiserate with him."

Pat and Jerry Brown have an entirely different relationship than Gene and John Tunney; the two famous father-and-son teams are often compared because the younger Tunney has been active in California politics. John Tunney says he has always had "a very close relationship to my father. I admired him tremendously. I still do. I've always used my father as a very positive symbol in my political life as well as in my private life, whereas Jerry makes a definite effort to disassociate himself from his father." It should be noted, of course, that John Tunney did not follow in the same field of endeavor as his father, which probably makes their relationship smoother.

Pat Brown and his son at least occasionally find it easier to coexist with a buffer zone between them. Cynthia Brown Kelly says that at the family's Thanksgiving dinners, which are usually held at her house, "I try to put them at opposite ends of the table because they both come on like gangbusters. You're dealing with two very strong personalities." Her husband, Joe, who has had an ideal vantage point for observing the two Edmund G. Browns during the past thirty years, commented, "I think they both respect each other very much. Pat has a real love and warmth toward Jerry. And I think Jerry has a real respect for his father. Jerry is not the type of guy that would jump up on his father's lap and give him a big kiss or anything. They may not agree on issues, but Jerry is as loving toward his parents as anyone." Cranston, who has had ample opportunity to view the father-son relationship from outside the family circle, says, "I think they really love each other, but they have trouble communicating."

According to Frank Mesplé, "I have always sensed in the ex-governor a tremendous desire to be close, to bring his old friends in to help Jerry, and I always had the feeling that Jerry didn't want the old friends too close around." Pat Brown has urged passage of a law that would provide for former governors to sit as ex-officio members of the state senate, as a means of putting their experience to good use. In spite of Pat Brown's obvious desire to be involved in his son's administration, he seems to have been shunted aside, say those who are in a position to watch the two men. "I sense a disappointment that he isn't called upon," Mesplé said, and added that at least one member of the present administration has told him that "if Jerry calls his father, oftentimes they're very productive and meaningful discussions. If his dad calls to get hold of Jerry, that usually doesn't work too well."

Alan Cranston remarked that Pat Brown has occasionally said to him, " 'Will you tell Jerry to call his mother?' or, 'Tell Jerry this, but don't tell him I told you.' " In a lighter vein, Pat Brown once told Cranston, "I'm thinking of backing somebody against him. I've got the perfect candidate, somebody who will listen to me—his sister Kathleen."

Jerry Brown does sometimes call on his father for advice and follow it, for example, in deciding to retain Roy Bell as state finance director. But, as usual, the younger Brown claims he can't credit a specific person for presenting him with ideas, which he professes to get from a variety of sources, including newspapers, books, magazines, people he talks to, dreams, and his subconscious. "It all is just a confluence of thought that has an impact," he says.

Pat Brown commented, "I wish sometimes he would consult with me a little more. He could have avoided some problems if he'd had an opportunity to talk to me." He said that although in general "Jerry has been an extraordinarily good governor, I don't agree with everything he does. I think he's appointed too many minorities. It's like reverse discrimination. He's done plenty [for women and minorities], and I think he should continue to do plenty. But somewhere along the line the white Anglo-Saxon Protestant male feels he's been discriminated against."

Pat Brown said he sees no justification for the criticism his son has received for getting involved in some decisions too late. "I think Jerry is far more intelligent than I was in that connection. I believed governors could change events. Jerry is a much better accomplisher of objectives in that he waits until things become critical, and then he'll come in and work out a solution."

Pat Brown does cite one instance of his son's taking action too late: his entry into the 1976 presidential race. According to Pat

Brown, "I got him on the telephone, and I said, 'If you don't run at least as a favorite son, I'm going to run as a favorite father.' " Pat Brown thinks that if his son had run against Jimmy Carter in the Ohio primary, he would have won there, and "that would have been the end of Mr. Carter." But he doubts "whether they would have taken Jerry" as the Democratic nominee. "That is highly problematical because of his youth." He speculated that Jerry Brown might have wound up as the vice-presidential candidate.

Jerry Brown has expressed resentment about his family life to some of the people who have been closest to him over the years. "Jerry had very, very intense feelings that he was used in his own household [as a political prop]," says Carl Werthman. "And he didn't want to put anyone through that," which is one reason he has not married. Bill Burman remembers that Brown had "a good deal of resentment to his father" for not being around. And, commented Leo Wyler, "I think [Jerry has] tremendous resentment against Pat's personality because he was always trotted out as the young boy, but Pat is not one to let somebody else shine. As Jerry grew up in the political circle, I think he got an antipathy toward the surface personal relationships that Pat had, being friendly to everybody." Furthermore, said Wyler, "I think that Jerry's perception of the office of governor really has an awful lot to do with his rivalry with his father."

Former Legislative Analyst A. Alan Post, who knew several governors, including both Browns, commented that "Jerry Brown has reacted against his upbringing. There's no question about it. He is an intellectual, and a great deal of what one finds in the political world is not intellectually gratifying. He seems to react very much against what he saw" during the years when Pat Brown was an elected official.

Jerry Brown's attitude toward his father and his father's career may explain why he was never very much involved in Pat Brown's campaigns, even in 1966 when Jerry Brown was a young lawyer in Los Angeles. In fact Pat Brown said that in mid-1977 he asked his son if he had participated in any of the senior Brown's races, and "he said he did something, but he didn't work too hard in them. I don't know why."

Speaking of his son's reaction toward his own administration, Pat Brown commented, "Jerry doesn't follow the traditional

things. He's got individual ideas about a great many things. I
think Jerry recognizes that I made some very serious mistakes as
governor. I let my emotions in a great many cases get away from
me. I don't think Jerry does that. He's much tougher than I am."
Pat Brown considers it natural that a child should both disap-
prove of and learn from what he sees as his parents' shortcomings. He says he could hardly bear his father's trait of laughing at
his own jokes. "You can't see that in yourself. You can't mirror
your own inadequacies," philosophizes Pat Brown.

Although Jerry Brown might often criticize his father, he does
not like to hear other people do so. In 1961, when Brown was a
student at Berkeley, his father assigned a staff member to show
him around the state so he could obtain a firsthand introduction
to California politics. The aide who conducted the tour says the
governor "very much wanted his son to see how he was perceived
by the party faithful. I think Pat always had an inordinate
interest in the kid. He was something very special to both" Pat
and Bernice Brown. Part of the trip covered rural areas of
Northern California, where "Pat was seen as the villain who had
helped steal water from the north and give it to the south" by
promoting the state water project, one of the major achievements
of his eight years as governor. The tour guide said that when
Jerry Brown heard criticism of his father, he became "somewhat
defensive. You can despise your father personally, but you can't
stand anybody else's negative observations." The trip helped
"restore Jerry's confidence because he was compelled to defend
pop. He had the kind of contempt a bright, well-educated kid
would have for someone who was Pat's age and who was an
accommodating politician who had to be nice to people that Jerry
believed were scum. He always believed that all the party people
around Pat were ward heelers, and he carried that prejudice, I
think, a long way."

Dealing with the governor's son was a task that few members
of Pat Brown's staff relished. According to Mesplé, Jerry Brown
"would ask a lot of questions, and I think that's what kind of
ticked off some of the staff people," whose attitude was: "Hell,
he's off somewhere else being something else, and then suddenly
he begins to probe and question. Why all the second guessing of
his dad or the staff?" Jack Tomlinson, another of Pat Brown's
aides, said, "Jerry never shared his thoughts except when he had

a bitch, which he expressed frequently. Jerry has never shied away from trying to get something done when he thought it should be done. Lots of times people thought that he was a genuine pain in the ass. . . . I'm sure he looked upon me as another one of the many professional political types around his father. He didn't respect them because he didn't respect the process and those who served in the process."

Another former member of Pat Brown's staff says that "the kid had a terrible reputation among the staff as the ballbreaker. He was really viewed in a very negative way as somebody who could undo in one afternoon what the staff had spent weeks trying to put together." The ex-aide said many staff members disliked Jerry Brown's "purist approach that came either out of the monastery or out of Berkeley."

Members of the governor's staff regarded the younger Brown as a meddler who did not share their own awareness that Pat Brown, and not his son, had been elected governor. The depth of their feeling was made clear by an incident that occurred while Jerry Brown was a student at Berkeley. One of Pat Brown's former assistants said the governor's son had wanted a highway patrolman who acted as a driver-bodyguard for Pat Brown to teach him to drive a motorcycle. The request was turned down as too dangerous and "members of Pat's staff offered to take up a collection to buy Jerry a motorcycle."

The dislike Pat Brown's aides felt for Jerry Brown was matched only by their affection for their boss. One after another spoke of him in the most glowing terms. Mesplé: "I adulated Pat, almost too much." Don Muir: "I knew him quite well, loved him dearly." Tom Hickey, who served both Browns, called working for Pat Brown "the best job I ever had." Bud Carpenter, the lobbyist who turned down several offers of high positions in Pat Brown's administration but who did advise him from time to time, termed Pat Brown "the best governor we ever had" during Carpenter's forty years on the Sacramento scene. "I think he had more guts in meeting the problems, whether it was a tax that had to be imposed or a decision that had to be made." Carpenter, who has also worked with Jerry Brown, added, "I have not had that kind of experience with this governor." And Bob Nance, who never worked directly for Pat Brown but knew him fairly well, said, "I will go to my grave with nothing but a strong platonic love for Pat Brown. He commands love from everyone."

Most of those who worked for Pat Brown had trouble transfer-ring their allegiance to his son. The majority of them either switched to other politicians or faded out of politics. Joe Cerrell, for example, moved into Hubert Humphrey's camp, and on August 22, 1977, wrote in a letter to *Newsweek,* "It is our country's loss that he [Humphrey] was never able to lead us as president." It is difficult to imagine anyone who worked closely with Pat Brown saying such a thing about his son.

Pat Brown also spawned a whole generation of political activists. Don Muir, Tom Hickey, Jack Tomlinson, and John Vasconcellos all earned their initiation into California politics as travel secretary to Pat Brown, who traveled extensively around the state, dropping in on local politicians, newspaper editors, police chiefs, and anyone else he thought might be informative or useful. Jerry Brown has no travel secretary because he goes on trips infrequently. When he does travel, he rarely drops in on people for casual, unscheduled visits.

Pat Brown was willing to listen to almost anyone who had a valid reason for wanting to talk to him. His son is much harder to reach. According to Mesplé, "When I was in Brown's office as legislative secretary, Christ, if [representatives of] the beer industry or the race tracks or anybody wanted in to talk to the governor, that was considered part of the process. You might disagree with them, but by God you sat down and listened to them. And I think there is a tendency on Jerry Brown's part to say, 'Well, I'm not going to listen to those characters.' " Mesplé suggests, "Hear 'em out and do what you think is right. I think [Jerry Brown has] always had a tendency [to believe] that there was a sort of innate corruption about that," probably because he saw "too much dealing, too much compromising, too much moderating" by Pat Brown when he was governor. Tom Hickey says Pat Brown "saw the role of governor as one where he had a responsibility to deal with issues that concerned interest groups within the state, whether those issues concerned him or not. He would respond to perceived needs that other people felt. Jerry is much more difficult to get to. He attends only to the problems that he thinks are important."

Hickey also pointed out that the two Browns faced entirely different circumstances during their terms as governor. In 1962, California passed New York to become the most populous state, and Pat Brown ordered a celebration to mark the occasion. The governor felt a sense of accomplishment because his progressive policies on education, highway building, and water development made it possible for the state to grow. Said Hickey, "Nobody had any concern about the impact these actions would have on quality of life ten, twenty, thirty, forty years later. We felt it was real progress. Now, ten years after Pat left office, we look back and say, 'God, how could we have been fooling ourselves?' " Pat Brown himself notes that when he was governor the emphasis was on growth, to the tune of 500,000 new Californians a year, but now it is on quality. Currently, he concedes, "Bigness is just like being fat. There's no virtue in it at all."

The foremost example of Jerry Brown's interference in his father's administration was the Caryl Chessman case. Chessman, known as the "Red Light Bandit," had separate felony convictions for rape and robbery and had been on Death Row since 1948 but had managed to use the legal system to avoid execution while Earl Warren and Goodwin Knight were in the governor's office. During his years in prison, Chessman had become an author, and his writings had evoked both notoriety and sympathy for his case. In February 1960, a year after Pat Brown took office, an execution date was set for the felon.

The night before Chessman's scheduled execution, Bernice Brown was at Squaw Valley as the state's representative at the opening of the 1960 Winter Olympics. The governor ate dinner at a restaurant with his clemency secretary, Cecil Poole, who was in charge of reviewing the cases of prisoners sentenced to die. Brown and Poole had a final talk about Chessman and agreed that the governor would not delay the execution. By that point, the most Brown could do for Chessman was grant him a temporary reprieve. Because Chessman had twice been convicted of felonies, only the state supreme court had the power to commute his sentence, and the court had already turned down Brown's request that Chessman be spared. Chessman's only hope was for the governor to order that the execution be stayed and then ask the legislature, which had refused to abolish capital punishment, to reconsider.

After his dinner with Poole, Pat Brown returned home alone. Late that night, Jerry Brown, a few weeks out of the seminary and a twenty-one-year-old student at Berkeley, called his father and asked him to spare Chessman's life and appeal to the legislature to ban the death penalty.

Pat Brown related his reaction: "I'll never forget this as long as

I live. I said, 'You've only got one chance in a thousand' " to persuade the legislature to overturn the previous decision. "He said, 'Well, if you only had one chance in a thousand, and you were a doctor, and you could save a man's life, wouldn't you try to?' I said, 'Jerry, I'll save him.'

"He couldn't believe that he had convinced me that easily. He wouldn't have been convinced that easily. He's not as subject to emotions as I am. I wanted to do it, anyway, just between you and me. The Chessman case always bothered me because he hadn't killed anybody." Also, Pat Brown said, there were so many errors in Chessman's trials that he had a reasonable doubt about the condemned man's guilt.

Pat Brown explained that the fact his son had until a few weeks earlier been a student for the priesthood made his argument on behalf of Chessman extremely persuasive. "I had a tremendous respect for his moral I.Q. at this stage of the game. So when he called me up and asked me to do that, it was more than a son calling, it was a man that had given three-and-a-half years of his life to God. He definitely and beyond peradventure of a doubt changed my mind."

Pat Brown also recalled the "very awesome power that a governor has to decide whether you live or die. When you've got the power of life or death, the thing that goes through your mind is, 'Gee, how can you let some guy die just to further your own political career? Am I so crass that I'll let a human being die when I don't believe he should die?' "

So Pat Brown granted Chessman a reprieve and asked the legislature to suspend the death penalty in the state for two years' further study. The legislators refused, Chessman's stays of execution finally expired, and he went to the gas chamber on May 2, 1960, but not before the episode had caused Pat Brown to be branded with names like "Tower of Jelly." Pat Brown now says, "The reprieve was kind of a silly thing to do because it just postponed the poor guy's agony. I knew that, but then Jerry said, 'You have one chance in a thousand.' "

Looking back, Pat Brown is convinced that the Chessman affair was the beginning of his downfall. "It hurt me terribly." His first year had been "fantastically successful," particularly in working with the Senate and Assembly. Mesplé said that during that first year Brown and the legislature had an excellent relationship because 1958 marked the first time in many years that the

Democrats controlled both the governor's office and the legislature. "The Chessman episode badly shattered a great deal of that because the legislature felt they'd been handed the hot potato, and why didn't the governor take the heat himself," said Mesplé.

The Chessman case also seriously damaged Pat Brown's popularity in part because the state supreme court as well as the legislature had made him look like the villain, ironically, because of his compassion. Brown said that after he asked the court to spare Chessman's life, Chief Justice Phil S. Gibson had told him, " 'Pat, not only are they going to turn you down, they're going to kick you in the teeth.' They wrote an opinion turning me down and criticizing me for asking, even asking, to commute a horrible man like Chessman." The decision against Chessman was four to three, with Justice Tobriner writing the dissenting opinion. One footnote to history is that the swing vote was cast by Thomas P. White, one of Pat Brown's appointees. Brown, who described White as one of "my loyal friends," named him to the court in August 1959 as a favor. White had agreed to resign after a few months, according to Brown, but "we had a hell of a time getting him off the court," at last succeeding in October 1962.

After his decision to try to spare Chessman's life, said Pat Brown, "Everywhere I went I was booed. I went to the Winter Olympics, and I was booed. I went to the ballgame [in San Francisco] in April, and I was booed. I never was before that. It affected my dobber, my psyche. My chief assistant, Fred Dutton, said to me, 'You had no right to reprieve this man. You were the trustee of the blind and the aged and the children. And you were doing a great job. And just for this wretch,' he said, 'you sacrificed it all.' "

Pat Brown said that because he gave in to his son's last-minute plea even though he had turned down Chessman's earlier requests, "I got a reputation of being a vacillator, of not being able to make up my mind, of changing all the time, when as a matter of fact, when I got into anything, I stuck to it. I never changed." Altogether, Pat Brown considered appeals from fifty inmates on Death Row and let thirty-six of them die, for what he calls "the most horrible crimes."

Bernice Brown says she, too, "was really upset about it because I didn't think it would do any good and it would hurt Pat, and I was right. And it was Jerry who was responsible.

"The press wrote it up as if he vacillated, but they didn't

understand he didn't have the power to commute him," Mrs. Brown added. "That was never made clear."

Although Brown defeated Richard Nixon in 1962, he lost to Reagan by nearly one million votes in 1966. Certainly, much of the huge margin reflected public dissatisfaction over riots in Watts and on the campuses, as well as the sentiment, as Muir put it, that "Pat Brown had run his course." Cerrell pointed out that "when you lose by almost a million votes, you know there was no single issue or factor that brought the defeat about." One obvious element in Pat Brown's humiliating defeat was that he and his aides badly underestimated Ronald Reagan, whom they dismissed as a lightweight without political experience. According to Mesplé, "There was literally dancing in the hallways when he won the Republican primary, because we figured, 'Christ, this guy has never had a second in public office.' So there was no real conception of the masterful campaigner he was," in a state where there is no substitute for being adept in front of the television cameras. But most of Pat Brown's supporters seem to agree with Senator Alan Cranston, who said, "Pat was to some degree, I think, undone by the Chessman case. That was the first big downer in his governorship."

On March 17, 1977, seventeen years after Chessman died, *San Francisco Chronicle* columnist Herb Caen reported that when someone told former San Francisco Mayor George Christopher, who ran against Reagan in the 1966 GOP primary, "What people forget about Chessman is that he never killed anyone," Christopher replied, "Oh, yes he did. He killed Pat Brown." Pat Brown shares Christopher's assessment: "I never fully recovered from the Chessman case."

On another occasion, Pat Brown did not take Jerry Brown's unsolicited advice because he could not. Pat Brown said that in August 1957, when his son, then in the seminary, learned he was considering running for governor rather than seeking reelection as attorney general, Jerry Brown urged his father to run for the U.S. Senate instead.

Jerry Brown wrote his father and said "he thought the U.S. Senate offered a far greater opportunity to serve the people and to serve God. It was a beautiful letter. I still have it. He went on to say that [a senator] really had an opportunity to work on antidiscrimination nationwide and to help the minorities and the poor and to maybe bring peace to the world. He didn't denigrate the governorship in any way at all, but he just thought that the Senate offered a far greater opportunity."

In his book *Reagan and Reality: The Two Californias* (Praeger, 1970) Pat Brown quoted from the end of his son's letter:

> God has endowed you with certain talents and abilities and has given you the opportunities to make use of them. And, just as it is true that you have been given these talents and opportunities, it is equally true that you have been given serious obligations right along with them.
>
> These obligations consist not only in a just and fair administration of your office, but in making positive efforts to spread and defend the natural law of God. How can the rights of minorities be protected if the entire concept of "inalienable rights" is being pushed aside by the protagonists of "situation ethics"?

"I was amazed, frankly, at the letter," Pat Brown recalled, "because it was such an analysis of the job of being governor. It's a letter that to this day I wonder. . . . He never had been a great student at school or a great scholar. I really thought one of the priests wrote it down there for him. It was that well constructed and everything." What Jerry Brown did not know was that Pat Brown had already agreed to support Clair Engle for the Senate seat in return for Engle's backing him for governor.

If the death penalty is the issue that helped destroy the first Governor Brown, at least the second Governor Brown approaches it with his eyes wide open. On July 20, 1977, after the senate had overridden Brown's veto of the death penalty but before the override in the assembly, Mervin Field released a California Poll showing that residents of the state favored the death penalty by a margin of seventy-one to twenty-three, the highest rate of approval the issue had received in the more than two decades public opinion had been surveyed on it, except for 1975, when the ratio was seventy-four to twenty-one. Previously, sentiment in favor of capital punishment ranged from a low of forty-nine to twenty-nine in 1956 to a high of sixty-six to twenty-four in 1972, the year the voters approved a death penalty initiative.

The U.S. Supreme Court struck down the death penalty

nationwide in 1972, finding it to be "cruel and unusual punishment," prohibited by the constitution. After California's voters overwhelmingly approved a death-penalty initiative that November, the legislature passed and Governor Reagan signed a bill reinstituting capital punishment. While state courts studied the validity of that law, no executions took place, and in December 1976, the state supreme court ruled that the 1973 law was unconstitutional because it made death the mandatory sentence for certain crimes without allowing mitigating circumstances to be taken into consideration.

One month after the California Supreme Court's decision, Brown reached the end of his 1977 address to the legislature and then added rather casually, "The Supreme Court has recently struck down the death penalty in this state. That is something that I thought about for a long time. My position is very clear on this subject. I respect each one of you. I respect the judgment of the people, but as you begin your deliberations, I feel it incumbent upon me to share with you what I believe. And for me this is a matter of conscience . . . if a [death penalty] bill should come to my desk, I will return it without my signature."

Brown's forthright declaration even earned him the plaudits of *San Francisco Chronicle* columnist Charles McCabe, generally the governor's most outspoken critic in the news media. McCabe wrote on March 1, 1977:

Jerry Brown got elected by projecting the idea that he was different from other politicians. He gave us his spacey version of Zen Buddhism, the radical ideas of the British economist E. F. Schumacher on lowered expectations, and some rather ostentatious frugality. Now that his administration is past its halfway mark, the emperor is naked, revealed as an entirely conventional power-grubber and wheeler-dealer, with a decidedly unattractive *persona*. Wherefore, his recent stand on capital punishment is all the more astonishing. Brown has practically never done anything that he did not think would bring him votes. . . . I have not had many good words to say about Jerry Brown. I recognized quite early in the game that he was brummagem material. But in this supremely human issue, he has stood on principle. He has done so at his considerable political cost, and he gets a handshake from me for it.

In May, the legislature passed a law that would have restored the death penalty in California, and on May 27, 1977, the governor vetoed the legislation, stating, "Statistics can be marshalled and arguments propounded. But at some point each of us must decide for himself what sort of future he would want. For me, this would be a society where we do not attempt to use death as a punishment."

Four months later, when I asked him if he would be able to ignore a condemned person's plea for clemency, Brown replied, "I don't know. I don't think you know until something happens. I've said I would carry out the law and serve my oath of office. The law was passed by two thirds of the people, two thirds of the legislature, and an executive repeal just doesn't strike me as the appropriate balance between the legislature and the executive. The law of clemency envisions a judgment to be made in each case, not some blanket pardon. I could pardon everybody in prison today. I don't think the law envisions that. People leave it to the good faith and good judgment of the chief executive to make judgments according to the letter as well as the spirit of the law. And certainly the spirit of the law at this point is that there be available the death penalty for the crimes enumerated and that the chief executive have the power of clemency in appropriate situations. I'll take a look at each case."

But, Brown added, "I think the death penalty has fundamental problems. I don't think it's appropriate. It doesn't serve the goal it intends, namely to protect society. I think it's arbitrarily imposed. It occurs long after the fact on an almost random basis and extinguishes a life in a deliberate way without the normal context that occurs in war or self-defense or heat of passion, which would seem more understandable, even if not particularly justifiable."

The bill that passed both houses of the legislature by two-thirds majorities after Brown's veto in May 1977 invoked the death penalty for sixteen types of first-degree murder, including the slaying of a police officer; murder during the course of a robbery, kidnap, or rape; killings by torture; mass murders; hired killings; and the murder of a witness in order to prevent testimony in court. This was the first time in Brown's term that one of his vetoes was overridden. The governor, who favored life imprisonment without possibility of parole for persons convicted of serious crimes, did not attempt to persuade legislators to refrain from overriding his veto. Instead, he urged them to vote their conscience, as he had. Paul Priolo, Republican leader in the assembly, and other GOP stalwarts accused Brown of actually wanting the legislature to override his veto so he could avoid the almost certain presence of a November 1978 ballot measure to restore the death sentence. Friends and foes of Brown agreed that if the death penalty were on the ballot when Brown was seeking his second term, it would hurt his chances of winning. But Marc Poché said, "If it turned out that the governor had to lose, I think he'd be willing to lose on that issue."

Ironically, Brown takes a much more dim view of human nature than his father, and is significantly more hard-line on all law-and-order issues except the question of the death penalty.

Soon after he announced he would veto a death-penalty bill, Brown demonstrated his position on crime by proposing to spend $94 million to expand the state prison system, declaring that his administration would be glad to spend money for more prisons "if the judges have the fortitude to provide us with the clientele."

Brown has signed legislation that imposes mandatory prison sentences for those who sell a half ounce or more of heroin; for people who use a firearm while committing robbery, kidnap, rape, assault with intent to murder, and other crimes; for former convicts who commit violent crimes while on parole; and for anyone who commits a violent crime against senior citizens, the blind, or the handicapped. He has also signed bills that make it a felony for terrorists to threaten anyone with death or serious injury in order to gain social or political ends and that direct courts to fine criminals to help compensate their victims.

When he signed the law that directs judges to issue prison terms for criminals who use firearms, the first mandatory sentence law in the state in ten years, Brown declared: "Whatever the circumstances, however eloquent the lawyer, judges will no longer have discretion to grant probation *even* to first offenders. This may not rehabilitate nor get at the underlying causes, but it will punish those who deserve it. The philosophy of this bill is based not on sociology or Freudian theory but on simple justice."

He expressed similar thoughts three days later, on September

26, 1975, when he signed the bill relating to heroin sales: "It doesn't matter who you are, [whether] you are rich or you are poor, or you have a good argument or a good story, . . . Right now for many people crime pays. . . . It takes a lot to get caught, it takes a lot to get through the [court] process, it takes a lot to get convicted, it takes a lot to get sent to prison. This bill in many instances will make it easier and quicker to send somebody to prison, thereby increasing the cost of crime and thereby deterring it." The intent of the bill, said Brown, was to show that "this is wrong behavior and that it is deserving of punishment irrespective of whether the punishment will deter, rehabilitate, or anything else."

At the same time, the governor announced that he would reverse Reagan administration policies, under which, he said, repeat offenders received shorter sentences than did first offenders. Brown declared that a career criminal should be made aware that "at some point he's never going to get out."

The governor also voiced strong opposition to California's indeterminate sentencing procedure, under which many criminals received sentences such as "from five years to life," and a parole board decided the actual release date, the main criterion being reports from experts and prison officials who observed the inmate. "There's been a philosophy that an expert group of people called psychologists and psychometrics and psychiatrists and various other assorted people were able to take a person and figure out what's in his head and then tell when he's ready to be released," Brown said at the September 26, 1975, press session on the heroin sales bill. "Now that philosophy is coming under serious question." As a substitute, Brown proposed "mandatory, certain sentences, whatever is in your head. Then we don't have to spend a lot of money on group gab sessions where you talk about what your mother did or didn't do to you. And I think that's a lot of what goes on in some of these places, and I personally sat in on a few. I once sat in on a group therapy session in Vacaville [correctional medical facility]. Very interesting, but I'm not sure what it produces."

Brown also took a law-and-order stance while he was a candidate for president. While campaigning in Maryland, he said, "Prisons don't rehabilitate very well, but they punish pretty good. We tell them that real early. We say, 'This is your punishment, and if you do it again, you're going to get more.' We have cut away a lot of baloney about if you go to prison you'll get psychotherapy and psychology and all that junk. It's not pleasant, and it's not supposed to be."

On September 20, 1976, Brown signed what he called the "most far-reaching criminal justice reform in the last fifty years": Senate Bill 42, which ended the indeterminate sentence. Instead, the new law requires a judge to choose the middle of three possible sentences for a given crime unless specific facts justify a longer or shorter term. Under questioning by Brown, Rodney J. Blonien, executive director of the California Peace Officers' Association, who was present for the signing of SB42, said that more anticrime legislation had been passed and signed during the less than two years Brown had been governor than during Reagan's entire eight years in office.

A year later, when I interviewed Brown, he explained, "I think it's reasonable to have clear laws to attempt to maintain reasonable security and safety in the society." Some crimes are "socially unacceptable, and certain reasonably severe sentences are appropriate. It's one way of setting forth what are the values of society and what are the sanctions for their violation."

Brown has said he would like to abolish the so-called Saturday night specials, or cheap handguns, but he told an audience at the University of Maryland during his 1976 campaign, "I would not try to confiscate every gun in the country." In September 1975, however, Brown did sign a law increasing from five to fifteen days the period someone buying a handgun must wait before taking delivery.

As of the end of 1977, the only significant laws signed by Brown that reduce criminal penalties are one authored by Willie Brown that legalized various sex acts between consenting adults in private and another by George Moscone that lessened the penalty for possession of up to one ounce of marijuana to a maximum fine of $100. When Brown signed the marijuana bill, though, he issued a stern warning that the sale or cultivation of marijuana, even less than an ounce, is still punishable by a prison term. "This new law . . . does not decriminalize possession of marijuana, as many suppose," declared Brown.

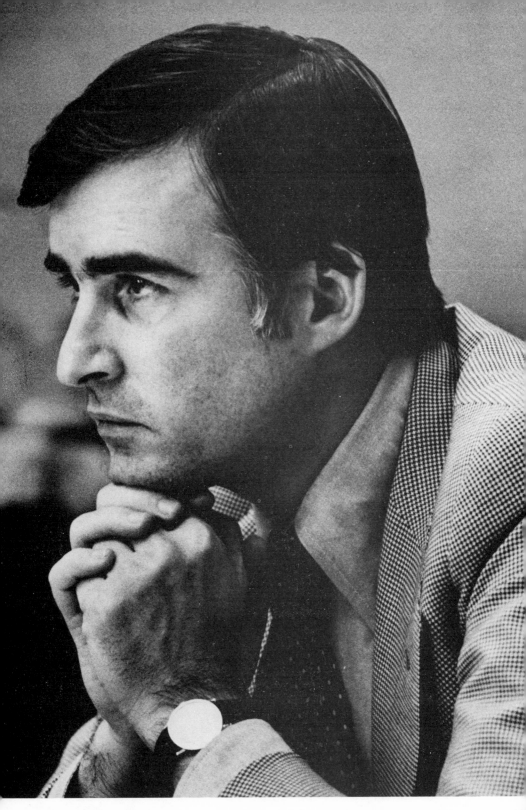

(Photo: *Sacramento Bee*)

LEFT: Jerry Brown as he looked at St. Ignatius High School's "Senior Fite Nite," Spring 1955. He was listed on the program as "Attorney General Brown," and according to the Tale of the Tape, he stood 5'8" and weighed in at 143½ pounds—a pound and a half lighter than his opponent, whom he solidly beat.

BELOW: Jerry Brown is fourth man back in left row in this photograph of the Sanctuary Society at the University of Santa Clara, 1955–56. Members of the group were responsible for conducting morning and evening masses for members of the university community. (Photo from *Redwood 1956*, the University of Santa Clara yearbook)

ABOVE: The University of Santa Clara debate team, 1955–56. Among those pictured are Father William Perkins, the coach (third from left); Frank Damrell (fourth from left); and Jerry Brown (third from right). (Photo from *Redwood 1956,* the University of Santa Clara yearbook)

CENTER: June 1956. Jerry Brown and Peter Finnegan, two months before they entered the Sacred Heart Novitiate at Los Gatos to study for the priesthood. (Photo: Peter Finnegan collection)

RIGHT: Bernice and Pat Brown, 1964 (Photo: California State Library)

LEFT: Running for governor, 1974: Brown with Houston Flournoy; and with Bob Moretti (below). (Photos: *Sacramento Bee*)

LEFT: Photos of Brown with singer Helen Reddy caused some people to ask, "Who's that man with Helen Reddy?" (Photo: Kathy Harter)

BELOW: In January 1974 the Brown family gathered in San Francisco to celebrate Mrs. Ida Brown's 96th birthday. Directly behind her is her son, Pat Brown. The man standing second from the right is Joe Kelly. Between Pat Brown and Joe Kelly is Cynthia Brown Kelly. (Photo: Cynthia Brown Kelly collection)

ABOVE: January 6, 1975: Chief Justice of the California Supreme Court Donald Wright swears in Edmund G. Brown, Jr., as the state's thirty-fourth governor. (Photo: *Sacramento Bee*)

OPPOSITE: Governor-elect Brown visits with Governor Ronald Reagan in the governor's office amid moving-day clutter. (Photo: *Sacramento Bee*)

BELOW: The Reverend Martin Luther King and Governor Brown meet after prayer breakfast. (Photo: *Sacramento Bee*)

ABOVE:
Rose Bird (Photo: *Sacramento Bee*)

CENTER:
Jacques Barzaghi (Photo: *Sacramento Bee*)

BELOW:
Marc Poché (Photo: Paul Bacosa studio)

ABOVE:
Gray Davis (Photo: *Sacramento Bee*)

CENTER:
Tom Quinn (Photo: *Sacramento Bee*)

BELOW:
Peter Finnegan (Photo: Ken Arnold)

Brown talks to reporters upon returning from his April 1977 trip to Japan. (Photo: *Sacramento Bee*)

CHAPTER EIGHT

THE NEW LEADERS *

Less than three months after he was sworn in as governor, Edmund G. Brown, Jr., told a group of reporters who were standing in a hallway at the Capitol, "My job is to make appointments, to set out overall policy for the executive branch, and appoint the best people I can. I do that." He outlined a similar view of the presidency while he was seeking that office. At a Sacramento press conference on May 4, 1976, Brown stated that "the chief role [of the president] is one of describing a vision, setting a direction, focusing on the most important things, and getting the kind of people whose philosophy will begin to permeate those large institutions that are there before the president arrives and remain long after he leaves."

Taken together, Brown's appointments constitute what is no doubt the most important action of his term in office. He has

* Portions of this chapter appeared in the *Los Angeles Times*, August 21, 1977.

brought about a genuine social revolution, transferring power from the white, middle-aged males who have traditionally held it to both men and women of all races, ages, and social backgrounds. As of January 4, 1978, Brown had made a total of 2,111 appointments during his first three years in office. Of those, 658 were women, 198 Chicanos, 167 blacks, 64 Asians, 30 American Indians, and 10 Filipinos.

Brown's most celebrated, and controversial, appointment, that of Rose Elizabeth Bird as chief justice of the state supreme court, illustrates his interest in naming women and members of minority groups to important positions in state government. This concern is far from new; as early as June 9, 1973, while Brown was secretary of state and almost eight months before he formally announced that he was a candidate for governor, he pointed out to a women's group meeting in Los Angeles that only one of the top 156 jobs in the Reagan administration was held by a woman. "There are countless women in California with imagination and energy whose talents must be used if California is to meet its great potential," said Brown. "It's time for an end to the stereotyped thinking that relegates women to the so-called 'feminine' occupations. No person should have his or her options limited by outdated thinking." Marc Poché, one of Brown's closest friends since the two met as students at Santa Clara University in 1955 and who served as director of programs and policy during the first eighteen months of the Brown administration, says that Brown's desire to bring to high-level positions people who have been shut out in the past because of their sex, ethnic background, or income level is "a very deeply felt thing. It's not a political thing. It comes out of his gut."

Brown once said at a press conference that "I just look at the individuals, look at the job, and make the best human judgment I can. That process is really the story of what my administration is all about. I want people who are open, who are bright, who have a sense of value and purpose." In March 1975, he told the *Sacramento Bee*, "I've put people in office who are very sensitive and committed to human beings first. Foremost, I don't have a bunch of businessmen."

When Brown was criticized for naming Adriana Gianturco, thirty-six, a former *Time* reporter and transportation aide in Massachusetts, as director of the state Department of Transportation (Cal-Trans), he responded by quoting from the teachings of Suzuki-Roshi, founder of the San Francisco Zen center, "In a beginner's mind, there are many possibilities and [in an] expert's very few.' Now Adriana happens to be far more than just that [a beginner]. I think she has a lot of training, experience, and certainly her record qualifies her every bit to be director of Cal-Trans as much as mine does to qualify me to be governor. If I wanted a technician then I wouldn't be looking for a director because we have the finest engineers and technicians in the world over there at Cal-Trans," said Brown at a press conference on March 16, 1976.

Many of those who have worked most closely with Brown during the past three years are young attorneys with backgrounds in public interest law, the American Civil Liberties Union, or as public defenders. Among them are Tony Kline, Brown's legal-affairs director; Rose Bird, who served two years as secretary of agriculture and services before she was named chief justice; Paul Halvonik, Brown's former assistant for legislative affairs; Mickey Kantor, who was Brown's campaign manager for the presidential race; Mario Obledo, who has been secretary of health and welfare for the entire Brown administration; and Robert Gnaizda, former deputy secretary of health and welfare and still one of Brown's sounding boards.

Also from this background is Jim Lorenz, one of the founders of California Rural Legal Assistance (CRLA) who headed the Employment Development Department during the first six months of the Brown administration until he was fired and replaced by another former CRLA attorney, Martin Glick. Lorenz sees the "old boy, old girl network of people who came through legal services and public interest law" as "the old school tie" of the Brown administration. According to Lorenz, Kline, who was a contemporary of Brown's at Yale Law School, plays the key role in helping Brown choose people for important jobs. Kline's influence, says Lorenz, has been "enormous. He is largely responsible for Jerry's excellent appointments to the administration."

In 1971, Kline, Gnaizda, and two other young lawyers formed Public Advocates Inc., the largest nonprofit public-interest law firm in the West. In its early days, the San Francisco-based firm represented La Raza Unida, a Chicano organization, and the Sierra Club in a suit against Secretary of Transportation John Volpe. The plaintiffs were able to halt building of a $100-million freeway that would have displaced 5,000 low-income persons, most of them Mexican-American, and destroyed three parks. Even more important, the court agreed with arguments by Public Advocates that the federal government, the defendant, should pay for legal fees and for the testimony of expert witnesses. The decision meant that public-interest attorneys would not have to rely so heavily on grants from foundations and that private lawyers would be more willing to represent clients who could not afford their fees. Public Advocates also launched the *Serrano* v. *Priest* action that resulted in a ruling that California's method of using property taxes to finance schools was unconstitutional because pupils in wealthy districts tended to receive a better education than did students in poorer ones. The firm also represented tenants and other residents in San Francisco's Yerba Buena redevelopment area and won 2,000 new housing units, whereas only 276 had been planned.

Traditionally, most appointees to top-level federal and state government posts have had to take hefty cuts in pay when they became public officials. This is one way in which many of the people Brown has brought to state government do not fit the norm. Kline notes that "being a public-interest or a poverty lawyer, we're among the few people who usually earn more money rather than less in government."

Brown's appointees cover a wide spectrum, including:

Women. Bird and Claire Dedrick, a leading environmentalist, were the first two women cabinet members in state history. Dedrick started the Brown administration as secretary of the Resources Agency, the state's equivalent of the U.S. Department of Interior. Dedrick became a trailblazer for a second time when, in June 1977, Brown appointed her as the first female member of the state's powerful Public Utilities Commission, which has authority to regulate the rates of gas, electric, and telephone companies, among its other duties.

Other women named by Brown to important posts are Elisabeth Coleman, Brown's press secretary since August 1976; Carlotta Herman Mellon, his appointments secretary, who is in charge of screening candidates for all openings the governor can fill; Gianturco; Janet Levy, director of the Department of Aging; and Virginia Mae Days, director of Veterans Affairs.

Blacks. In February 1977, at the same time Brown named Bird to be chief justice, he appointed Wiley Manuel to be the first black on the high court. Manuel had previously worked for twenty-three years in the state department of justice and since January 1976 had served as an Alameda County superior court judge, a post for which Brown had also selected him. Manuel, the son of a dining-car waiter, said at his swearing in that "at the time I graduated from law school, I could not aspire to this bench." Prior to the appointments of Bird and Manuel, a total of ninety-one justices had been members of the supreme court since its founding in 1849. All ninety-one of them had two traits in common: They were white, and they were male. Brown did choose a white male, Frank Newman, a distinguished professor at Boalt Hall Law School at Berkeley, for the third opening on the court he filled in June 1977, after the forced retirement of Justice Marshall McComb.

When Bird left her post as secretary of Agriculture and Services, Brown picked the first black to serve in the cabinet in California history, Leonard Grimes. At the same time, the position Bird had held was divided in two, with a State and Consumer Services Agency, which Grimes was named to head, and a separate Agriculture Department. In essence, Grimes was given an upgraded rank and title, although his new job was little different from the one that had been his during the first two years of the Brown administration, director of the Department of General Services.

Information that Brown had named a second black to his cabinet turned out to be both false and embarrassing to the Brown administration. On June 24, 1977, Brown picked Huey Johnson, a conservationist, to succeed Claire Dedrick as secretary of Resources. One of Brown's aides, making an incorrect assumption based on the new secretary's name, reportedly informed various people in the Capitol that Johnson was black. Circulation of the story came to an abrupt halt when it reached the ears of Assemblyman Willie Brown, who, as one of the leading black politicians in the state, makes it his business to know who is black and who is not.

On December 13, 1977, Brown appointed Doris Alexis, a black

woman, as director of the Department of Motor Vehicles. Alexis, who had gone to work in the department in 1952 as a $1.33-an-hour temporary employee, would earn $41,000 a year as head of the agency, which has 7,000 workers.

Mexican-Americans. Mario Obledo, Brown's secretary of Health and Welfare, is the first Chicano to serve in California's cabinet. He was formerly head of the Mexican-American Defense Fund, as was Vilma Martinez, whom Brown chose in March 1977 to replace the ultraconservative Catherine Hearst on the University of California Board of Regents. Brown said he wanted a Mexican-American on the Board of Regents because "I am not satisfied that UC is open enough for all citizens." Herman Sillas, first vice president of the same Chicano organization that produced Obledo and Martinez, served as director of the Department of Motor Vehicles from the beginning of the Brown administration until near the end of 1977, when President Carter named him a U.S. attorney. Brown also appointed Cruz Reynoso, a former director of CRLA, to the state appellate court, the next highest judicial level to the supreme court, and Reynoso is said to have a good chance to be picked for any future vacancy on the supreme court that might occur while Brown is governor.

People of Oriental descent. In June 1977, Brown appointed Yoritada Wada as the first Asian-American on the University of California Board of Regents. He has also named Jerry Enomoto head of the Department of Corrections (or prisons), and Taketsugu Takei director of the Department of Consumer Affairs.

American Indians. Fred William Gabourie, a former actor and movie stunt man, was appointed to the Los Angeles Muncipal Court in Jaanuary 1976. He is believed to be the state's first full-blooded Indian jurist.

Brown's appointments have resulted in several cases in which an official's job was uniquely suited to his background. The family of welfare director Obledo was on welfare when he was a child; Enomoto, who runs the state prison system, spent eighteen months as a teen-ager in a Northern California relocation camp for Japanese-Americans during World War II; and Ed Roberts, the director of the Department of Rehabilitation, which operates programs for the handicapped, is a quadriplegic.

Obledo, forty-five, was one of twelve children. His father, a housepainter in San Antonio, died when Obledo was five, and the family spent several years on welfare. Obledo thinks the experience helps him relate better to the 1.5 million Californians who are on welfare.

Enomoto, fifty-one, says that although "there was no conscious link between the fact that I was locked up under those circumstances at one time in my life and the fact that I subsequently went into the corrections business, . . . I feel like that experience gives me some feelings about people and about what we do with and to people that help me in terms of this kind of business." Enomoto, who has worked for the Department of Corrections since 1952 and was formerly superintendent at Tehachapi State Prison, is in charge of a prison system that has 21,000 male and female inmates and 9,000 employees. He pointed out that even though he is not black or Chicano—blacks and browns make up 54 percent of the state's prison population—"I am a minority. I have been kicked around. I have felt discrimination and all that stuff. I have had places that wouldn't rent me an apartment. So I have some personal feelings that make me understand where people are coming from, some link of feeling between people who, through their own behavior or a combination of a lot of factors, find themselves in trouble." Enomoto does not conform to the stereotyped image of the hardbitten prison official, and he will talk to anyone who might have solutions to prison problems, even representatives of prison-reform groups. "I got nothing to lose by listening to anybody," he says.

Two of Brown's more innovative appointees are white males, Phil Favro and Dr. Jerome Lackner. Favro, a classmate of Brown in high school and for the year Brown spent at Santa Clara University, is state fire marshal. He was a lieutenant in the San Francisco Fire Department, a rank low enough to ensure that he actually rode to fires on fire trucks when Brown tapped him as the state's top firefighter in October 1975. The day after Favro's appointment was announced, Brown responded to criticism about his alleged lack of qualifications for the job by stating that the qualities he was seeking were "intelligence, courage, and honesty." He went on, "I wanted a man right off the fire engines, not out of bureaucracy."

Favro said that in addition to his background and his friendship with Brown, which some people thought injected cronyism into the choice, his appointment caused Brown to come under criticism from some firefighting organizations because he failed to follow tradition and consult them in advance. "There was a lot of flack," said Favro. But, "I was a firefighter that he knew and trusted. When he asks me questions about something, I'll tell him what I think. I'm not technically qualified to do a lot of the code work that's required, but that's what I have two deputies to do."

Favro sees his role as trying to make his department more responsive to the public. He has created citizens' committees that meet several times a year to discuss regulations covering building safety, explosives and flammable liquids, fire extinguishers, and fireworks. "We have sought input from the people who are being affected by the regulations," says Favro. "I don't think that's been done before. Typically you regulate by saying this is what you should be doing, and the experts will tell you how to do it. I find that amateurs, if you will, have an awful lot to contribute simply by opening their mouths and saying something because we bureaucrats have a tendency of talking only to ourselves." Favro has instructed his staff to respond to citizens whenever possible by telephone instead of by mail, which he considers "kind of a cold way of communicating with people, especially some of the letters that bureaucrats write. So I've tried to put a stop to that." Favro has found his method to be effective. "People appreciate telephone calls. If they took enough time to sit down and write you a letter because they're concerned about something you're doing, I think it's worth my time to get on the phone and call them back."

And then there is Lackner, the head of the Department of Health, who calls himself a "liability" to Brown and has proof to back up his claim. In March 1976, Lackner proposed that federally funded clinics should dispense heroin at no charge to addicts, which caused a controversy and drew an almost immediate public rebuke from Brown. Lackner explains that current methods of treating drug addiction have failed, and "I want to put the underground out of business by using a purely business approach, not a medical approach." Lackner says that giving heroin to any addict who wants it would not result in the creation of new addicts because "junkies make new junkies, dealers don't. The user sells himself to the dealer, not the other way around." Lackner is quick to add, "However, the governor disagrees with that one hundred percent."

Lackner, fifty, no doubt would have been a poverty lawyer like many of Brown's other appointees had he chosen to practice law. He has degrees in both law and medicine but decided to be a doctor instead of an attorney. Unlike most physicians, he belongs to a union; he was a charter member of the Union of American Physicians. Cesar Chavez and Marc Poché were among his patients before he joined the Brown administration. During a peace march in San Francisco in 1965, Lackner heard that Chavez's United Farm Workers needed medical care, and he traveled to UFW offices in Delano in California's Central Valley, where he set up the first clinic for farm workers. Lackner's office in San Jose was broken into twice during the late 1960s, and in the wake of 1976 revelations about political burglaries aimed at the UFW, he now assumes that whoever entered his office was looking for Chavez's medical records, which Lackner had filed under another name.

Like Favro, Lackner has an unusual outlook for an administrator. "I have a funny attitude toward groups that hassle us," says Lackner. "I feel they perform a useful function, getting government off of dead center. It's almost a partnership." Lackner readily admits, "I'm not an administrator. I'm a health professional." As a result, at Brown's urging, Lackner hired Raymond Procunier, former head of the Department of Corrections, to be his chief deputy and to take Lackner's place as an administrator. Lackner emphasizes, "I come strictly from outside the establishment."

In addition to sex, race, and socioeconomic background, many of the people Brown has named to office are unique because of their youth and their potential for leaving their imprint on state government far beyond his term as governor. Chief Justice Bird, for example, was only forty when she moved to the supreme court, and although she has said repeatedly that "I don't look upon this as a retirement job," the fact remains that she could head the court for several decades. Even if she should resign, she will most likely continue to be very influential for many years simply by virtue of having been chief justice.

Bird says that "in a very real sense he [Brown] has jumped a generation in terms of governance. He has appointed an awful lot of people in their thirties, when ordinarily the people holding

those positions would be in their late forties, fifties, and sixties."
Among those who were in their thirties or younger when Brown
appointed them to high posts are Gray Davis; Tony Kline; Donald
Burns; Robert Gnaizda; Tony Dougherty, who replaced Poché as
Brown's top legislative assistant; Elisabeth Coleman; Carlotta
Mellon; Tom Quinn; Richard Maullin; and Jacques Barzaghi.

Bird also commented, "Where other people in politics have
talked about putting minorities and women into positions of
authority and power, I think he's one of the few that's really
done something about it."

There are those, of course, who are not so enthusiastic about
Governor Brown's appointments. "He has gone a little overboard,
in my opinion, in the appointment of women and minorities,"
says State Senator Alan Sieroty (D, Los Angeles), who is generally
supportive of Brown's policies. "And I think it is resulting in the
overlooking of many people who are very well qualified."

Democratic Assemblyman Daniel Boatwright (D, Concord)
concurred. "I just feel that there needs to be a better balance.
You know, just because you are a white Anglo-Saxon Protestant
male . . . does not mean that you are not sympathetic to the needs
of the people of the state of California."

One observer with an admitted bias, Houston Flournoy,
believes that Brown's appointments have been "cruddy. Except
that statistically and politically they look good."

According to Appointments Secretary Mellon, "Our basic goal
is to try to get the best people appointed, and within that to try to
also increase the representation of people who traditionally have
been excluded from government." Mellon, a former college
professor of women's studies, concedes that Brown wants her to
be on the lookout for qualified women and minorities, "but I
don't think [we] say, 'that's a slot for a minortiy and that's a slot
for a woman.' "

Brown outlined the philosophy of appointments that he had
applied during his first three years in office: "I would say I'm
trying to find a diversity of human talent for government, and
because of the fact that in many places in government women
and minorities are not as well represented or recognized or
sought after, their place in my administration is more visible. I
am determined to try to open up the places within government
and within the private sector to the extent that I can do that, and

I see it as an important part of the survival and the continued well-being of the state and of the country. What I mean by that is that there is a tremendous amount of talent that is needed for the well-being of the society that is being excluded and untapped because of stereotyped images, and those images should be broken down. It's not that one group should be preferred over another or that categories should be created but only that the society doesn't adequately assimilate the diversity of people and talent that it has within it, and therefore positive efforts have to be taken to break down these barriers. But the breaking down of the barriers is only a means to an end, which is a more open and diverse and opportunity-filled society.

"I don't think we should get hung up on the temporary changes that we have to go through in order to achieve that goal. I've got a lot of women, a lot of individuals who are defined as being members of groups that are not normally seen in positions of power. And that will continue to be so. I don't want a club, just an old-boy network to run government. The opening up will actually help the institutions that are now resisting it. I think they will come to understand that, especially in the corporate world," where Brown hopes his hiring policies will cause "a ripple effect. That's my goal."

In spite of Brown's policy of seeking minorities and women for government jobs, Willie Brown criticizes him because "there is nobody in Jerry Brown's administration who is black at the upper-echelon level. There are no black Tony Klines in Jerry Brown's administration. And I don't think Jerry Brown would be totally comfortable with a black Tony Kline or a black Bob Gnaizda or even a black Rose Bird." Willie Brown is of the opinion, as are most other people, that Leonard Grimes does not have nearly as much stature within the administration as did Bird, who was known for her willingness to say whatever she pleased, and to have the governor listen with respect. According to Willie Brown, the governor "did not have a black at cabinet level until Rose Bird left, and when Rose Bird left, he then stripped that cabinet level job of much of its authority and then he gave it to a black. That really grinds on me . . . I've got to have some reservations about where Jerry Brown is really coming from when it comes to black folk."

Willie Brown also spoke angrily about Mervyn Dymally's treatment at the hands of Governor Brown, who has generally ignored his lieutenant governor except when he was trying to woo black voters during his bid for higher office in 1976.

Responding to Willie Brown's charges, Governor Brown said, "People have as much authority as their ideas warrant. Authority comes from the intrinsic value of someone's thoughts and their ability to communicate them and their access in which to do both. Most of the special-interest groups will always want a little more authority, and their official spokesmen will always have to be somewhat discontent because that's their job. If everything were done, then they'd be out of a job."

Rose Bird is about six feet tall and lean. She has very fair skin and brownish-blonde hair that she usually wears piled on top of her head, which makes her look even taller. Her appearance, combined with that of her fellow justices, has prompted Herb Caen of the *San Francisco Chronicle* to refer to them as "Snow White and the Six Dwarfs." She has a girlish giggle and a pleasant demeanor, but those who know Bird well say that in private she can play hard ball with the toughest politicians and administrators.

Bird met Jerry Brown at International House at Berkeley in 1960 and kept in touch with him over the next dozen years, during which she graduated with honors from Boalt Hall Law School at Berkeley, was the first woman to serve as clerk to the Chief Justice of the Nevada Supreme Court, the first woman to be hired by the public defender's office in Santa Clara County, and the first woman to be a member of the faculty at the prestigious Stanford Law School, where she taught part time while she worked in the public defender's office. As a public defender, she wrote a landmark brief that was adopted by the U.S. Supreme Court in the case of *People of California* v. *Krivda*, which involved the search of a garbage can to gather evidence of a crime. Bird argued successfully that when a state supreme court had made a ruling based on the state's constitution, the U.S. Supreme Court should limit its jurisdiction and not apply the federal constitution to the case.

In the summer of 1974, Bird worked as a volunteer in Brown's gubernatorial campaign in San Mateo County, south of San Francisco. She recalled, "I did everything from stuffing envelopes and licking them to trying to set up more of a grassroots campaign," which the candidate lacked. When Brown was campaigning in her area, Bird sometimes acted as his driver.

Right after Brown was elected, he called Bird and asked her to come to Los Angeles to help him plan the new administration. "In his usual way, he wanted me to come the next day, as though you could drop your whole life and just immediately come." Bird may have established a precedent that would affect her future working relationship with the governor: "I went, [but] not the next day." She said she wanted to continue practicing law, and "I didn't have a real interest in staying [with Brown]. I just thought it would be interesting to see a government in transition."

However, the offer to be a member of Brown's cabinet intrigued Bird. "I had a strong feeling that he was going to be a very different kind of governor, and it might be exciting to work with him. I think he has a kind of vision that a lot of people in politics don't have. And I think he has an ability to put very disparate things together that are happening in a society and see the whole when everyone else sees just a small part, sort of in the way that a prophet can see the future."

When Brown spoke of government's limited ability to solve problems, it struck a responsive chord with Bird, who as a public defender had witnessed "the stupidity of a lot of government programs. You saw young people coming in, and you knew that they were going to graduate from Juvenile Hall into the municipal courts and then the superior court and end up in San Quentin or some part of the prison system, and there was no way to stop it."

Bird finally accepted Brown's offer. Technically, she was the first woman he appointed to the cabinet since he announced her selection two days before he disclosed Claire Dedrick's.

Two years later, when Brown revealed that he was nominating Bird to be chief justice, the news created a storm. Appointments to the supreme court must be confirmed by the state Commission on Judicial Appointments, a three-member panel that at the time of Bird's nomination consisted of Acting Chief Justice Mathew Tobriner, Justice Parker Wood of the state Court of Appeal, and Attorney General Evelle Younger, a Republican with plans to run for governor in 1978. Typical of adverse reaction to Brown's choice was an editorial in the *Los Angeles Herald-Examiner* on February 18, 1977: "Only the Commission on Judicial Appointments, by refusing to confirm Ms. Bird, can save the state from

Brown's serious mistake." The *Los Angeles Times* gave the opposite view, editorializing in favor of Bird's confirmation by the commission on February 15 and March 6, 1977.

It quickly became apparent that Tobriner, the old friend of the Brown family who had once picked Jerry Brown to be his law clerk, would vote in favor of Bird's appointment and that Wood was opposed, leaving Younger in the no-win position of casting the deciding vote. Most Republicans, including Younger's two major opponents at the time of the GOP nomination in 1978, San Diego Mayor Pete Wilson and Los Angeles Police Chief Ed Davis, were against Bird's nomination. But a vote against Bird could antagonize women as well as many independents who might vote for Younger in 1978.

Fuel was added to the fire when Bishop Roger Mahony, the former chairman of the Agricultural Labor Relations Board who had worked closely with Bird and was thought to be an ally of hers, wrote the Commission on Judicial Appointments:

> My opposition to her appointment as Chief Justice centers on her questionable emotional stability and her vindictive approach to dealing with all persons under her authority. I experienced personally her vindictiveness on many occasions when the ALRB, an independent state agency, chose to pursue a course other than that desired by Ms. Bird.
>
> She has a personal temperament which enables her to lash out at people who do not agree with her. Her normal approach is to become vindictive, then to transfer her feelings to a long phase of noncommunication. She would refuse to take or return telephone calls or to acknowledge any attempts at communication.
>
> I am gravely concerned that the future Chief Justice of our State Supreme Court be a person of balanced emotional stability, of judicial temperament, and of coresponsible collaboration with the other justices. In my experience and opinion, Ms. Bird fits none of these requirements.

Those who were opposed to Bird's nomination pointed out that an important qualification for a chief justice is previous judicial experience and that Bird had none, while her supporters responded that neither U.S. Chief Justice Earl Warren (a former governor of California) nor Roger Traynor, a former justice and chief justice of the California Supreme Court, had been judges before they embarked on distinguished careers as jurists.

Boatwright believes "there were people a lot better qualified to become chief justice of the supreme court" than was Bird. "Perhaps she should have been considered for justice of the court, but certainly I don't think [for] chief justice. I'm talking about purely knowledge of the law and nothing else." An associate of both Brown and Bird before Bird's nomination thinks appointees to the high court should be persons of "great stature and great commitment," and that measured in these terms, the nominations of Bird and Manuel by Brown were "not very impressive." But labor leader Blackie Leavitt, who has no reason to be protective of Brown, says, "I think that was one of the finest appointments that he could have made because Rose was the only one in his administration that you could get her ear and get an answer from her. I think that's one of the biggest things he's done as governor."

Bird had unquestionably exhibited a forceful personality as a member of Brown's cabinet and had clashed with a number of people, including fellow cabinet member Don Burns. After Burns wished Bird a happy birthday on November 2, 1976, Bird reciprocated the next day, Burns' own birthday, by sending him a note and a present. Her gift to Burns, who like Bird is not known as a shrinking violet, was John Dean's book, *Blind Ambition*.

Ben Bycel, who as an aide to former Senator George Moscone had often crossed swords with Bird, offered a humorous footnote to her nomination. While the appointment was under consideration by Tobriner, Wood, and Younger, Bycel, who had moved to Santa Barbara and opened a law office, received a call from one of Bird's aides. Bycel, who said Bird "was less than friendly to me" when he worked for Moscone, was informed by her assistant that the governor and Bird remembered him as "a strong advocate" and would like to appoint him to a state post. "I nearly fell off my chair laughing," said Bycel. "I viewed it as an attempt on their part to clean things up." Subsequently, Bycel did receive an appointment—to the State Cemetery Board, a position that carries with it the pay of $50 per day while on state business. "They obviously thought they could buy me off cheap," said Bycel, chuckling over the incident. In spite of apparent fears by Brown and Bird that Bycel intended to urge that she not be confirmed, Bycel said, "I wrote a note saying that Rose would make a great Chief Justice, which quite frankly I intended to do, anyway, because I thought she was about the best appointment he could have made."

Younger ultimately voted to approve the nomination of Bird, and a previous action by Bird may have helped Younger decide in favor of her. Bird regards her two principal achievements during her two years with the Brown administration as having helped create the Agricultural Labor Relations Board and having lobbied successfully for legislation that requires regulatory boards to include representatives of the public without expertise in the field being regulated.

The public-members legislation, according to Bird, "was a major accomplishment because it overcame tremendous power within the legislative branch. When we started out, even Willie Brown laughed at us and said, 'You know, there's no chance, you're not going to make it on this one.' That legislation was very important because it meant opening up government to the citizens again."

When Governor Brown signed one of the public-members bills in September 1976, he declared that its passage was proof that "the legislature recognizes that ordinary citizens are as competent to make public policy in the regulated areas as the professionals themselves." And at the time he swore in several dozen public representatives on various boards in February 1977, Brown told the new board members that their role was to be that of "lobbyists for the people."

Bird's fight to put public members on state agencies may have played an important role in Younger's decision to vote for her. One of the bills required that six people who are not attorneys be added to the State Bar Board of Governors, which previously consisted of fifteen lawyers. When the Board of Governors cast an advisory vote on whether or not Bird was qualified to be chief justice, the vote was twelve in favor of Ms. Bird; three against; five abstaining, and one absent. The vote of individual members of the board was not made public, but during open hearings on the nomination, board member Joseph Cummings, an attorney, said that only six of the fifteen lawyers on the board had voted for Ms. Bird, implying that the six other favorable votes came from the public members. Younger voted for Bird's nomination with obvious reluctance. Had the six public representatives not been on the Board of Governors, Younger might have been able to vote against Bird and argue that at least eight of the fifteen members of the board had not found her qualified to be chief justice.

One aspect of Brown's appointments policy that has been widely criticized is his nonappointments; Brown has failed to fill many positions for which he could have chosen people. Most vacancies existed early in his term as governor, when Brown personally interviewed many potential nominees, even for the most obscure positions. Appointments secretary Carlotta Mellon concedes that such criticism was at least in part justified at the start of the administration, although she says such attacks are no longer valid. Daniel Boatwright charges that "when he doesn't make appointments, I think he is really not fulfilling part of the oath of office. There is no justifiable reason for failing to make appointments after two and three years to these various boards and commissions. None." Boatwright added, "It really is, I think, crippling the work of a lot of these bodies. . . . Some of them can't even get a quorum because the governor has failed to appoint."

According to Peter Finnegan, "It's like Jerry's constipated. I truly do believe Jerry does have this feeling that once he's made an appointment, he's given away a little power. It's cockeyed thinking." One of Brown's early actions as governor was to name Finnegan to the Alcoholic Beverage Control (ABC) Appeals Board, which has three members. When one member resigned, leaving only Finnegan and one other person on the board, Finnegan tried to persuade Brown to fill the vacancy but was unsuccessful until he threatened to "go public. I told the governor in formal communications," said Finnegan, that unless Brown filled the opening, he would post notices in the legal newspapers in Los Angeles and San Francisco announcing that the appeals board "would cease holding hearings for lack of a quorum. That prompted him then to get on the stick" and name the third member. Finnegan admits that his job, which pays about $20,000 a year and requires very little work, is "the highest-paid sinecure in the state of California." And one old friend of Brown and Finnegan, with Finnegan's appointment in mind, said, "If I were Peter Finnegan, I could never say anything bad about Jerry."

In August 1976, one of Brown's most severe critics, Assembly

GOP leader Paul Priolo, issued a report that showed that of the
3,349 jobs subject to being filled by the governor, 565, or 17
percent, were vacant. Priolo publicly called on Brown to "fulfill
his responsibilities of office and take action to fill the 565
appointive vacancies presently slowing down the governmental
process within the state of California." Priolo also said it was
"most distressing that California's governor has neither the time
nor the interest to fill these appointive positions. It is rather
ironic that while Jerry Brown was cavorting around the nation
espousing his philosophy of greater public participation in
government, his home state was left to suffer from his unwillingness to fill the appointments which would make greater public
participation possible within California."

Priolo's compilation of openings, however, showed that while
the vacancies might seem impressive in sheer numbers, few jobs
of consequence had not been filled. For example, 149, or more
than one-quarter of the vacancies cited by Priolo, existed on local
medical quality review committees, and many of the other
openings were on such agencies as the Law Executive Board of
the Job Development Corporation, the Resource Conservation
Commission, local Hospital Advisory Boards, the Health Facilities Commission, the state Design Awards Committee, the
Advisory Committee on Emergency Medical Services, and the
Intergovernmental Board of Electronic Data Processing. In most
cases it is likely that Priolo himself had never heard of these
agencies until his researchers discovered that vacancies existed
on them.

In addition to his own staff, the most important posts that a
governor of California must fill are judgeships and trustees of the
state's colleges and universities. Priolo's study revealed that the
vacancy rate on these bodies was only 2 percent, although Priolo
did not mention it.

According to Mellon, "The Governor feels that you don't just
make an appointment because the appointment is there. There
should be a reason. You've got a darn good person you want to
put in, or there are some policies you want to enact, and you
ought to make some positions, or they don't have a quorum, or
enough people are saying they want an appointment to the
Contractor License Board, so you make one."

Betty Werthman says that Watergate proved that "when you
allow someone else to appoint your people, you don't know who

you're getting," and that Brown feels "to assure the people that they get the best, he has to talk to" potential appointees. "It slows the process down, but what do you want: a fast process and no-good people?"

Joe Kelly, the governor's brother-in-law, recalls a family gathering that occurred while Brown was being criticized for the number of unfilled jobs; Brown went around the room asking his relatives and friends, "Do you think your life has been less full or complete because there's a vacancy on the Horseracing Board?"

Don Muir's experience in Brown's 1974 campaign did not leave him with any reason to go out of his way to say nice things about the governor. But Muir commented, "He has done some unconventional things that I kind of applaud. For example, sometimes when he says, 'You know, maybe I just won't fill this vacancy for a long time.' I saw this under his father," whom Muir served as travel secretary for several months, "the tendency for the agency head to come running and say, 'Well you got to [fill a particular job].' What job?" said Muir, "is the question that should have been asked. What effect does it have on the state if nobody is appointed? How does it affect people? In most cases where he [Jerry Brown] hasn't appointed, I can't see that it affects anybody, except that maybe there's one less job filled in California."

As Brown's legal affairs secretary, Tony Kline is responsible for keeping track of judicial vacancies and of candidates to fill them. The number of openings on the bench was higher than usual immediately after Brown took office because the Democratic-controlled legislature had held up creating about fifty new judgeships until Reagan left office, so that a governor from the Democratic Party could fill them. "I went in there [to Brown's office] after he'd been governor for a couple of weeks," said Kline, "and I said, 'Look, we ought to fill all these vacancies.' And he said, 'Why?' Frankly, the question had never occurred to me. The vacancies are there, and I just assumed they've got to be filled. He said, 'Well, what does a judge cost the taxpayers? Is appointing more judges the best way to deal with the problem of court congestion? How big is the bench? Do we have a big bench, little bench, do we have more judges per capita than other jurisdictions?'

"So we looked into those issues," Kline said, "and found some very interesting things," including the fact that each judge costs the state about $250,000 a year in terms of salary, office space, a staff, and a fully stocked library.

"We found that California has got the largest judicial system in the world. There is no nation in the world that has more judges than the state of California. We have, for example, three times as many state judges here as there are federal judges in the entire United States. We found that we have nearly as many judges in Los Angeles County alone as there are in England, although England has four times the population of Los Angeles County.

"We found that there is no significant jurisdiction in the world that has more judges per capita than California. So that the real problem" turned out to be "that Californians are the most litigious people in the world, that more disputes are brought for resolution in the courts here than is the case anywhere else in the world. And that maybe what needs to be done is that some things need to be taken out of the courts that don't need to be there."

Armed with this information, Brown said at a press conference on April 2, 1975, in reference to appointing more judges, "I'm troubled by the fact that judges have an automatic cost of living [increase] and relatively handsome salaries. And their pension system is unfunded. I want to take a look at the work load there and [see] whether or not income meets outgo."

Late in 1977, Brown said that although some of the comments about vacancies are valid, "oftentimes I'm not satisfied that I've found the right person or that I understand the potential of a given office. I'm not prepared to make an appointment pending that understanding. I would prefer to see the matter just continue with whatever momentum it has. Most of the time the government bureaucracy just grinds on, and unless I really see something, why bother?

"The system conspires against openness . . . and one way to short-circuit that circuitry is often just to do nothing and say, 'Well, we're going to wait and let new people emerge,' and that's exactly what I've tried to do. Sometimes a vacancy is openness, emptiness. If nothing happens, who's affected? I have often intentionally left vacancies to stimulate awareness, consciousness and discussion. I think it gives greater potential for constructive change if one allows a pause until we find out what we are trying to do."

If on occasion Brown can be slow to choose a person for a job, he can also be very quick. About one week before Brown's inauguration, Don Burns, who had been working on the transition team but had not yet learned what job, if any, he would have in the administration, had dinner in Los Angeles with Brown and several other people. After dinner, Brown and Burns happened to be walking together, and Brown said, " 'How are you enjoying it? Have you given any thought to what you might like to do?' So," Burns recalled, "I said, 'Well, you know, I think I might like to try being Secretary of B and T [Business and Transportation].' He says, 'Fine, you got it.' That was the entire conversation."

Burns later learned that Brown had long before decided that Burns should be his Business and Transportation secretary but had not told him because "he wanted the person to develop the idea that they wanted to do the thing and felt that they could do it before he offered it to them. Which is probably not a bad idea."

CHAPTER NINE

THE
GOVERNOR'S STAFF

Going to work for Jerry Brown is not recommended for anyone who is not in perfect health, who requires more than six or seven hours of sleep a night, who needs either private praise from his boss or public recognition for his accomplishments, who is in the habit of following a schedule, or who likes to have authority delegated through a normal chain of command.

Among those whose bodies rebelled against Brown's regimen of freeform work days lasting fourteen hours or more, six and seven days a week, are Carl Werthman, Tom Hickey, and David Jensen. Werthman spent the first eight months of the administration as a special assistant to Brown, working as a troubleshooter in health, criminal justice, and other areas. His stint as an aide to Brown ended after he suffered a heart attack and underwent open-heart surgery. Reflecting on his time with Brown, Werthman says he thinks his health was impaired by the long hours, the irregular eating schedule that Brown's method of management by crisis often necessitates, and the pressure of the job. Hickey was able to keep up with Pat Brown during his two years as the elder Brown's travel secretary, but ninety days as an aide to Jerry Brown left him with pneumonia and hepatitis. Jensen developed an ulcer after working for two years as a press aide to Brown. Each man was in his thirties and in reasonably good health at the time he joined Brown's staff. After recovering, Hickey returned to the business world, Werthman went back to teaching, and Jensen, a former wire-service reporter, joined the staff of the *Sacramento Bee.*

Alan E. Rothenberg succumbed to Brown's repeated requests and accepted the position of secretary of Business and Transportation as Don Burns' interim replacement in early 1977. Rothenberg, only thirty-one at the time, refused to stay longer than the ninety days he had agreed on and often walked out of late-night meetings during his time in Sacramento "because I like to sleep." Brown had hoped three months on the job would convince Rothenberg to sign on permanently, and although Rothenberg found his post extremely exciting and viewed the power at the top levels of government as "a powerful narcotic—when you're up it's hard to come down," he remained firm in his resolve to quit and resume his banking career, his life with his family, and a more normal work schedule.

Of the rewards of working for a politician, perhaps the greatest one is the opportunity to participate in decisions that affect large numbers of people and in some cases to initiate those actions. Gray Davis and Mickey Kantor have had more first-hand experience with Brown than anyone else during the last three years. Davis, as executive secretary throughout the Brown administration, has played by far the more significant role. On a day-to-day, hour-to-hour basis, no one has been in more direct contact with Brown since November 1974. As Brown's presidential campaign manager, Kantor has been the governor's chief political aide since the 1974 election, even though his involvement lasted for only about four months, and his authority was diluted by the power Davis retained, as well as by the presence of Tom Quinn. It is no coincidence that Davis and Kantor chose almost the same words to describe the means of having any influence with Brown. Davis: "If you're going to be chief of staff, you have to be here when he's here, and he's here most of the time." Kantor: "You have to be with Jerry every day or you're just not with him."

Because of his work habits, being at Brown's side requires a renouncement of outside activities, which has proved difficult for Quinn, Kantor, Marc Poché, Paul Halvonik, and others with family responsibilities.

Former Secretary of Resources Claire Dedrick will never forget the three-day "holiday" weekend early in the administration when she, Brown, and several others wrestled with problems relating to the timber industry. She said the group worked at least sixty of the seventy-two hours with about three hours of sleep a night until "the stroke of genius arrived sometime late Sunday afternoon. We damn near starved to death," said Dedrick because the meetings lasted until the early-morning hours and by that time no restaurants were open. Dedrick was temporarily living at the Senator Hotel across the street from the Capitol at the start of the administration. She subsisted on crackers, butter, and the cream that other guests had not used in their coffee, which the bellhop would save for her "dinner" when she got back from Brown's office. Dedrick said one of her friends gave her a copy of George R. Stewart's book *Ordeal by Hunger* and dedicated it to the Brown administration. But Dedrick, an ardent admirer of Brown, considers the hard work she did with him "the most incredible learning experience of my life."

There are those who do not have such fond memories. Dan Lowenstein says he has often wondered how Brown can attract so many talented aides in spite of the fact that "he doesn't treat people very well." According to Ray Fisher, who took a leave of absence from Tuttle and Taylor to work for Brown for several months, "His greatest liability is his coolness, his difficulty in relating to people at a human level. There are times when he's just tactless and rude, and you feel like saying, 'Why don't I get at least a pat on the back for my hard work?' He just uses people up."

Frank Schober says he once told Brown that "a lot of his success could be attributed to a very fine group of galley slaves." Robert Gnaizda points out that it is "a good Zen paradox" that Brown is "entitled to love his job and deny everyone else the opportunity to love their jobs. What he's done is he's locked up most of the potential of the people he's brought to government" by blocking their talents. Gnaizda cites Mario Obledo, Tony Kline, Ed Roberts, Jim Lorenz, Marty Glick, and Rothenberg as examples.

Although Peter Finnegan has never worked directly for Brown, he has noticed that the governor's office under his friend "is not a fun place to work." Finnegan stated, "If you find one person in Sacramento that's working in the governor's office that can tell you that they enjoy working for him, . . . they're bullshitting you. I mean, everybody just wants out. You know, that tells you something about the whole operation, and it goes directly to Jerry. I think it's very disturbing."

"One of the things about Brown," said David Jensen, "is that he's not the kind of guy who pats you on the back and tells you what a wonderful job you're doing. But you'll hear it when you do something wrong. So if you're a person that has to live on kudos and praise, you don't work for him for very long because you'll become very unhappy. And he expects an awful lot, I think far more than anybody else I've ever worked for. He's a yeller. He always tends to raise his voice."

Brown supporters Dedrick, Poché, and Bob Nance say the governor is grateful for what his aides do for him, for the hard work and the long hours, but as Dedrick says, "He doesn't utilize conventional techniques of expressing that." She believes Brown shows his thanks by doing "substantively, positively helpful things. If you've got a personal problem, he'll do something, never admitting that it's got anything to do with the fact that he knows you're feeling lousy." The sixty-year-old Nance, who fills in periodically as Brown's press assistant, said Brown often voiced concern that Nance might be getting tired and once made tea for him. Discussing Brown's alleged lack of interest in the comfort of his staff, Nance said, "To me if anything it's just a goddamned front Jerry Brown puts on. I think he's one of the most compassionate guys I've ever known." Poché said Brown "assumes a very high level of professional skill, loyalty, dedica-tion, and competence. If you know him well enough, you can see thanks in his eyes.

"I can understand someone coming in the governor's office and watching him operate for two or three hours. . . . I can see how somebody could walk out of that and say he's not compassionate. I can see them saying he's abrupt," said Poché. But "I found him one of the easiest people in the world to work with. I think he has almost too much personality."

Gray Davis, thirty-five, graduated from Stanford with honors in 1964 and from Columbia Law School in 1967. He served as a captain in the army in Vietnam and was awarded a Bronze Star.

At first glance, it might seem strange for Brown, the war protester, to have a former combat officer as his top aide, but Davis says he, too, was opposed to the Vietnam War. "I had an obligation to respond to the dictates of the system until I could persuade enough people to change the system," says Davis. "I believe in the system. I think the system is pretty responsive." Davis joined ROTC at Stanford in the early 1960s, before the United States was deeply involved in Indochina, and so was obligated for future military service. While in the army, from December 1967 until December 1969, he spent much time and effort doing the same thing that Jerry Brown, whom he had not yet met, was doing in California: trying to talk people into voting for Eugene McCarthy.

After his discharge, Davis went to work for one of the five-name Los Angeles law firms. "It's as conservative as the name suggests," he said. During his three years there, he served as a volunteer in several campaigns, including John Tunney's 1970 senate race. In late 1972, as Tom Bradley was launching a drive to become the first black mayor of Los Angeles, an aide called Davis, who "had never raised a nickel in my life," and asked him to be campaign finance director. Davis requested a leave of absence from his law firm but was told he would either have to stay on or resign. After thinking it over for a month, he quit and joined a campaign that culminated with Bradley ousting Sam Yorty from the mayor's office in May 1973. "To this day, the most satisfying election experience I've had is participating in his victory," says Davis. He regards his entry into politics as a natural product of his training at Columbia Law School, where he says he learned more about how policy is formed than about the effect of the policy. "The effect on me was to cause me to become a policy junkie," declared Davis.

Davis described his role as Brown's chief aide as "a very wearing undertaking. This job requires a certain kind of intellect and more emotional staying power than presiding over a department," which was his first choice. "I think it's the best and worst job," said Davis, using exactly the same words David Jensen used in describing Davis's position. Davis said he likes the opportunity to generate ideas that can be put into practice "if you can convince just one person." On the other hand, Davis must monitor the flow of paper and people and decide which of both gets to Brown. "That's the part of the job that I find not terribly satisfying."

One of Davis's suggestions was to find a more equitable way of allocating pay raises to the one hundred members of Brown's staff than a simple percentage increase, under which the highest paid aides, such as Davis, would receive the largest raises. During Brown's first year in office, the salaries of Davis and other top assistants were cut 7 percent, while clerical workers received a raise of five percent. In 1976, all state workers, including those on Brown's staff, were given a pay hike of $70 a month. In 1977, members of the governor's staff got a raise of $35 a month plus 5 percent of their pay, which amounted to nine percent for clerks and six percent for Davis and others at the top. "Our intention was to provide some economic assistance to the lower-paid employees in the office who don't get the recognition that some of the others of us do," Davis said.

The most unsatisfactory experience as a member of Brown's staff, from the viewpoints of both Brown and the aide involved, was that of Jim Lorenz, who directed the Employment Development (or unemployment) Department (EDD) during the first six months of the Brown administration in 1975. Lorenz, the same age as Brown, is a Harvard Law School graduate who helped found California Rural Legal Assistance, a poverty law group. He researched issues for Brown during the gubernatorial campaign in 1974. After the election, Tony Kline, a friend of Lorenz who was the de facto personnel director for the incoming administration, asked Lorenz if he would like to head EDD, and Lorenz said he would. "The conversation must have taken all of fifteen seconds," said Lorenz. Soon after that Brown called him "and said, 'Lorenz, why don't you take the Employment Department?' and I said, 'Okay.' "

Several weeks after Brown's inauguration, Lorenz visited an unemployment office in San Francisco to see how it operated. He had planned that the trip be unpublicized, but *San Francisco Chronicle* columnist Herb Caen found out about it and complimented Brown and Lorenz for the visit. The praise bothered Lorenz, who did not believe the state's unemployment policies should be lauded when California's jobless rate was about 10 percent, and almost a million people were out of work. Brown, however, appreciated Caen's story, according to Lorenz. Lorenz was further troubled by Brown's attempt to take credit for creating new jobs on his first day in office when, said Lorenz, no new jobs had been produced. Lorenz said he had difficulty pretending to be enthusiastic about such things. "I would say that I tended to be one of the more skeptical people in the administration about Brown," said Lorenz, who added that the governor seemed to sense how he felt.

Lorenz's usefulness to Brown came to an end shortly after Lorenz proposed that the state spend $175 million to fight unemployment by creating nonprofit community organizations that would hire thousands of jobless people. Lorenz had not intended that the plan, which he had offered simply for consideration by Brown and others, be made public. But the conservative *Oakland Tribune* obtained a copy of his memorandum, attacked it with a headline in red ink, and called for him to be fired.

The EDD was part of the Health and Welfare Agency, of which Mario Obledo was secretary. Soon after the *Oakland Tribune* story broke, Obledo told Lorenz he had lost his effectiveness and suggested he resign. "Knowing Mario, that didn't sound right to me because Mario doesn't initiate anything," said Lorenz. "At that point, if Jerry had called me and asked me directly, I think I would have resigned. But he wasn't man enough to say it to me directly. I was insulted. I didn't like this shadowboxing, and so I didn't submit my resignation. I just waited, and Mario got a little more agitated each day."

After ten days Lorenz tired of "this fencing at long distance" and requested a meeting with Brown, who agreed to see him and asked Davis and Poché to be present. Poché said he was extremely reluctant to participate since he hardly knew Lorenz and had had nothing to do with his agency. At the meeting, Brown asked for Lorenz's resignation, and Lorenz said he wanted more time to think it over. According to Lorenz, "We talked about the state of the world, very philosophical, until I started communicating that I was still resistant to quitting, and then he became more impatient and walked out of the room and left it to Gray Davis and Marc Poché to try to persuade me to leave. What a difficult position for them to be in."

A few hours later, Brown called Lorenz and told him he was being fired. The governor issued a statement in which he said, "Jim is a man of high ideals with a commitment to serving people. But despite his considerable talents, I don't think he can adequately manage such a large department of state government and effectively help meet the state's responsibility to the one million unemployed people in California."

Lorenz attributes his dismissal to the fact that he offered Brown political advice, which the governor did not want, and to the familiarity that had developed between the two men during the campaign, which Lorenz said made Brown uncomfortable after he became governor. Lorenz said he in turn had trouble living with the "political charade" under which department heads were not supposed to give explicit political suggestions but were expected to take politics into account in any proposals. Basically, Lorenz feels, the governor does not share his commitment to action.

Brown is reluctant to discuss Lorenz other than to say, "I have to have people I can have confidence in. I didn't think he was doing the best job. I wanted someone better," and to point out that Marty Glick, who succeeded Lorenz as EDD director, also replaced Lorenz at CRLA. That precedent, said the governor, shows he is not alone in believing that Glick is more effective than Lorenz.

In retrospect, Lorenz said, "On a comparative scale to what kind of job governors are doing in this country, he is doing a good job. That doesn't mean I don't have reservations about him." Lorenz said he voted for Carter in the 1976 California primary, but he expects to vote for Brown for governor in 1978 and might contribute money to his campaign.

Many others who have worked closely with the governor take issue with Lorenz's faultfinding. "I never could understand," said Rose Bird. "I've read some reports and comments that he surrounded himself with yes people and that he liked people to agree with him. I think once you know the governor, that's not true at all. One of the things I really admire about him the most is that he gives you the freedom to be yourself, which not many bosses do. When I worked for him, I could be quite blunt in my criticism, and I think rather than give me demerits, he seemed to like that." According to Poché, Lorenz had hardly any direct access to Brown during the period he worked for him, and would not be able to make valid criticism.

Roy Bell, Phil Favro, and Jerome Lackner have jobs comparable to Lorenz's in rank, and all three reject the idea that Brown likes to have yes people around him. The governor makes the decisions, but he wants opinions as well as facts from his aides, according to Favro. "I haven't had any occasion where he said, 'Just give me the facts, and we'll make the decisions up here.'" Finance Director Bell said, "He would normally expect a recommendation from us, but he would not automatically accept it, and he shouldn't."

Lackner likes "the freedom I have to go over to Brown's office and bounce any wild idea off the wall." Brown "doesn't want people who see only his point of view or support his point of view. He's an incredible governor because he permits you to argue with him." Of Lorenz, Lackner said, "I think Jim's methodology was maybe at fault. I think he was easily frustrated with a no and maybe even personally hurt with a no."

Lackner's press secretary, Bob Nance, offered another aspect of dealing with Brown: "You can go to him if you are running out of money for a program that is working well, especially if it is your own fault that the money is running out, and tell him, 'We fucked up, and here is what is going to happen to all the people who depended on the program because we fucked up.' It's not fair to throw the burden on the people who benefit from the program for our mistakes. And if you can convince the governor—this is not a pleasant conversation in any way—that the problem was your fault and the program was worthwhile, he will release general fund money to continue paying for the program."

If Gray Davis is Brown's surrogate on administrative and substantive matters, it is generally agreed that Jacques Barzaghi is Brown's intellectual alter ego. The governor has called Bill Burman his "confessor," at least at one stage of his life. Perhaps it is no coincidence, then, that the last time Burman saw Brown, ten years ago, Brown introduced him to Barzaghi.

Barzaghi is the only person on Brown's staff who also worked for him in the secretary of state's office, although Barzaghi played a minor role there. With Poché, Bird, and Burns gone, Davis, Barzaghi, and Tony Kline appear to be the only members of Brown's staff who do not have to ask permission from someone else in order to see or talk to the governor.

Barzaghi, the same age as Brown, expresses unusual thoughts with a French accent. For several years, he had a shaved head. He is Brown's primary link to the worlds of Zen, new art forms, and different ideas, or as Peter Finnegan puts it, to "the crazies, the weird people." Barzaghi's first name was once Lorenzo, but he changed it to Jacques, which gives him the same initials, JB, as Jerry Brown. Descriptions of him range from "benign bullshit artist" to "the Guru Governor's Guru" to "sinister."

Tony Kline discounts much of the speculation about Barzaghi. "I don't believe he's a Rasputin or an evil, malevolent force around here," he said. "The reason he is so fascinating for some people is that he speaks with an accent and didn't come to Sacramento wearing leisure suits and white shoes." Kline was quoted in a two-part series about Barzaghi that appeared in the *Sacramento Bee* on May 11 and 12, 1977. The *Bee* reported that according to records of the Central Intelligence Agency, Barzaghi was suspected of being a Chinese Communist sympathizer who helped foment student riots in Paris in 1968. In addition, the *Bee* said, Barzaghi had trouble gaining permanent resident status in the United States until he attached himself to Brown in the early 1970s. Then, according to the *Bee*, Brown advised Barzaghi to marry an American woman and intervened with U.S. Immigration authorities on his behalf. Barzaghi has four children by three wives, each an American woman.

Barzaghi, who in 1977 was in the process of becoming an American citizen, denies accusations that he is a Manchurian Candidate type or that he exerts a Svengalilike influence on Brown. He blames the *Bee*'s decision to investigate him on personal differences between him and one of the two reporters who worked on the story, Nancy Skelton. Barzaghi believes the facts did not warrant the *Bee*'s insinuations; he asserts that the paper ran the stories because it is "more interesting" to write that someone is sinister and give play to the reader's imagination than to write that he is not that much different from anyone else.

Just who is Jacques Barzaghi?

He was born in Beausoleil, a small town in the south of France. His parents split up when he was young, and he was raised by his grandmother, a working woman who was away from home much of the time. "So basically I was by myself," he recalls. Barzaghi grew up poor. Later, he traveled the world as a sailor in the French merchant marine and served in the French army in North Africa. His first wife, Tanya, was the daughter of American-born actor Eddie Constantine, whom Barzaghi describes as the Frank Sinatra of Europe. After living for six years in Paris, where he was involved in filmmaking, Barzaghi moved to the United States in mid-1968, a few months after the student riots and labor strikes that brought France to a standstill.

Jacques and Tanya Barzaghi and Ann Campbell, like Tanya, an American woman who had been living in Paris, settled together in Los Angeles for a short time until Tanya and her two daughters by Barzaghi returned to Paris. Campbell bore Barzaghi a third daughter in 1970 and married him in 1971. Shortly afterward, the U.S. Immigration and Naturalization Service granted him permanent-resident status.

Several months before the Immigration Service action, Barzaghi met Brown at the Laurel Canyon home of Rolando and Linda Klein. Barzaghi and Klein had worked together on an American Film Institute movie that was never released. The Kleins became close friends of Barzaghi and one day invited him to dinner, telling him that the secretary of state would be present. Barzaghi remembered that "secretary of state in my mind was probably fifty-year-old man with three-piece suit and very conservative, I mean, that was my French view of government since I was not aware of government in this country." Barzaghi spent forty-five minutes talking to a young man in jeans who had been introduced to him as "Jerry." He recalls the conversation as being a "very open" discussion of such topics as art, movies, American Indians, and human relations. According to Barzaghi, after about three-quarters of an hour, "I said, 'Hey, when your secretary of state is coming? Because I'm hungry.' " Following some nervous laughter, Barzaghi learned the full identity of the "Jerry" he had been talking to.

Shortly after he met Brown, Barzaghi visited the secretary of state's office in Los Angeles and commented that the pamphlets produced by Brown's staff were not very attractively designed. "Jerry just snapped back at me and said, 'Well, if you have any ideas, just let me know.' " Barzaghi then went to work with Tom Quinn and Brown aide Llew Werner on redesigning the pamphlets, and "Here I am today. That was the beginning."

Barzaghi appreciated the informal atmosphere in Brown's office, and the two quickly became friends. "Within Jerry's office," said Barzaghi, "there is no such thing as a relationship between the boss and the worker. There is people working together. That's what attracted me: the openness. I never got that feeling that somebody wanted to say something but that they didn't say it because Jerry Brown was the boss, which basically is the same now. I don't see any difference. There is no such thing around him of people you call yes men or no men. When people want to say something, they just say it."

Barzaghi began as a trainee clerk, but by 1974 he had gained Brown's confidence to the extent that he was entrusted with the crucial job of producing television commercials for the gubernatorial campaign. Barzaghi said this task was assigned to him in part because a professional campaign advertising agency would have cost a fortune, and Brown wanted to limit spending so he could limit his fund raising. "Jerry doesn't like to ask for money," said Barzaghi. "He knows the political implications of asking for money, which is not a nice one. A big company with a lot of money would give twenty-five thousand or fifty thousand or one hundred thousand to one candidate. I don't view it as clean as every citizen giving a dollar. There is a possibility" that the donor may say, " 'Hey, I gave you one hundred thousand dollars, but since I'm in business, maybe sometime, somewhere, I will ask you for something.' We have to live with it, that's the way the system works, but that doesn't mean it is a good system."

Barzaghi believes Brown is much less likely to be corrupted by the "system" than are other politicians because "Jerry Brown is what I classify as an honest person in terms of the way he responds to his responsibility. I know Jerry will not sign a piece of paper unless he understands it fully. To me, Jerry Brown is what I classify as within the marketplace, which is—on one side you have the church and on the other side you have the marketplace. I believe it's very easy to be an honest man within the church but not within the marketplace." As evidence of Brown's resistance to temptation, Barzaghi cites an incident that occurred when Brown was a seminarian and the novice master ordered coffee removed to prevent novices from drinking it. Brown argued unsuccessfully that leaving the coffee where it was and giving the novices a chance to refrain from drinking it would be a better way to build their character. Commemorating the incident, a sign next to a large coffee pot in Gray Davis's outer office suggests that staff members bear in mind Brown's advocacy of self-discipline before they indulge in the drink.

Barzaghi now has the title of cabinet secretary. He is also Brown's special assistant for the arts. He earns $25,000 a year and tends to be a jack of all trades. Brown considers him an astute judge of character and often asks him either to interview or to sit in on interviews with people who are seeking anything from high-level state jobs to a few minutes of Brown's time. In such situations, Barzaghi said, his function is to determine "what the person is looking for. I don't focus myself on the technical part. I'm not saying that person is a good administrator or a bad administrator. That's not really my interest." Instead, Barzaghi looks for "how that person will relate to other people," which is what he believes government is all about.

Discussing his relationship with Brown, Barzaghi expresses doubt over "who's giving and who's receiving. My tendency is, I'm probably taking more than I give. I'm probably learning more myself than what I can give." Barzaghi credits Brown with teaching him "something else than what was in my life before, which was very narrow. Suddenly, by talking to him . . . I find out there is a world, which I'm part of and which is beautiful, which I enjoy, and how can I make that world be better? Hey, I have to say thank you Jerry because I don't know what I give to him, but what he gives to me has no price, no price whatsoever."

Barzaghi views as an important part of his job the setting of examples for other people. That is why, he declares, his fourth child was born to his present wife Connie at home, with Barzaghi assisting.

As long as he is close to Brown, there are likely to be people who believe, as does Peter Finnegan, that Barzaghi is somewhat sinister. Says Finnegan, "Jacques bothers me. I consider Jacques dangerous. I always have. I don't like the way he thinks. . . . I think Jacques is a supreme con artist. . . . I have the feeling that Jacques is not truly a democrat with a small d. He certainly has never understood the American government. I also don't think he believes in the democratic process. I wouldn't be surprised if he's a Maoist. I've always had that perception of him. And that scares the shit out of me. This guy has input into appointments, into policy. There's been very little policy, to be honest, thank God."

Barzaghi emphatically denies such allegations. He says he loves his adopted land and cites an experience he had immediately after landing in the United States for the first time. In the men's room at Kennedy Airport, says Barzaghi, another man offered him a drink from a bottle of whiskey, a sharp contrast with his childhood memories of riding on trains in France and watching hungrily as other passengers in his compartment ate their brown bag meals and refused to share any with him.

"I've been through everything," Barzaghi comments. "When

you talk about going to school hungry with no food, I did it. When you talk about suffering, I mean, I did. When you talk about loneliness, I have it. When people talk about riding bicycles, I mean, that's the only thing that was available in my town. So it's like all the program that Jerry's bringing out, I know about it, and I have no problem with it." By limiting his consumption of material goods, he says. "I feel like I'm not losing anything."

Barzaghi speaks of his father's desire to come to America, a dream destroyed when his father died on Tahiti before he had the chance to travel to the United States. Then Barzaghi's mind drifts back a decade to New York, to Kennedy Airport, to a public rest room and a proffered drink: "Something happened there, I don't know what it was, but I felt, I'm in paradise. It just blow my mind. I couldn't believe it. Probably was exceptional. Probably will never happen again. But that moment. . . ."

CHAPTER TEN

FACING THE PRESS

Virtually all observers of Jerry Brown, including his friends, his foes, and journalists who are supposed to be impartial, agree that he is extremely adroit at dealing with the press. Unlike most other politicians, of course, Brown had a firsthand opportunity to learn the importance of the press as he grew up by watching his father's career.

Although Brown surpasses most other politicians, both those within California and those in other parts of the country, in his understanding of the press and his ability to use it, anyone who seeks statewide office in California must be able to take advantage of the chances the press offers to reach the public. The size of the state, in population and territory, makes it impossible for any candidate to meet personally with a significant number of voters even for the brief time it takes to shake hands or kiss a baby. Also, California's political parties are much weaker than their counterparts in other states, especially those in the East and

Midwest. As Tom Quinn explains, "The party structure in California is not horribly significant in terms of campaigns. The party certainly didn't play a role in Jerry's campaigns. The people are the ones who cast the votes. And California is not a place like Cook County [Chicago] where there's some kind of a political organization that will be able to communicate directly with people and influence votes.

"What is the party?" Quinn continued. "The party's a little office on Wilshire Boulevard or something like that with three or four people. The only way the party would reach the people is through the media. The party does not have any kind of a grassroots organization in this state. Every candidate starts from Ground Zero and creates his own campaign without a party structure to assist. So if you want to do commercials, you do your own. The party," he said, is "a paper organization."

Houston Flournoy learned the hard way that what Quinn says is true. "I must say in all honesty, although I resent it deeply, that if I ever were going to run again, I would pay a hell of a lot more attention to the media and a hell of a lot less attention to the people," he stated. "Quinn's specialty," Flournoy added, was that "he worked the radio news shows, and they are probably about as irresponsible a segment of the press as there is. You can call them up in a campaign, and they'll ask you, 'What do you want to say?' and you can say it, and they'll put it on at the commute hours. By the time the other guy finds out about it, it's three o'clock in the morning. No editing, no verification, no nothing. Just pump it out."

Bert Coffey, chairman of the Democratic party in California during 1977, also agrees with Quinn. Coffey said Brown's habit of reaching people through the news media and practically ignoring the party structure has weakened the Democrats in California. But, he said, the trend toward emphasizing media over party dates back almost twenty years, to John F. Kennedy's 1960 campaign for the presidency. Although Brown's attitude toward the party has angered many Democratic regulars, Coffey observed, the governor's support "seems to have eroded with everyone but the people—judging by the polls—and that's all that counts."

Joe Cerrell, who earns his living by helping Democratic candidates, is critical of Brown's tactics. According to Cerrell, "When you win by a narrow margin," as Brown did in 1974,

"you need everybody. I do think the party has a real claim on
Jerry's victory. But he feels that they need him more than he
needs them." Cerrell considers Brown's lack of interest in the
Democratic party "unhealthy. He makes a mockery of it. It could
come back to haunt him."

Brown's view is that parties have not been much of a factor in
the state for most of the twentieth century. He also believes that
political organizations throughout the country "are breaking
down" since the spread of the presidential primary system.

Charles Manatt, chairman of the state Democratic committee,
concurs. He says California has "less of a governor-dominated
party" than many other states but adds, "I don't think the party
is a lot weaker or stronger than it would have been otherwise
because of Jerry's activities."

Brown seems to have a deep curiosity, if not fascination,
regarding the press. Doug Faigin, who first met Brown when he
interviewed him for Radio News West during the 1968 McCarthy campaign, recalls that he found himself answering more
questions than he asked. Brown wanted to know all about the
process of producing radio news, and he questioned Faigin
closely about what would happen from the time the interview
was recorded until it was broadcast.

Betty Werthman was impressed by Brown's voracious appetite
for news one evening when Brown, a date, and the Werthmans
went out together. Brown, then secretary of state, "would pick up
newspapers on every corner and read them," according to
Werthman. "I couldn't believe it." However, she added, Brown
may have been driven to the newsstands that night because his
date seemed intent on relating her conversations with plants.
Don Burns, noting Brown's compulsion for print media, commented, "I think he's going to die of lead poisoning from the
newsprint."

To keep abreast of current reportage, Brown scans several
papers a day, receives a daily news summary, and checks the
Associated Press and United Press International wire machines
in his press office. The daily news summary is a collection of
several dozen stories that are clipped and sent to Brown, with
copies to other key members of the administration, such as Gray
Davis, cabinet officers, and agency heads. Included are articles
about Brown, the legislature, state agencies, the environment,

and other subjects known to interest Brown and the other readers. In several instances, one high-ranking member of the administration has asked the staff member who prepares the summary to omit stories that presented the official unfavorably, asserting that such articles could damage his credibility with others who have access to the briefing but promising to make sure that the governor sees the deleted story. Usually, the request has been granted.

To prepare the summary one of Brown's aides reads the major newspapers in the state (including the *Los Angeles Herald-Examiner, Los Angeles Times, Oakland Tribune, Sacramento Bee, Sacramento Union, San Diego Tribune, San Diego Union, San Francisco Chronicle, San Francisco Examiner, San Jose Mercury,* and *San Jose News*), as well as out-of-state papers such as the *Washington Post* and *New York Times* and dozens of magazines. Several times each day the wire-service stories are sent to Brown and Davis, and once in a while the governor stands over the wire machines, reading the copy as it comes in. On rare occasions, members of his staff will call the wire services to offer corrections or explanations of material in wire stories before they are printed in newspapers or broadcast over radio and television.

Brown's background and his interest in the media have combined to make him what Charles Manatt calls "certainly on today's standards . . . the best there is" at dealing with the press. Manatt attributes Brown's success with reporters to his "fundamental knowledge and understanding of what's important to the media." State Senator Alan Sieroty remarked, "I think that the governor has some excellent skills in communication. . . . He's able to articulate ideas very carefully. He puts into a few words a great deal of meaning. He says a lot and he says it well."

Others see Brown's relations with the press in rather Machiavellian terms. One such critic is Nancy Skelton, who has been on the Brown beat for the *Sacramento Bee* during most of his term as governor. On April 11, 1976, at the beginning of Brown's try for the presidency, Skelton wrote:

Brown is minutely careful with the media. He uses them. Calculates them. Manipulates them when he can. Indeed, the record shows, they have been his most reliable tool in making the enormous jump from junior college board member to viable presidential contender in seven political years. He knows better than anyone else, if it weren't for television, radio and the press, he wouldn't be where he is right now. Not so popular. Not such a curiosity. Not so pleasingly mysterious, like a half-buttoned blouse. Brown has totally depended on the media thus far to carry his presidential message across the country. Wire service stories, television broadcasts, newspaper columns, magazine articles—they've been leaving the state on a regular schedule since Brown became a candidate. Brown has yet to [travel outside of California since he became governor].

Brown says, "I'm just pretty much myself" in front of reporters. As for being a manipulator of the media, he retorts, "That's Nancy Skelton. She invented that phrase. I don't know what that means. I could say the media manipulates the candidates. It's a circuitry. The formulas that are adhered to by the media are somewhat limiting: 'The critics have said.' There are some very narrow, stylized formulas in which the exchange between the media and the public official is carried on."

But there is no doubt that Brown sees the relationship between the press and the politician as an adversary situation in which he can more than hold his own. People such as Vic Biondi and John Jervis, who have gone from reporters to state officials; Fred Epstein, Brown's campaign press secretary in 1976; and David Jensen, another of Brown's former press aides who is now a colleague of Skelton on the *Bee,* share her assessment even if some of them do not use the phrase "media manipulator."

Brown defines his dealings with the media as a "game" in which the reporters are "always" trying "to get the public official tied down before he wants to be." Journalists, according to Brown, "all want to get in the middle of the thought process before I feel that I'm finished thinking. That's been a constant tension around here. They want a half digested thought so they can be the first to write a story. And I want to think about [a subject], I want to mull it over, I want to meditate on it, and until I'm finished thinking about it, I don't have an announcement to make because I may decide to do something else or not do anything at all. I don't consider a decision made until I announce it."

Those who have had the most contact with Brown respect his tactics. "I think Jerry's success with the media is because he has an intuitive sense of how to communicate with people very well," says Tom Quinn. According to Gray Davis, Brown "has unique clarity of thought and speech that comes across in the media, which mirrors him. There is nothing so powerful as a clear idea. He is capable of communicating. It's as simple as that. You can call that media manipulation, but if you do, it misses the point. Most public officials seem to talk in a foreign language. There is no clear idea transmitted from sender to receiver. Jerry also tends to provide insights to people that they hadn't previously received." When asked whether Brown is a creation of the media, Llew Werner, who once worked for City News Service and has since served as a press assistant to Brown, answered with another question: "Isn't everybody in politics [a creation of the press]? Everybody is because the only way you reach people is through the media."

Don Burns recalled the time when he was secretary of Business and Transportation and he had only twenty minutes, minus frequent interruptions, to brief Brown on a very complex topic: redlining, the practice insurance companies and banks use to eliminate poor neighborhoods in which they don't want to invest. Burns was afraid Brown was not well enough prepared, but "he went out there [in front of the press], and he just wowed 'em. It's an incredible talent. Jerry doesn't like me to say this, but he can put things in a very punchy way. One of his talents is, you can go to him with something he's never heard about before, but three minutes later he can go out and there'll be a bunch of reporters, and he will say something that's very quotable, you know, it's headline material. It's amazing. And then people question him, and he's good on the answers."

Brown had shown his shrewd media sense as early as October 20, 1973, after the famous "Saturday Night Massacre." At 8:25 P.M. Eastern time, or 5:25 P.M. in California, it was announced that President Richard M. Nixon had ordered the firing of Special Watergate Prosecutor Archibald Cox; both Attorney General Elliot Richardson and his deputy, William Ruckelshaus, had resigned rather than carry out the command. When reporter Ken Reich, an old friend of Brown, heard the news bulletin on the radio, he rushed to his office at the *Los Angeles Times* to help put together a story for the Sunday paper. As he reached his desk, the telephone was ringing: It was Brown, saying he wanted to issue a statement calling for Nixon's impeachment. Reich tried to talk him into waiting until the next day so the *Times* could use the story on Monday, but according to Reich, Brown insisted, "Everybody is going to be saying this tomorrow. I want to say it tonight." Reich said Congressman Jerome Waldie, also a candidate for overnor, was the only other California politician with the sense to comment on Nixon's actions that Saturday night. The timeliness of Brown's move proved "he has a very good political antenna," Reich said, and as further proof mentioned that Brown had been the only person he knew who thought Eugene McCarthy was going anywhere several months before McCarthy humiliated Lyndon Johnson in the 1968 New Hampshire primary.

One example of Governor Brown's impact on journalists, at least on those who do not cover him daily, was offered by television reviewer Terrence O'Flaherty of the *San Francisco Chronicle*, who wrote on October 7, 1975:

California's Governor Edmund G. Brown Jr. made his first appearance on NBC's "Meet the Press" Sunday afternoon. Questions fired at him by a panel of political reporters were answered immediately, directly and with far more candor than I have seen displayed by a politician on this show in years. And he did so even when the questions were ludicrous—as many of them were.

Like President Kennedy, Brown not only understands how the press operates but also seems genuinely to enjoy matching wits with reporters. When a reporter opened Brown's press conference on August 15, 1975, by saying, "I expect the first question is, To what do we owe the honor of this meeting?" Brown responded, "I think it is appropriate that we normalize our relations. That is what they say in international policy." Brown's news conferences are often interrupted by widespread laughter among the press corps over such quips.

An example of Brown's gamesmanship with reporters occurred on April 12, 1977, when he returned from Japan. He told media representatives who met his plane at Sacramento Airport, "One of the reasons I paid for my own trip is so I wouldn't have to answer so many of your questions." Brown then went to his office, and within fifteen minutes of his arrival, press aides were rushing around gathering stories that had appeared during his four-day trip because Brown's first wish was to see what had been written about him.

Brown thinks that as a rule press aides are superfluous because they do work that reporters should be doing themselves. At least that is what he said at a September 26, 1975, news conference: "They do a variety of functions, information officers, but . . . we can cut back on that. . . . I think you people can ferret out what you need to ferret out and not get a prepackaged version, . . . so I've got my doubts about information officers." But Brown still has a four-person staff in his press office, including a press secretary, an assistant press secretary, and two clerk-typists. In the words of John Jervis, "He's got people who meddle with the press much more than Reagan or Pat Brown ever did. Including himself."

Both the governor and Gray Davis keep a watch over the press office, as Brown has done throughout his career in public office. "He likes to keep very close tabs on what the press operation is doing, more so I would say than [he does] some other sections in the governor's office," said David Jensen, who was associate press secretary during the 1974 campaign and through Brown's first year and a half as governor. "During the gubernatorial campaign, he approved every single press release, and he would edit them severely," Jensen said, even down to "minor word changes. During the campaign, every press release was okayed by him personally, word for word. We had to go to some lengths to get a copy of the press release to him, especially when he was traveling around." Usually, Llew Werner would accompany Brown on trips, and either Werner would call the press office, or the news staff would call him. Then it was Werner's responsibility to grab Brown and bring him to the telephone so the latest news release could be read to him. Jensen added, "Initially, as governor, he was looking at every press release, also," until after a few months Brown stopped reading the more routine ones. "I've always thought that he would have made a hell of a good editor or reporter," said Jensen, "because he just incessantly questions. He was a very demanding guy to work for."

Peter Finnegan said that soon after Brown's inauguration he came upon the governor "sitting there editing some routine press release, and I just said to him, 'You've got to be out of your fucking mind. Either be a governor or be an editor, but don't be

both. I mean, you know, govern for Christ sake. You're supposed
to be governor.' It's absurd. Besides, how do you think Bill Stall
feels—felt?" Stall, a former Associated Press reporter, was press
secretary for the first year of the Brown administration, then
joined the *Los Angeles Times*.

Says Brown, "My words and my thoughts are what I'm
contributing, and I don't want some faceless person to be
misrepresenting to the public what purports to come from me. If
they want to know what I think, I'll tell 'em. That's the reason I
got rid of the signature machine. I do not let other people write
language that purports to come from me but doesn't. That's been
one of my strict rules. I am offended, and I've always been
disenchanted by reading speeches and utterances from presidents
and politicians and governors that aren't their own.

"I view the government and leadership as educational, persua-
sion, communication. So words are very important. Language is
very important. That's what we work in. We're not manufactur-
ing durable goods here. I'm communicating ideas. That's what
I'm getting paid for, to apply my brain to problems that are there.
What else do they get for their forty-nine thousand dollars?"

Bob Nance, press secretary in the State Health Department,
usually fills in as Brown's acting press secretary when Brown is
between news secretaries or the incumbent is on vacation. On
August 28, 1975, Nance distributed a press release from the
governor's office in which he used the phrase "at the detriment
of." The next morning, when Nance arrived at work, there was a
copy of the press release on top of his desk with "at" scratched
out and replaced by the word "to," along with the inked initials
"EGB." Two years later Nance explained that he had been
grinding out a number of news statements on deadline and had
not had a chance to proofread the offending one before he sent it
out. Nance, who describes himself as "a rock bottom, far-out
conservative—shit, Attila the Hun is a flowing liberal compared
to me," is a great admirer of Brown. "For one Goddamned
reason," said Nance, a retired air force major and former prison
guard who seems perpetually harried except when he is relaxing
at his favorite watering spot with two drinks set before him. "He
tries to accomplish that that can be accomplished with existing
resources. When it comes to trying to get a dollar's worth of value
out of a dollar, which is impossible in bureaucracy or govern-

ment, Jerry Brown is going to get you six, seven, eight cents more" than anyone else. The press release that Brown corrected and initialed is framed and hung on the wall in Nance's office.

Brown did not always exhibit such respect for the niceties of the English language, according to Father William Perkins, the Jesuit priest who was his high-school debate coach and freshman English professor at the University of Santa Clara. "He was great on ideas, and he was lousy on grammar" as a college freshman, said Perkins. "I told him once, 'Jerry, whatever you do, you'd better have a good secretary because you sure are lousy at the mechanics of the English language.' I used to give him two grades. I'd give him a grade for his content . . . and a grade for the mechanics. And it would be A and F, and I'd say, 'All right, that averages out to a C.' So I'd have this big debate after every paper I'd hand back. He'd come up, and he'd want to argue about his grade, and I'd say, 'Jerrrry, what you said was great, but the way you said it was lousy.' He was just careless about anything and everything, you know. Incomplete sentences, dangling participles, split infinitives, putting periods at the end of a sentence—he didn't care much about that." Usually, after arguments that both pupil and teacher apparently enjoyed, Perkins would raise Brown's grade to a B, and several months after Brown took office Perkins saw him and told him, "I gave you Bs, but today with inflation and everything, they'd probably be worth As," which caused Brown to laugh.

Brown's timing in two separate instances led *Los Angeles Times* reporter Ken Reich, Brown's old friend, to "become increasingly disillusioned. He's not a very principled man in my opinion." The first occurred on April 23, 1975, when Brown signed a bill that repealed a smog-device requirement for 1966–70 cars in the Los Angeles area. According to Reich, when Brown was running for governor, he had said he would do everything he could to return blue skies to California and had called the mandatory smog-control devices an important step toward cleaner air. At 7 P.M. on April 23, Brown opened a public hearing in downtown Los Angeles. At 10:46 P.M., fourteen minutes before the 11 o'clock news started on most major Los Angeles television stations and with live cameras present, Brown announced he would sign the bill that repealed the smog-control law. Both Howard Berman and Llew Werner had told Reich before the hearing that Brown would sign the law—Werner even suggested that Reich arrange with the *Times* to have a photographer present for the signing—but when Brown arrived at the hearing, he said he was still undecided. "I regarded the entire thing as a tremendous charade," said Reich. "He timed the actual moment of his decision for the television cameras. This was the first concrete instance that I felt that he had clearly taken a decision for political reasons and had not been candid about the means of taking that decision. He had insisted that his mind was not made up."

When asked if he had, in fact, timed his announcement for television, Brown called the suggestion "crazy" and explained, "If I was going to do that I would have done it earlier and done it for the six o'clock news." Brown cites the smog-device issue as a case in which "the decision is not made until the act is done. In that meeting, I wanted to give everyone a chance to say their thing. Certainly I was moving very strongly in the direction of signing that bill. But I hadn't closed the door to someone proving to me that this thing was worth all the problems it was creating. I don't like to close off argument or discussion prematurely, and so I give people a chance. In my own mind, it's not only important to make a decision but to base it on something rational and publicly explainable. We're supposed to be dealing in public information. Why not have a public debate? What's wrong with that? That's openness."

The apparently casual manner in which Brown announced he was entering the presidential race also struck Reich as phony. By mid-March 1976, dozens of reporters had been following Brown around for several weeks, asking whether he intended to run for president. At a press conference the afternoon of March 12, he refused to say whether he planned to become a candidate. About 6 P.M. he invited four reporters into his office for coffee. One of the four, Doug Willis, an Associated Press political reporter, described in an AP story what happened as Brown sat in seemingly idle conversation with the reporters:

"Everything ought to be re-examined, but re-examined in the light of furthering certain principles that come out of a certain liberal, humanistic tradition," Brown said. "The ideas of a tough, questioning process may not have a dramatic ring to it. But when you apply it to something like a freeway program or an art program or a criminal justice program or education, it is a very real thing. That forces a certain dialectic and dialogue that has been characteristic of my administration. That kind of philosophy and approach is what I think is necessary, and my entry in the primary will tend to give that approach a hearing," he said. That was the announcement.

Brown's manner was so matter of fact, Willis later related, that one of the reporters present, not realizing what he had said, asked a question on another issue, and the other three had to sit and squirm while Brown answered. Then they asked if they had heard him correctly, and Brown confirmed that he was in the race. Willis wrote in his story that "Brown grinned at the excitement as dozens of reporters, Capitol aides, and members of his staff crowded into his office, each asking if it was true." Willis also reported that one journalist who arrived soon after Brown's "announcement" thought the whole thing was a joke, and another said, "I can't believe it. Not even Jerry Brown announces he's running for president this way."

More than a year and a half later, Brown insisted that he had intended to make his announcement at either the press conference or a reception that afternoon, but "no one asked me. I was waiting for them to ask me." Then he conceded, "Maybe I wasn't as accessible" as he should have been. He also said he wanted to avoid making the announcement at a formal press event where there would have been "the full fanfare and hoopla of a campaign. I just was turned off by that. I just wanted to discuss it in a normal, non ping-pong, reporter-candidate kind of format."

David Jensen, who was in charge of the press office at the time, could chuckle over the incident more than a year after it happened, but he recalled, "It was a bone of contention for me." Jensen, who was a UPI reporter before he joined Brown's staff, said he had advised Brown to make the announcement at a time and place that would allow "everybody an equal shot." He had also told Brown that making the declaration before noon would be best for most of the reporters. "We could have done the traditional media number," Jensen said. "We could have made all the networks and everything . . . and it would have been on national television that night. Well, instead he does it at six o'clock on Friday which is actually in traditional thinking the worst possible time to do it. All of a sudden he mumbled something about he was running, and it was just incredible. I sort of flinched," said Jensen, who was present when Brown said he was running only because a secretary in the governor's outer office had called him to say that Brown was speaking with several reporters, and something important seemed to be taking place.

Reich has never thought it a coincidence that Brown's "casual announcement" occurred exactly one hour before Jimmy Carter attended a fund raiser at the home of Los Angeles business executive Max Palevsky, for many years an important bankroller of Democrats. By announcing for president when he did, Reich said, Brown made sure that the top news story that night and the next day would be about him, not about Carter's visit to California. Carter had just won the Florida primary and was establishing himself as the front runner for the nomination. "The appearance of sort of a casual, offhanded approach by a person who I know through much past experience carefully considers every move for literally months before making it was, I thought, telltale," Reich said. "The 'casual announcement' was clearly timed to upstage Carter." Since then, Brown and Reich have had virtually no contact, except when Reich has been assigned to write about his former friend.

Bill Stall, by then Reich's associate on the *Times,* wrote on March 17, 1976, that Brown's announcement, which was "sort of like saying, 'Gee, it's a nice day out,' " ought to

serve as a warning to national political reporters who will descend on California this Spring to cover the state's primary. They are used to advance texts of a candidate's speeches, of having everything carefully prearranged, and perhaps, above all, of being assured that the candidate isn't going to drop some "bombshell" announcement out of the blue, or in some casual conversation. They may have to work a little harder in California. But Brown, with his Jesuit training, has never thought that that's a bad idea for anyone.

When Jensen went to work for Brown in mid-1974, he found that Brown "had a very highly developed sense of what was right and wrong in terms of press and how it would appear to the public. He has good instincts there, good judgment, generally speaking, with the exception that he doesn't really appreciate the need to be on time for news conferences. I guess it's just part of his personality that he can't keep appointments right on the nose."

Jensen said many members of the Sacramento press corps were angered by Brown's way of announcing his candidacy after they had followed him around fruitlessly for weeks. "There were a number of people who were enraged" either because Jensen could not reach them to get them back to the Capitol, because they had put in a long day and were looking forward to a relaxed Friday night, or in the case of Los Angeles television stations, because the announcement came after their six o'clock news shows and made it difficult to shoot film and get it to Los Angeles in time for the eleven o'clock news. "Those reporters think they're important," said Jensen. "And they *are* important. And you don't want to just unnecessarily create bad feelings."

Brown continued to keep reporters on their toes throughout the presidential campaign. Fred Epstein, Brown's press secretary for the race, said the candidate's personal style made his visit to Maryland chaotic for the tremendous number of reporters who were following him. Some 150 journalists, who filled two press buses, were issued credentials for Brown's first trip to Maryland, according to Epstein, "because he was a phenomenon. It was a huge event.

"Sometimes he can make things difficult for the press corps," said Epstein. "He refused to be kept to deadlines and press releases and all the Mickey Mouse stuff. He's a very strong-willed individual. He rebels against that kind of management. There was some resentment that he was in the driver's seat and could make the reporters do what he wanted."

Epstein said Brown was amused by "the death watch," which requires reporters from major news agencies to keep near a candidate at all times in case an assassination attempt occurs.

In spite of Brown's condescending attitude toward the media circus his campaign created, he quickly became a darling of the press, according to Epstein. "Very seasoned Washington press people were comparing him to Bobby Kennedy and Jack Kennedy. They hadn't seen anything like it [Brown's effect on his audiences], certainly not that year and not since 1968."

Epstein, who had managed Gray Davis's unsuccessful bid for state treasurer in 1974, learned that "it's a tough job" being

Brown's press secretary, "given Jerry and Gray and everyone else. You don't have complete freedom. The traditional role of a press secretary is to tell a candidate what to do and how to do it. Mainly, you don't tell Jerry what to say and what to do, where to stand. He doesn't lend himself to that type of management."

The frustration of being Brown's press secretary was brought out by a story in the *San Francisco Chronicle* on December 24, 1977, which said Elisabeth Coleman had threatened to resign unless she were given more responsibility and Davis agreed to stop interfering in her domain. At the time, Coleman had served for a year and a half as press secretary—the same period in which her two predecessors, Stall and Jensen, had served combined.

Brown's preference for casual, unplanned meetings with the press over formal, structured news conferences, which he considers inhibiting, also makes covering him or being his press secretary difficult, said Jensen. In general, reporters would rather deal with scheduled events. But Brown "keeps the press off balance," pointed out John Jervis. "He will say things of import while walking in the hallway while someone takes notes."

There are those who think that Brown, who has lived by the press, will die by the press. For example, Houston Flournoy predicted that "the media will be a part of his defeat. Because I think the media is more wise to Jerry Brown than maybe the general public is. And little things mean a lot over the long haul. You don't keep the Capitol press corps sitting around for an hour and a half waiting for a press conference very many times before they're going to find a way to ding you." Carl Werthman agrees that "Jerry's a genius at playing the press. But that can backfire." An observer well versed in Democratic party politics in California believes that "Jerry is fortunate to have arrived at a time when political parties are dying, and therefore the party can't punish him for his lack of partisanship or his lack of loyalty.

"The new-style politics is basically media politics," he continued. "It's the six o'clock news, and it's heavy saturation of commercial television and radio and to a limited degree billboards and mailing devices, all impersonal methods that don't really permit the public to ever really be in contact with the candidate at any stage. Jerry is a master at the utilization of the one-shot press release . . . where there's no story behind the headline."

Brown's lack of personal friendships, particularly among party activists,. means he has few people to rely on in a tight situation, according to this source, "and the implications of it are horrendous in terms of political sociology. It just means that he is nothing more than a face on the tube" without anyone to protect him if his popularity begins to slip. The observer said that the closest thing Brown has to his own constituency is the UFW, but he said the UFW sees Brown as a vehicle, "and that's a very dangerous position to be in politically, because when they're finished with you, they toss you in the trash barrel," as happened to Brown's political mentor, Eugene McCarthy, after the 1968 election. "Brown never learned the process on the way up. And he's not been doing much except running for office since he was a kid. He ought to get his ass kicked and in the process grow and mature," but because of his dependence on the news media Brown "may get hurt worse than he deserves."

Brown puts little stock in such theories, stating, "It's a strange thing that people feel so guilty about the technology of communication when it's an integral part of our culture. It's there like a chair. Or oxygen. There's twenty-two million people out there. How can you reach them? The world is a world of communication. Everyone's got a television, everyone's got a telephone, a radio, you're using a tape recorder." In addition, says Brown, people can learn more about a politician by watching him for five minutes on television than they could if he passed through a crowd saying, "Hi, how are you?"

In early 1977, there was evidence that the press was getting wise to Brown's style. The governor called a news conference on February 3 to announce that "California will loan approximately ten billion cubic feet of natural gas to weather-stricken Eastern and Midwestern states this month." The state's two major gas companies, Pacific Gas and Electric Company and Southern California Gas, had already volunteered to divert some natural gas East, a matter over which the state has no jurisdiction, and had announced the shift several days earlier. Reporters present, sensing that Brown had made a colossal mistake, pounced on him with such questions as: "The ten billion cubic feet of natural gas, what have you done to get that back there, or is that somebody else's project?" "But you have no power to order that it be done, right?" "Aren't you announcing the same thing that the PUC [Public Utilities Commission] announced two days ago?"

"Wasn't this shipment of gas going to go East regardless of whether Governor Brown did anything at all?" "Are you taking credit for something that was going to be done, anyway, to help these dying people? For something that was already done? That the president announced last night?" After a barrage of such questions, Brown lost his patience and asked a question of his own: "What is this, a debate?"

Brown still insists that he had no intention of misleading the press that day or of taking credit for something he had not done, but he admitted that his staff had made "a couple of mistakes" in the writing and editing of the press release that was handed out before the news conference. The experience strengthened his dislike for the distribution of advance press releases in situations in which, in Brown's words, "people are going to be Talmudian scholars about things."

One of the reporters at that press conference, Bob Schmidt of the *San Jose Mercury-News,* wrote in a column five days later:

> The press is a sensitive social organ, and when it is charged with having been manipulated, it reacts with some violence. It reacted with violence Thursday, at a press conference called by the governor. Political leaders since year one have followed a custom of identifying themselves with commendable efforts in which the government they head is engaged, and disassociating themselves from activities producing an adverse public response. . . . Now the press had him up there in front of them, vulnerable. At least part of what he was saying was suspect, and the reporters chose that time to show, by gosh, that they were not simply tools of Jerry Brown. . . . There was open hostility.

Six months later, Schmidt wrote that some of the reporters "seemed to take an unprofessional relish in having the usually unflappable Brown so obviously on the defensive." He also noted that Brown had not held an open-ended news conference since that February confrontation and said that the situation was "too bad" for the press, the public, and "for the governor, because while his celebrated sense of what concerns the people of California may be merited, the questions from a roomful of reporters representing newspapers and radio and television stations from all parts of the state can certainly serve to increase that awareness."

Jim Lorenz, former Employment Development Department director, said the announcement of the natural gas shift was unpleasantly reminiscent of Brown's declaration of January 6, 1975, a few hours after he was sworn in, that "in his first major act as chief executive," he was signing an order to implement the federal Comprehensive Employment and Training Act (CETA) in California, which would create 1,500 jobs (at a time when the number of unemployed people in the state was 845,000). Earlier that day, Brown had said in his Inaugural Address, "Very shortly I will sign an executive order requiring every state agency and department to actively participate in federally funded public-service employment programs. Before the month is out, hundreds of men and women who are on unemployment or welfare will be performing meaningful jobs."

According to Lorenz, "In actuality, that program was already in place. In other words, the announcement was nothing more than a packaging deal. It was describing in a different way what already was happening. There wasn't a single new job that was actually added to the labor force" as a result of Brown's signing the order.

Relating the events of January 1975 and February 1977, Lorenz declared, "The press finally picked him up on the natural-gas thing. That was actually a trick that Tom [Quinn] and Jerry had done for years."

In the opinion of Carl Werthman, the press is "how politicians communicate with each other." Just as Brown uses the media to convey his thoughts to the public, the press is one of the best ways to get a message to him. Stephen Reinhardt remembered two occasions when Brown contacted him after news stories had reported Reinhardt's criticism of the governor. In 1970, when Brown was running for secretary of state, "he made some efforts to separate himself from the rest of the ticket because it looked like a bad year for the ticket," according to Reinhardt. Reinhardt criticized Brown for disassociating himself from other Democrats, his remarks got into the press, and the next day Brown called him to discuss the campaign.

In 1975, despite Reinhardt's key role in helping Brown become governor, Reinhardt had not heard from him for several months after the inauguration. Then, in an interview with the *Wall Street Journal*, Reinhardt said it was too early to assess Brown's performance as governor, but that one of the most important guidelines would be his success in resolving the state's farm labor problems. Shortly thereafter, Brown called Reinhardt and asked him to come to Sacramento to help draft the Agricultural Labor Relations Act. "Soon after I got there, he mentioned that 'I read what you said about me in the *Wall Street Journal*,' " said Reinhardt. "That may have been what brought me to mind with Jerry. Sometimes I have a feeling Jerry forgets people for large periods of time."

According to Lorenz, Brown often will not deal with a situation until "it gets in the media, and then it has a reality of its own." For example, at one point news stories reported that the governor's failure to appoint a fifth member to one state board had kept the board from making a decision. The next day, Brown made the appointment, said an article in the *Chronicle* on June 1, 1976.

Brown realizes that because of the built-in tension between office-holders and the media, he is likely to be damned no matter what he does. In the fall of 1977, he pledged to begin holding less highly structured press conferences again, as Bob Schmidt had suggested in his column. Brown said he hoped to have them often enough to suit the press. But he was resigned to the outcome of his gesture: "See, if I have a weekly press conference, then I'm trying to get too much exposure, and if I don't have it, then I'm not accessible enough, so either way you can write a story. And that is the bottom line. Which is production. Production of information."

CHAPTER ELEVEN

THE SEPARATION
OF POWERS

"The legislature legislates and I govern."

GOVERNOR EDMUND G. BROWN, JR.,
March 11, 1975

Jerry Brown's strict adherence to the constitutional separation of powers between the executive branch and the legislature may be unique in this age of imperial presidents and governors, but it is sincere. For example, at a March 11, 1975, press conference, when a reporter asked Brown if he was telling the legislature to delay passage of a bill, the governor responded:

"No, I'm not telling them to do anything." He added, "I always tell people to vote their conscience. They should vote whatever they think is best for the constituency they represent. I'll do the same. That's all. I mean, we do have two branches of government, and I think it is a healthy thing. I don't see that I have to, you know, try to prelegislate everything. The thing should go through; if it gets to my desk I'll make a decision. . . . I think that's a healthy interaction. Some [bills] make it; some don't. Some get signed; some get vetoed. That's what it is all about around here."

After Brown had been governor for almost three years, he expressed his philosophy of executive-legislative relations in similar terms: "I think that a mistake chief executives often make is they lay the gauntlet down, and they just push the legislature. It doesn't work that way. It's a relationship, and the more it can be joint and cooperative, the better it is. If the chief executive attempts to push too hard, then the resistance stiffens on the part of the legislature, and therefore it's necessary to maintain a balance between legislative and gubernatorial initiative. It's not only necessary, there's no other way."

Brown added that "the chemistry" of executive-legislative relations "makes it very difficult to exceed a certain quota of legislative activity." He points out that he pushed only one major piece of legislation in each of his first three years in office: the creation of the Farm Labor Board in 1975; a law to protect the coastline in 1976; and a new method of school financing in 1977. "But to try to put all these things in one year, people in the legislature will not accept it. So important bills often get through because they're perceived as being high on the priority of the legislature as opposed to being high on my priority.

"I often am involved in the process, but I may not actively assert my participation," said Brown, particularly on "those bills that have adequate legislative momentum without me. I may hold back and let it go and then get involved later. There just seems to be in the interrelationship a necessity for some bills to pass and some bills to fail. So sometimes the failure of one bill will make possible the success of another. There will always be a certain number of successes and failures, and there can never be all successes, just as there is usually not all failures.

"The art of governing," Brown declared, "is the art of knowing how much to inject one's self in the process, how much to let others take the lead, and how to balance these two elements." He is aware, just as he is about his relations with the press, that no matter what he does, he will be criticized: either for becoming involved in the legislative process too soon and usurping the legislature's role, for which Willie Brown, George Zenovich, and others attacked him in connection with the drafting of the

Argicultural Labor Relations Act, or if he chooses not to participate early in the legislative process, for failing to exercise leadership. As Brown told reporters on March 19, 1975, there are approximately 5,000 bills introduced each year, and "only in rare cases will I take a hard position."

When Brown took office, Democrats controlled the Assembly fifty-four to twenty-five and the State Senate twenty-four to fifteen, with one vacancy in each house, and many Democratic legislators were looking forward to working with a governor from their own party after eight years of Ronald Reagan. George Moscone says Reagan regarded the legislature with "utter and open calumny," and Assemblyman John Vasconcellos commented, "I think Ronald Reagan was not liked by almost anybody of either party. He was a prudish, righteous, pompous guy who always talked down to everybody, even [members of] his own party."

According to Senator James Mills, the president pro tempore of the senate, "If Reagan went out on the front steps to have his picture taken with us, he would in offhand remark indicate how it was a kind of unusual occasion to be with the legislature and not have anybody trying to stab him between the ribs." At one photo session, said Mills, who would stand near the governor on such occasions because of his own rank, "there was a beautiful girl who was brought by the photographer" as a means of making his subjects smile. "And she was dressed in a bikini, and she was gorgeous, and Ronald Reagan said, 'Well, it's nice to think about just once all these guys are trying to do it to somebody else instead of doing it to me.' That's the way his mind works. On one occasion, he said to me, 'I know what you'd really like to do. You'd really like to take me out and put me up against the wall and shoot me.' " Mills said Reagan made this comment in the presence of several other legislators, including some Republicans, "and they were all embarrassed because Ronald Reagan was showing his true face. He went through life in Sacramento thinking that the Democrats in the legislature had one thought in mind: to try to ruin Ronald Reagan. It never occurred to him that there might be people serving in the legislature who might have purposes at least as worthy as his own. And in my opinion they were a great deal more worthy because he was concerned about only one thing, and that was his ambition. I think most members of the legislature are reasonably ambitious men, but most of them realize that they have probably risen as high as they are going to rise, and this is an opportunity to serve the public."

Even Howard Way, a Republican who served in the Senate for Reagan's entire term, as well as during Pat Brown's last four years and Jerry Brown's first two, says that Reagan "sort of regarded us upstairs as mortal enemies" because he "was always running for president or something."

Many legislators perceive similarities between Reagan and Jerry Brown. Assemblyman Robert Cline, a Republican, says that if Reagan had gone out of his way to befriend members of the legislature, he would "have been able to get virtually anything he wanted. But Ronald Reagan was like Jerry Brown. He came into politics from the top." The most powerful member of the legislature, Speaker of the Assembly Leo McCarthy, said Jerry Brown and Reagan both favor "a restrained role for government in many areas. On Governor Reagan's part, I always had the sense that it was just a very fundamental basic distrust of government as an instrument of problem solving. With Governor Brown, it's more a selective use of government for problem solving but not a fundamental distrust that the whole thing is an oppressive structure, rather that it can be if it's not kept accountable." George Moscone commented that at the beginning of Brown's term, "One thing that troubled me was that he didn't seem to trust the legislature," but from what he has heard since he left the senate to become mayor of San Fransico, Moscone believes Brown's attitude has improved over the course of three years.

In Brown's seven-minute inaugural address to the legislature, one of the briefest in history, he called for more jobs for people of all backgrounds, pledged to keep state taxation "at a level no higher than it is today," and asked the legislature to send precedent-setting farm labor legislation to his desk. Brown concluded the speech by saying that the task facing the state "is not the work of one person. It is the work of all of us working together. I ask your help. Thank you very much. We have a lot of work to do. Let's get to it." His comments were hailed by members of both parties.

The honeymoon continued for many months. On August 14, 1975, Assemblyman Willie Brown, who would soon become a severe critic of the governor, said, following a meeting between the legislature's black caucus and Governor Brown, "I frankly think that Jerry Brown has the opportunity to make the best governor the state of California has ever had," according to an Associated Press story in the *Sacramento Bee*.

Marc Poché, Brown's top legislative aide for the first year and a half of the administration, said it was inevitable that the legislature would become discontent because "the job now is deciding who *doesn't* get what instead of the way it used to be, deciding who gets what. Gray Davis declared, "We institutionally disappoint around here." Davis added that a governor's duty to veto some bills that many lawmakers favor "breeds more disappointment than it does joy."

Seven out of every ten bills introduced relate to finance matters, and many liberal Democrats had assumed that Brown's popular identification as a liberal Democrat and his heritage as Pat Brown's son would result in his viewing appropriations bills favorably. Liberals had their hopes shattered when Jerry Brown turned out to be much more like Ronald Reagan than Pat Brown on fiscal matters. But Brown's pledge to avoid any general tax increase dictated that he would have to hold the line on spending because California, unlike the federal government, is prohibited by its constitution from deficit spending.

A. Alan Post, who retired in September 1977 after almost thirty years as the state's nonpartisan legislative analyst, has a unique perspective on recent governors. Post, whose job required that he study the state budget more closely than anyone else, says that while Reagan often talked about holding down taxes and spending, "Jerry Brown not only talks fiscal conservatism, but he is even more conservative, I would think, than either Reagan or his father."

Roy Bell, finance director under both Reagan and Jerry Brown, made this comparison of the two governors: "I think they looked at issues in completely different ways. Governor Reagan was trying to save dollars. This governor wants the dollars spent the most effective way and doesn't necessarily feel that just spending more dollars means too much. He's looking more at the program and its effectiveness than the dollar that's spent." Said Bell, "It may end up looking the same from an external viewpoint, that both guys look like they're real tight with a dollar, but there are entirely different reasons."

Howard Berman, who is often regarded as Brown's closest and perhaps only personal friend in the legislature, says the governor's fiscal conservatism causes "some resentment" among liberals but notes that his financial policies are "politically popular, which works in some ways to the benefit" of all Democrats, both liberals and conservatives. "So the irritation is mollified to some extent."

George Moscone claims that "the idea that he would be tight with the pursestrings didn't surprise me because, don't you know, that's the new wave of liberal politics: Somebody decided that the people really could have their spirits upraised, and that was as good as giving them a job or something else. And if you said the right things, you were really performing. And if at the same time you were cutting back money and saying that we have to have a sense of self-determination and government shouldn't be in your lives, and look how they've screwed it up and Watergate and Southeast Asia and everything else, you in effect could get away with political murder in the sense that you could come off as a fiscal conservative, have the rhetoric of a liberal, and be a great friend of the so-called unwashed. That's the new wave of politics," which Moscone says both Brown and President Carter represent.

Outlining his philosophy on taxes in late 1977, Brown said, "I want people to get used to limits. There's so much money in the till, why add more? We're not making wise enough choices as it is. That's my view." Refusing to increase taxes is "a limit. It's a constraint. It's a perimeter. It gives definition to an amorphous world of expanding services. So we need some perimeters. And just taking the tax revenues as they are instead of always adding to them is a way to do that. One of the ways of sweeping away some of the dead wood is to hold the line on taxes and try to force out inefficient or ineffective programs with new ones."

Brown's fiscal conservatism has moved even Ronald Reagan to say, in an April 1976 interview with the *Los Angeles Times,* "I am, of course, gratified by his approach to spending."

In May 1977, Finance Director Roy Bell revealed that Brown's rein on spending had resulted in surpluses: $1.5 billion for the

1976–77 fiscal year on a budget of $13 billion and a projected $2.5 billion for 1977–78 out of a budget of $14.5 billion. Although Brown was under pressure from all sides to spend a substantial part of the surplus, he declined to do so, saying that the extra funds would come in handy if the state fell on hard times.

Bell also reported that in 1976–77 the state would receive $155 million more in personal income-tax revenues than had been anticipated, which would be followed by an expected $215 million excess in 1977–78. The increase arose mainly from the state's method of computing taxes: As a person's income increases, he moves into a higher tax bracket and pays higher tax rates. Many legislators, led by Assembly Minority Leader Paul Priolo and other Republicans, said that Brown's public claims of avoiding tax increases are a sham because income-tax bracketing amounts to an increase in taxes. The Republicans called on Brown to support income-tax indexing, under which tax rates would be adjusted to take inflation into account so that taxpayers could earn more money without falling into higher tax brackets; but the governor refused. When an editor of the *Los Angeles Herald-Examiner* questioned Brown on the subject in April 1977, he replied, "People want more services, more of everything. We've got to live within our means, but I think that if we start reducing income taxes, we'll have to reduce services. I think just avoiding a tax increase is quite an accomplishment in itself." Priolo promised that income-tax bracketing versus indexing would become an issue in the 1978 gubernatorial campaign.

As is the case with most bicameral legislatures, the two houses of the California legislature are entirely different. The upper house, the senate, consists of forty members who serve for four-years. Their terms are staggered so that half of the senators are up for election every two years. The highest-ranking member of the senate is the president pro tempore, who is often elected with bipartisan support from his fellow senators, and his political power is relatively limited. The assembly has eighty members, each of whom must stand for election every two years. Its top official, the speaker, is chosen by legislators from the majority party. In the words of Ray LeBov, an attorney who works for one of the legislative committees, the assembly is "essentially an imperial dynasty with the speaker having the power to give and to take away" in such matters as committee assignments, chairmanships, and money for reelection campaigns.

The present speaker, Leo McCarthy, is a youthful-looking man of forty-seven who was born in Australia but has spent most of his life in San Francisco. Like Brown, he received a Jesuit education and is an attorney. His San Francisco home is in the same block as the house where Brown was raised and where Brown's sister and brother-in-law, Cynthia and Joe Kelly, now live. McCarthy was an aide to a former state senator and served for five years on the San Francisco Board of Supervisors before he was elected to the assembly in 1968. He has been speaker since June 1974, when his fellow assembly Democrats chose him over several other candidates, including Willie Brown.

Although McCarthy does not consider Governor Brown a personal friend, the two have had a good working relationship, so good that Willie Brown commented, "Without Leo McCarthy, Jerry Brown's legislative program would be a wreck. He should thank God for Leo McCarthy. He should be worried if Leo McCarthy ever gets a cold. The speaker is Jerry Brown's best, most trusted, and most savvy ally, and Jerry Brown ought to remember that." Willie Brown thinks the governor is correct to allow McCarthy to handle the legislature for him because Jerry Brown "would only mess it up if he tried. He doesn't know who he should be dealing with in the senate, so he wanders around over there as a lost soul. He does not have a Leo McCarthy in the Senate."

Willie Brown's assessment is widely held. According to Jim Lorenz, McCarthy "at this point is more responsible for Jerry's success than any other person in California except Jerry himself and possibly his father and mother. But in the last two or three years Jerry owes Leo McCarthy more than anybody else in the state." Lobbyist Mary Bergan says, "I think if it weren't for McCarthy, Brown would be up shit creek with the legislature right now. You can't be at odds with those guys all the time, or you aren't going to get your programs" passed. She says Brown does "stroke" individual legislators from time to time, "but it's normally when he wants something instead of getting" their good will "in reserve." Alan Sieroty, a member of the assembly from 1967 until March 1977, when he was elected to the state senate, commented that "the governor's relationship with the legislature has been primarily with Leo McCarthy."

McCarthy said Brown "deals with me as I guess he would deal with whoever was speaker because of the unique powers" inherent in that position. "I don't want to be characterized as his right-hand man. 'Political ally' is all right, 'good working relationship' is all right."

Brown himself calls McCarthy "a very important person in Sacramento and a major part of the leadership structure in the state." However, Brown stated, "I deal with others. Most of those legislators, if pressed, will tell you they've had more contact with me than they did with Reagan, even Republicans." What he says is true.

Like Brown, McCarthy is a strong believer in the separation of powers. "While we seek as much common ground as possible," McCarthy said, "I think we have to be constructive adversaries to make sure that the legislative and executive branches in government in a more than theoretical way are checking each other for the general public interest." Each week, the governor meets with McCarthy, Berman, Mills, and other leaders of the legislature, as well as authors of major pending legislation. McCarthy thinks these sessions have helped Brown "learn through an evolutionary process . . . that leading a legislative house is a lot different than leading the executive branch. He's the only elected official over there. Here I've got to deal with seventy-nine other elected officials in this house and have a working relationship with forty state Senators, each of them independently elected."

Frank Mesplé says, "I don't know where Brown would have been if he hadn't had McCarthy sort of protecting his flanks." McCarthy, who did not endorse a candidate in the 1974 gubernatorial primary because the vote for speaker followed immediately after Bob Moretti relinquished the job of Speaker by running for governor, observed that Brown ultimately took office with two strikes against him: First, he had run against two very popular members of the legislature, Moretti and Moscone; and second, when Brown "was campaigning for political reform, he sort of painted the legislature with a broad brush, and a lot of very ethical, very clean, very public-service-oriented legislators were offended." Furthermore, McCarthy said, many legislators "just viewed him as sort of young, inexperienced, and trading on his father's name."

Commented one Democratic official: "The public loves the mattress on the floor and the Plymouth. But a lot of politicians came up the hard way, and they view some of those extra benefits as the perquisites of political office. For some legislators it's a big deal to rent the state car. It may be the first new car they've ever had even though they don't own it, and Jerry's made it kind of sinful and mean and bad for them to do that anymore. This kind of puritanism infuriates these guys."

John Jervis, staff director of the state senate's Democratic caucus, said that when Brown took office, the attitude of some Democratic senators was, "I don't want to see anything that the governor is spouting coming out with our letterhead. In other words, we are going to be totally independent of the little bastard."

Said McCarthy, "When he started out as governor, there were a lot interested in taking some of his blood. Particularly during the first year, I was very protective of his position on the basis that he deserved a chance to learn something about the awesome job of being governor of California."

The first fund-raising event Brown attended as governor was a $125-per-person testimonial for McCarthy in Los Angeles in September 1975 that brought in about $100,000. McCarthy later said the dinner was probably the most successful fund raiser in history for a member of the legislature. He distributed the money to the reelection campaigns of his friends in the assembly as a means of preserving his job as speaker.

McCarthy can, and frequently has, used his authority as speaker to protect Brown from being embarrassed. McCarthy guides bills that Brown does not like, but does not want to have to veto, to the Assembly Ways and Means Committee, where they usually die a relatively quiet death. "That was the arrangement," said Ray LeBov. "Any bill that Jerry wanted to not have to deal with would die in Ways and Means." According to Alan Post, the chairman of the Ways and Means Committee has traditionally been approved by the governor and has tended to regard himself as someone who looks after the governor's interests.

The present chairman, Daniel Boatwright, forty-eight, an attorney from Concord in the Bay Area, confirmed that his committee, which includes one-quarter of the assembly members, has often killed bills, especially spending measures, that Brown felt he could not approve and did not want to have to veto. One example was James Mills's 1976 proposal for a one-cent-a-gallon gasoline-tax increase to finance public transit.

"The governor did not want it on his desk; he wanted it killed somewhere before it got there," said Boatwright. "The last place that could kill it was Ways and Means, and it was killed in large measure because Governor Brown said if it got to his desk, he would veto it, and he would prefer it not get there. We just felt that we shouldn't put the legislature at odds with Governor Brown during the first couple of years of his administration." John Jervis noted that "they pulled that Ways and Means trick" on Mills, and as a result, "Mills and the governor have a rather cold relationship."

Alan Sieroty, who was an influential member of Ways and Means when he was in the assembly, said, "You can see that after eight years of the Reagan administration, Democrats had a lot of ideas about programs they wanted to see put in effect." But there was "a Democratic speaker who wanted the legislature to act in this way and not embarrass the governor and not place this tremendous amount of spending before him." Sieroty estimated that the Ways and Means Committee, at McCarthy's insistence, defeated spending bills totaling almost $1 billion during the first two years of Brown's term.

A public breach, although a temporary one, occurred between Brown and McCarthy in June 1977, after Brown accused the legislature of "foot dragging" on one bill and said he would veto proposed salary increases for seven state officials, including a $16,000 raise for the governor. McCarthy declared that Brown was making "wholly inappropriate comments" and "shooting from the hip" with his charge of "foot dragging." As to Brown's threat to veto the pay raises, McCarthy told reporters, "It's not useful to engage in self-flagellation," as seminarians do. "I would address that comment to anyone in public life who feels that you have to eat humble pie in order to win the favor of voters."

Torpedoing James Mills's proposed gas tax may have been Brown's riskiest move in his dealings with the legislature in view of Mills's stature as president pro tempore of the senate. When a reporter asked Brown at an August 15, 1975, press conference, "Do you consider a gasoline use tax a general tax?" The governor's reply was brief: "Looks pretty general to me." The

definition of what constitutes a *general* tax raise is a bone of
contention between the governor and the senate leader. "The
governor has said that he is against any general tax increase,"
said Mills. "The gasoline tax has never been considered to be a
general tax increase. It's a special fund. It doesn't go into the
general fund. In effect, the gasoline tax in California is a toll."

Mills, fifty, is a bald man who wears a mustache and whose
dark-rimmed glasses give him the look of the historian he was
before being elected to the assembly in 1960 and the senate in
1966. As the senate leader since 1971, he has made alternatives
to the automobile, such as rail transit and bicycles, his primary
interests. Many of his colleagues regard him as an egghead given
more to the fussiness of a college professor than to the rough-and-
tumble ways of politics. One person who attended a strategy
session that included the governor, Leo McCarthy, Mills, and
other legislative leaders told how the meeting was brought to a
virtual halt when Mills pulled a cup of yogurt from his brown
bag lunch, took the top and began licking off the yogurt that had
collected there, while Brown, McCarthy, and the others surrep-
titiously watched the whole performance. Mills has also carried
on a lengthy battle with an airline that services San Diego, where
he lives. In a letter to the president of the airline, Mills
complained that no matter what kind of shoes he buys, the
airline's metal detector consistently detects the metal in his soles
and sounds an alarm. Mills wrote that other passengers don't
have the problem and that when he flies on other airlines his
attire causes no alarm.

Mills said he learned at least one lesson from his discussions
with Brown about the proposed gasoline tax: "A general tax
increase in the state of California is apparently whatever the
governor wants to call a general tax increase. It's just a matter of
being in a position to say what's a general tax increase and what
isn't, and he's decided to define it in certain terms. He's in a
position to call the shots on this, so I'm in a position of having to
be patient."

Another legislator's pet tax proposal, an alcoholic beverage tax
proposed by Senator Arlen Gregorio (D, San Mateo), to raise $35
million a year for prevention and treatment of alcoholism,
managed to get through the legislature but was vetoed by Brown
on September 14, 1975. Explaining his action, the governor said,
"I pledged to veto all general tax increases proposed during my

first year in office, and this looks very general to me. . . . Not every disease has a cure. But whenever the state can help, I believe it should. We now spend twenty-seven million dollars combating alcoholism. Yet there is hardly any data to show the impact of so much effort."

Gregorio, forty-seven, a liberal who has served in the senate since 1971, was surprised when he discovered that Brown opposed his proposal and echoed Mills in saying, "The whole question was what he meant by no general tax increase." Gregorio argued unsuccessfully that a tax on alcoholic beverage sales is not a general tax increase because 15 percent of California's citizens drink 75 percent of the liquor, beer, and wine consumed in the state, so a relatively small group would have borne most of the tax burden. Brown "was simply concerned about the whole question of whether or not this section would be perceived as a tax increase," according to Gregorio. The governor soothed him somewhat by including enough money to fund the alcoholism program that Gregorio wanted in the 1976–77 budget, making an alcohol tax increase unnecessary. Still, Gregorio was frustrated by the governor's veto after he had finally gotten his bill through the legislature. His attempts to secure passage of similar legislation had been defeated by opposition from the liquor industry. One Senator, who is friendly with both Gregorio and Brown, Jerry Smith (D, Saratoga), called the veto "an awful act in principle."

Both Mills and Gregorio have stated that they believe Brown's vetoes of their measures were motivated, at least in part, by his desire to keep his campaign promise to the letter and thus increase his popularity with the voters. One of California's leading consumer activists, Kay Pachtner of San Francisco, said a tax increase would not hurt the governor politically "as long as it's qualified and going for human needs." There is little doubt but that both of the proposed additional levies would have been felt much more directly by consumers than would other taxes, such as those on property and income.

In spite of widespread opposition to his fiscal policies, Brown has remained firm in his resolve to avoid raising taxes. As he told the *Sacramento Union* on September 19, 1976, "If I wanted a tax increase, it would be very easy to just give the word, and the spending bills would come down like torrents of rain. There's no doubt of that, but because of the collective commitment of Leo

McCarthy, Dan Boatwright, Jim Mills, and others in the senate"
few tax measures are approved by the legislature.

Brown's habits and prejudices occasionally hurt him in his
legislative dealings. Howard Berman says many legislators are
unhappy that "it isn't the starting assumption on appointments
that he's going to fill positions with people that are being
requested by legislators." McCarthy said another aspect of
Brown's appointments policy that sometimes upsets legislators is
his occasional failure to notify them in advance when he is
selecting someone from their district for a job. Such oversights
cause embarrassment for the lawmaker involved, says McCarthy,
"that, repeated many times, will antagonize a lot of legislators. I
think he's much better than he was when he came into office.
He's about halfway to where he has to go."

Even Brown's admirers admit that his reserved personal style
costs him chances to ingratiate himself with members of the
legislature. "He doesn't have a locker-room mentality," Gray
Davis commented. On the other hand, noted Preble Stolz, a
former legislative assistant to both Pat and Jerry Brown, the
current governor often does "things that blow their mind. He
goes up to *their* offices and sees them in *their* offices" instead of
making the legislators came to him.

Brown has also broken with tradition by not hosting parties for
lawmakers during his first three years in office, except for one
picnic during the summer of 1976. And of course, senators and
assembly members can no longer look forward to being enter-
tained in the Governor's Mansion.

In spite of his tightfisted approach to spending, Brown did
approve salary increases for members of the legislature. During
an appearance on NBC's "Meet the Press" on October 5, 1975, he
explained his thinking: "I viewed that five-percent salary increase over two years, compared it with the eight- and nine-
percent salary increases of most public employees, then gave
proper deference to the coequal branches of the legislature,
recognizing the need to work with them next year, and I signed
the bill."

Two pieces of legislation that cost the Brown administration
points, at least in some quarters, were a bill to limit judges'
salaries, a pet project of Brown, and a privacy law, which the
governor vetoed.

According to Ray LeBov, a joint legislative committee studied judicial reform for more than a year before hammering out a plan to restructure the judiciary. In essence, the measure would have established a one-tier system in place of the present two levels of trial courts: municipal court for the more routine cases and superior court for the relatively complicated civil suits and serious crimes. But LeBov said Tony Kline, who represented the administration during consideration of the bill, was so determined to place a lid on judicial salaries that "he singlehandedly, although it wasn't his intent, scuttled the whole effort."

LeBov said Kline, in his "monomaniacal" dedication to the limitation on salaries, "reminds me of Captain Ahab." LeBov went on to say that although he agreed with Kline in principle, "to think that in a state where unemployment is running at ten percent . . . that *that* [the limit on judges' salaries'] is the most important and the only important issue facing the state of California . . . is crazy. I think it's a function of the fact that he [Kline] perceived himself as being in a position where he could get even with those bastard judges who screwed him over when he was a practicing attorney."

LeBov described the court restructuring plan, which he worked on, as a "momentous, historic proposal" that should have lived or died "on its own merits, not on the basis of does it or does it not include a lid on judicial salaries." But Kline, according to LeBov, said the administration would support the bill only if it included the limit on salaries. "That was the *quid pro quo.* The governor's office would support it if it had that and if it had mandatory retirement for judges in it. And that was the start of the process which killed the bill."

When the court-reorganization bill failed to pass, said LeBov, Kline "ultimately hijacked" another act, tacked the salary limit on to it, "and he finally got his pound of flesh."

Senator Alan Robbins, who, as a member of the Senate Judiciary Committee, was involved in the attempt to reorganize the courts, said the limit on judges' pay was far from being the most important part of the package, but it "was the part they [the Brown administration] could probably get the most public mileage out of. Politicians run on public mileage," said Robbins. But, he added, Brown and Kline "could have displayed a little bit more concern for the rest of the package, what the court system would be like."

Kline said the attempt to limit judges' salaries may well have been his single most difficult battle during the administration. In his opinion, the provision was important because the public will not be willing to make sacrifices unless judges and other leaders do. Kline, a bald, black-bearded, intense individual, declared that judges who feel they are not making enough money "can always return to" private practice. "You are not sentenced to sit on the bench. There is no dearth of people who want to be appointed to the bench. Believe me, there is no dearth. The idea that judges have to be highly paid is predicated on the unarticulated assumption that the best judges come from the most highly paid elements of the bar, which I reject out of hand. That would eliminate district attorneys and public defenders, for example."

The bill that the legislature finally passed froze judges' pay from January 1, 1977, until July 1, 1978, after which judges may receive an annual cost-of-living increase of up to 5 percent. When the bill was passed, judges earned from $45,000 for municipal court to $67,000 for the state's chief justice and received an automatic cost-of-living pay raise each year, which amounted to 13 percent in 1975 and 9 percent in 1976. When Brown signed the new law on September 22, 1976, he noted that California judges were the highest paid in the world except for those in Alaska, where the cost of living is much higher, and that judges were the only state employees with a statutory right to automatic raises. Brown called the legislation "a major step that I've been working on. This was the fourth attempt, and I'm very happy to see that it was passed finally so that people who work for the people [do] not . . . keep getting more and more." As a result, Brown said the discrepancy between the lowest paid and the highest paid would diminish instead of grow.

Brown, who makes $49,000 a year and has strenuously resisted several attempts to raise the governor's salary both before he took office and since, cut his top aides' salaries by 7 percent in one of his first important acts as governor. Klein, Gray Davis, and Marc Poché were among those whose pay shrank. "When we talk about tightening our belts, I think we've got to look at those with the largest belts," Brown said when he announced the pay cuts. Three weeks earlier, in his inaugural address, Brown had proposed a 7 percent decrease in his office budget, declaring that "every branch and department of state government must reexamine itself with a view toward eliminating expenditures not absolutely essential to the well-being of the people."

The Information Practices Act, also known as the Privacy Bill, seems at first glance like one that a liberal such as Brown would routinely sign. The bill, first introduced in April 1975 by then Senator George Moscone, would have prohibited state and local government agencies from gathering secret personal records on individuals; allowed citizens to inspect, copy, and correct their files; banned disclosure of information in someone's file in most cases unless the individual consented; and created a five-member Information Practices Commission to regulate the collection of personal information by government agencies. The act, drafted in response to a 1972 ballot measure approved by the electorate that added privacy to the rights protected by the state constitution, passed the legislature overwhelmingly, with bipartisan support. Then Governor Brown vetoed it. Brown's veto, issued at 11:58 P.M. on October 1, 1975, two minutes before the act would have become law without his signature, surprised and angered Moscone and Ben Bycel, the American Civil Liberties Union (ACLU) lobbyist who had drafted the legislation.

Bycel, a lawyer and former reporter, said, "All the time we kept communicating with the governor's office [and asking], 'What do you need' " in the way of information about the bill, " 'What do you want?' " At one point, said Bycel, one of Brown's aides, Paul Halvonik, himself a former ACLU official and a friend of Moscone, said the governor objected to the creation of another commission and would sign the bill if the provision that called for the commission were taken out. But when Moscone asked Halvonik to confirm that promise in writing or to testify that Brown agreed to the compromise, Halvonik refused. On the night of October 1, just a few hours before Brown had to make a decision, Bycel and Moscone were asked to give the governor's office phone numbers where they could be reached. About 9 P.M., Marc Poché called Bycel and asked him to state by telephone reasons why Brown should veto the bill. Bycel refused to play what he considered a law-school game in which he would have been arguing the opposite side of his own case, saying he could only tell why Brown should sign the act. He also asked for a chance to talk to Brown personally but was rejected.

When Brown vetoed the bill, one reason he gave was that the law was too complicated. Bycel's response: "I agree. It was too complex to read in ten minutes at eleven-forty-five. My frank impression of what happened is that Brown never knew what was going on" until shortly before midnight, because of foul-ups by his staff. Bycel declared that the experience showed "a lack of organization and a lack of systematic approach to legislation" within the governor's office.

Moscone shares Bycel's opinion. "I didn't have great success in getting through" to Brown to discuss the pending bill, he said, adding, "It was too big a bill [for Brown to assimilate] on such short notice."

One month later, Moscone was elected mayor of San Francisco, and in 1976, Senator David Roberti (D, Los Angeles), introduced a bill similar to Moscone's. The Roberti measure, also written by Bycel, omitted the Information Practices Commission on the assumption that this was the part of the act Brown found most objectionable. But on September 30, 1976, the governor vetoed this bill, too, saying the estimated cost of administering the law, $4 million initially and another $13 million each year, was too high. Instead, he issued an executive order that guaranteed individuals access to their files and included many of the other provisions of the two information privacy acts. Brown said this order would "do most of what is essential in this bill at a fraction of the cost. If, with experience, the executive order proves deficient in ways which cannot be corrected by administrative action, we can then consider legislative action."

In September 1977, after Bycel had departed Sacramento, Brown codified the information privacy law by signing a bill authored by Roberti that was very similar to the 1976 executive order. Asked why he had vetoed similar laws to the two previous years, Brown said he had done so because they created "a bureaucratic nightmare." He said he often vetoes laws because there are already too many on the books. "Why mandate? Let's persuade. Let's inspire. Let's go with what we've got," he said.

Bycel attributes the 1976 veto to a vendetta against him by Rose Bird, who told Bycel the administration wanted to draft its own privacy legislation. Bycel said he told Bird, "I think you're going to miss the point if you're going to have government write a bill that will curb government." Bird's response, according to

Bycel, was that if he and Roberti went ahead with their own bill, "We'll blow you right out of the water."

According to one source, the Roberti bill was one of those that was to have died in the Assembly Ways and Means Committee "because Jerry didn't want to have to veto it again, given that it was now in the form that he said it should be in." However, the observer said, "McCarthy's lieutenants forgot" to kill the Roberti law when it got to the Ways and Means because of "a mixed signal." The source added that Bird "took it as a personal affront that somebody [Bycel] didn't automatically accede to what she wanted" and instead "tried to negotiate with her."

Brown has also vetoed legislation that would have prohibited state agencies from checking the background and character of applicants for important jobs, calling the bill "irresponsible." On the other hand, he struck a blow for privacy on August 28, 1975, when he vetoed an act that would have eliminated the confidentiality of some discussions between a doctor and a patient when a death becomes the subject of a coroner's investigation. "This society collects too much data, often at the detriment of a person's right to privacy," Brown said at the time. (This was the message drafted by Bob Nance that wound up framed and on the wall in Nance's office, as described in Chapter Ten, "Facing the Press.")

Brown has received wide praise for carrying out his inauguration pledges to work with the legislature to eliminate the oil-depletion allowance, increase taxes on capital gains and stock options, lower from two-thirds to a simple majority the vote needed in the legislature to increase business taxes, and repeal a law that resulted in reduced taxes for many insurance companies. (The legislature passed the last two as constitutional amendments, which must be submitted to the voters. Each amendment was approved in the June 1976 primary.)

One major law passed through Brown's skill in dealing with the legislature was the California Coastal Act of 1976, which curtailed development along the state's 1,000-mile coastline. Brown drew much acclaim for his role in creating the coastal bill. He stayed out of the legislative infighting until the very end. Then, when the bill had passed the assembly but was in trouble in the senate, the governor hammered out a compromise among the various factions, including legislators who had sponsored rival bills; the construction industry; labor; and conservationists. After Brown negotiated with the involved parties for several hours in his office, drafted a list of compromises, and publicly handed the new agreement to Senator Jerry Smith, the sponsor of the bill, it passed the senate by a vote of twenty-five to fourteen. Until Brown's intervention, Smith had been able to get only eighteen senators to commit themselves to voting for the coastal act, three less than was needed for passage.

Smith recalled, "the coastal bill certainly was not a piece of legislation that he was in the forefront of until the very end, and then he was an asset." Howard Berman cited Brown's performance on this act as proof that "sometimes delay turns out to be the shrewdest political move." Preble Stolz, the member of Brown's staff who was most involved with the coastal bill, said unequivocably, "It could not have been done without his help." Stolz felt the coastal legislation was in some ways even more difficult to produce than was the Farm Labor Act because it involved more groups with competing interests. Stolz said Brown allowed the interest groups to fight among themselves early in the legislative process before he stepped in because he realized that "a governor can only lean on a limited number of people." Tony Dougherty, who assisted Brown, Stolz, and Marc Poché in working out the coastal agreement, called Brown "a master of timing," and said, "There was this whole process going on upstairs [in the legislature] that had to run its course. Everybody had to beat their brains out on the coastal bill. He got into it at exactly the moment that he was needed. I think that Smith bill would have failed if he had not intervened at that moment."

On August 25, 1976, after Brown secured passage of the legislation, the *Sacramento Bee* editorialized, "Thanks to a stunning display of leadership by Governor Brown, another battle has been won in the continuing campaign to save California's coastline." Brown's performance on the coastal act also attracted praise from newspapers as distant as the *Washington Post* and the *Wall Street Journal,* which said in an editorial on September 14, 1976, "Governor Brown did not merely sign this bill, he personally lobbied it through the legislature."

The energy legislation that President Carter had considered his top priority during his first year in office failed to pass, and during an interview with reporters in Washington on December 13, 1977, Vice President Mondale offered an explanation: "One thing that we found out in this first year was that one must be careful not to overcrowd the institutions, to try to solve too much too rapidly. There is a concept in missilry where you fire too many missiles too close together and they kill each other off—fratricide," said Mondale. He conceded that the Carter administration's pace was "a little too strong in the first year" for Congress to keep up with.

Even though Jimmy Carter and Jerry Brown have both served as governors, Carter apparently did not learn in Georgia what Brown has in California. More than two months before Mondale spoke to reporters on Carter's behalf, Brown told me:

"There are only so many issues that the legislature can digest, and there are only so many gubernatorial initiatives that the legislature can assimilate in one year. It's just a fact that it's very important that the initiative and the responsibility be shared with the legislature in order to get the maximum amount done. Because if it's perceived that undue amounts of initiative or authorship or momentum are coming out of my office, then it begins to pick up committee pressure as it goes through the legislative process. So one of the things I try to do is to make sure that the legislature has a very full share of any initiative, and I also recognize their coequal role."

CHAPTER TWELVE

THE GOVERNOR
AS PHILOSOPHER . . .

As a rising young politician, Jerry Brown was initially identified as a liberal. Since then, he has received mixed responses as it has become clear that Brown's philosophy challenges the usual definition of liberalism. In fact, in some areas, particularly his fiscal policies and his outlook on life, he strikes many observers as conservative.

Traditional liberal philosophers such as John Locke (1632–1704) and Jean Jacques Rousseau (1712–1778) have held an optimistic view of life and of human nature. But theorists who are identified as conservatives, among them Niccolo Machiavelli (1469–1527) and Thomas Hobbes (1588–1679), were pessimists. Typical of conservative thought was the sentiment expressed by Hobbes in his *Leviathan* (1651) that without a strong sovereign to check man's natural inclinations, there would be "continual fear and danger of violent death. And the life of man [would be] solitary, poor, nasty, brutish and short."

216

It is another of Jerry Brown's many contradictions, then, to find a consistent pattern of pessimistic statements by him:

"I think any historical examination will show that every civilization that has risen has also fallen. Do you need to say any more?" (On William F. Buckley's "Firing Line," October 11, 1975.)

Brown stated he "doesn't think mankind ever really improves itself. Therefore, we have to take the darker side in account of all that we do." (Associated Press interview, October 1975.)

"Life in itself has a rather tragic dimension. We have to recognize that . . . life is tough! Life is a struggle. And it's going to get tougher." (Interview with Walter Cronkite, CBS News, March 29, 1976.)

"Life is a vale of tears, and I don't think that is going to change, with or without technology." (National Catholic News Service, April 30, 1976.)

Poor people "whose voice is so mute on Capitol Hill still have the potential to pull this system apart as [their discontent] grows, and I think that's a realistic assessment." (Speech before National Press Club, Washington, D.C., June 18, 1976.)

"In another five years, we will need the army, not in the Panama Canal, but in the cities of our nation to defend ourselves against the people who have lost hope." (Nationwide television address paid for by Brown for President Committee, June 25, 1976.)

Father William Perkins, Brown's former teacher, says, "I think anybody who sits back and reflects seriously sees the disasters we have around us. Priests and ministers and psychologists and psychiatrists are probably more aware of that because that's the type of people they see. The people who drift in here to talk to me are people whose life is a disaster. . . . The world is really screwed up in many ways. This is a tough world to live in. Just to hold yourself together as a human being is tough." According to Perkins, Brown "has the perception that this is a disturbed world we're living in. It's not the simple agrarian society of the past." Even though Brown did not complete the study for the priesthood, the evils of life would have been made much more clear to him than they would be to a person who did not receive a Jesuit education, said Perkins.

Assemblyman Lou Papan (D, Daly City), who is concerned by Brown's pessimism, observed, "To predict that it's all going to be downhill from here on in, I don't even have that kind of pessimism in my family among my youngsters who are confronted with present-day shortages. So I think he's somewhat of a pessimist as a person. It's not the kind of quality for a leader."

Brown dismisses such comments, saying, "I never thought I was pessimistic." Nevertheless, Brown says, no one can "just mold human beings into anything you want." There is no "technological fix" that "will sweep away the accumulated wisdom of the ages."

Then he outlines his basic philosophy as he approaches forty: "The inherent riddle of existence and the problem of life doesn't go away. It just is there, and we have to come to terms with it and try to understand it, and that's what religion is all about.

"Life begins, life ends; during the pilgrimage there is joy, there is sorrow. There is suffering, there is pain, there is pleasure, there is ecstasy, there is boredom. It's all part of life. I don't think that melodrama changes, however you want to look at it. Jewish, Christian, Hindu, modernistic—there seems to be a unity of human thought since the beginning of time.

"I don't think the basic equations change because the irreducible reality is that at a given point human beings are born and at a given point they die. And that cycle is unchangeable. I don't think that's optimism, and I don't think it's pessimism. It's just a fact.

"I think it's important to realize that you don't just change the world with a new tax or a new bill or a new regulation. A lot of it begins within the individual, and without that there can't be very much. That's [E. F.] Schumacher's point in his recent book [A Guide for the Perplexed (Harper & Row, 1977)]. Politics is not life, it's a part of life, and fundamental change must begin with the individual. . . .

"I guess some of my cautionary comments come in response to the politics of overpromising . . . holding out bureaucratic or political solutions to profound human questions that in fact are not answerable with a government program but must be lived with and through as just part of being a human being. I still think government has an important role, it should do a lot, but at the same time we shouldn't overstate its capacity to effect fundamental changes."

Brown says that in response to "the politics of overpromising," he is "trying to bring a greater clarity and integrity to the language of politics. There's so much verbal garbage that is collected in the political process that it's no wonder people have a low opinion of political activity. I'm trying to rebuild the credibility of the process, and I think it's important to be careful about the language that is used. . . . Holding out the promise that a bill with a few million dollars, or a few hundred million dollars, is going to profoundly alter family structure, the relationship of various groups in the society, is just not true. . . .

"What we have to do to survive in this struggle. I'm interested in laying that before people, understanding it. I want to understand the world, and I want to communicate that understanding to others and work together with the people to try to make for a better society."

Discussing ways to plan realistically for the future, Brown quotes, " 'In a beginner's mind, there are many possibilities, in an expert's very few.' I like that. It's very true. So how can you keep a beginner's mind in a world of experts? That's the trick."

The general reaction to Brown's philosophizing is favorable. Even Assemblyman Alister McAlister (D, San Jose), who is not usually complimentary of Brown, praises the governor for having "a contemplative nature and a certain intellectual bent. I think that's good, whatever other difficulties he may have."

Daniel Lowenstein, Brown's aide when he was secretary of state, said his former boss "has very unconventional and unusual insights into some of the things that are going on in this society and a good ability to communicate them. And I think that puts him above almost any other political leader you can name right now."

Brown is reluctant to identify himself with any particular interest group or philosophy. Ask him what groups he sees as his natural constituency, and he hedges somewhat at first, then lists the various elements of the Democratic party plus those independents and Republicans who agree with his views. Or as he told the *National Journal* on May 14, 1977, "I'm not a person who is a member of some camp, that if I deviate from the party line, I am thereby changing my attitude."

Ask him which politicians or philosophers have especially influenced him, and Brown responds, "I can't say that there's any particular historical figure that I'm trying to emulate. My ideas come from a variety of people." The only person Brown mentions by name is the late E. F. Schumacher, who is often referred to as his intellectual mentor. Brown quotes the subtitle of Schumacher's classic, *Small Is Beautiful* (Harper & Row, 1973): "Economics as if People Mattered." "That's important insight," says the governor.

Marc Poché described Brown as an "eclectic pragmatist. I think he takes bits and snatches of other people's philosophy and welds them into his own, and his own is whatever works in a particular situation."

It is generally agreed that at least until Brown ran for president in 1976, his style was to say what was on his mind without giving much consideration to trying to please his audience. Says Llew Werner, "Basically Jerry said, 'I'm going to run. I'm going to tell you what I think. If you like it, vote for me. If you don't like it, don't vote for me, but that's it. I am who I am.' "

According to restaurateur Frank Casado, "Jerry doesn't worry about being reelected. He could care less. He can always go back to the seminary. He's got a lot of things going for him." Mario Obledo said he was interested in working for Brown because he "told me he had made no commitments to any special groups, but he had made a commitment to his own person, and that was to open government up to all peoples of all backgrounds. I thought it presented something new in America." Don Burns gave similar reasons for his willingness to serve in Brown's cabinet: "It was really mind boggling that someone of that sort would be in a position of that kind." Burns, who previously worked as an attorney in Washington, added, "I had been rather appalled by what happens in Congress, for example."

Father William Perkins, who knows many politicians and political activists, commented, "The first thought most politicians have when they get elected is how they're going to get reelected. Now I don't see that in Jerry at all." As proof of his theory, Perkins cites "the fact that he was, I won't say ungrateful, but the fact that he so neglected all the people that helped get him elected." Several months after Brown was elected governor, Perkins asked him, " 'Why don't you do more politicking and that kind of thing?' 'Well, he said, 'if the people like what I've done, they'll reelect me. If they don't, they won't.' He said, 'I don't believe in the creamed chicken and peas dinner sort of thing, and I don't go the circuit because that's a waste of my time.' So he really had this idea that he wanted to do a job, not start to run for the next term the day he was elected."

* * *

Dave Dawson and Bart Lally, both former classmates and old friends of Brown, are Republicans. And both express approval of Brown's politics. "He's doing a very Republican job," said Dawson. "He's more Republican day by day. The message I think he's running on now is that you can't label people Democrats or Republicans." Lally's comment is, "I'm very comfortable having him as governor. He's a Republican." Robert Cline, the Republican assemblyman who served with Brown on the Los Angeles Junior College Board, agrees. "The people of California are essentially fiscally conservative," Cline believes. "He has taken the financial ball away from our team and has been running with it himself."

One Democrat, State Senator Alan Sieroty, defends Brown for presenting "a very personally constructed program. I think that's something in his favor," says Sieroty, even though Brown's ideas "don't come out of any Democratic party book." Another Democratic observer, Jack Tomlinson, Pat Brown's former aide, says of the current governor, "I don't think he's doing a Republican job. I think he's doing a political job, and it borders on genius. I also think if we called him up tomorrow morning and told him, 'You can't be a Democrat anymore, you have to be in the Platypus party,' it wouldn't bother him a bit."

Perkins persuaded Brown to give the commencement address at Santa Clara University in the spring of 1975, and "it was kind of a typical Jerry Brown speech. He could have been Barry Goldwater in one sense, and he could have been [John F.] Kennedy in another sense. He really covers the spectrum."

According to Poché, "I think you can be a liberal without having all sorts of liberal social programs. The job of a liberal now, I think, is to make these programs more efficient. If that doesn't save enough, then you simply choose between programs. I think that's where the so-called new Democrats are going to come from, and I think Carter and Brown may be in the same mold."

Frank McCulloch, managing editor of the *Sacramento Bee,* pointed out that classifying Brown is difficult not only because his words and actions defy categorization but also because the terms "liberal" and "conservative" are becoming outdated. Brown is "a very skillful politician," said McCulloch, "and he'll make whatever use serves him best from both a liberal and a conservative philosophy, whatever those are. . . . In a lot of ways he's an utter pragmatist, and he's able to put it [any philosophy] to good political use. Now that's the context I think you've got to understand him in." McCulloch, fifty-seven, was a news executive with *Time,* the *Los Angeles Times,* and *Life* before joining the *Bee.* Asked if he would compare Brown to any other politicians he has known, McCulloch suggested Brown's former mentor, Eugene McCarthy. Like McCarthy, says McCulloch, Brown is "remote, arrogant, and elitist, and yet succeeds in presenting himself as the only champion of the unwashed. . . . They don't suffer fools gladly, either one of them; both are inactionists in the sense they'd much prefer to ask questions rather than push; and they're effective, bitter critics of the power structure as it now exists."

Like McCarthy, Brown takes pride in discovering new directions and giving them a public forum. As Gray Davis puts it, "A new toy to Jerry is a new idea, a new publication, a new movement. He likes to be aware of things before other people are." According to Ray Fisher, Brown "likes the intellectual gamesmanship of dialogue and reasoned discourse." James Straukamp recalls Brown as "great for disputes. He likes to play intellectual games."

Brown is quick to grasp an apparently minor detail and build it into a new idea. His press office is tape recording our interviews, and at one point he drops the subject at hand to note, "We're automating our staff. Normally, when you interview somebody, you have their press assistant or some other person standing there. Here we have just a little machine. I find that just an interesting example of the age of cybernation."

One intellectual exercise he does not like to engage in is defining the causal connection between events. "You have to understand the process of my mind," he says. "I see the world in very fluid, contradictory, emerging, interconnected terms, and with that kind of circuitry I just don't feel the need to say what is going to happen or will not happen. Generally, I see a range of possibilities, and within that range I will make my choice.

"The Newtonian physics that object A collides with object B and moves it to point C, I don't see the world in those terms. That's one way of looking at it, but it's the circuitry of semiconductors and computers and electronic interconnections, that's what's happening today."

When asked if he feels a necessity to try to outdo his father either in terms of accomplishments or at the polls, Brown replies,

"I don't think the periods are comparable. Shakespeare once said comparisons are odious, and I think there's a lot of truth to that." Seeking to win by a larger margin than his father did would be "relating to a past. Trying to relate the 1960s with the 1970s, what's the point?"

When Brown is reminded that most people do care about records and, for instance, that Babe Ruth's home-run total has been a point of reference for half a century, even though 1977 is an entirely different era than was 1927, Brown's answer is "Sixty home runs, I'm not in the record business. Report cards and records, I got out of that after I graduated from college." He ignores the fact that every time a politician's name is on the ballot, he in effect gets a report card.

"Man is small, and, therefore, small is beautiful. To go for giantism is to go for self-destruction." So said E. F. Schumacher in the book that has so extensively shaped the thinking of Jerry Brown (*Small Is Beautiful,* Harper & Row, Perennial Library edition, 1975, p. 159). The similarities between the philosophies of Schumacher and Brown abound:

• Schumacher advocated "the development of a life-style which accords to material things their proper, legitimate place, which is secondary and not primary" (p. 294). He also pointed out that "infinite growth of material consumption in a finite world is an impossibility" (p. 122). "An attitude to life which seeks fulfillment in the single-minded pursuit of wealth—in short, materialism—does not fit into this world, because it contains within itself no limiting principle, while the environment in which it is placed is strictly limited" (pp. 29–30).

As Brown says, "Excessive consumption should be tempered. That's an important idea that has to be communicated." In his annual report to the legislature on January 7, 1976, Brown stated, "The country is rich, but not as rich as we have been led to believe. The choice to do one thing may preclude another. In short, we are entering an era of limits."

• Schumacher wrote, "Fossil fuels are not made by men; they cannot be recycled. Once they are gone they are gone for ever" (p. 16).

In his nationwide television address on June 25, 1976, Brown declared: "There are certain things that don't come back. When you've used a barrel of oil, it's not coming back again."

• In *Small Is Beautiful,* Schumacher declared, "It must be clear that, change being a function of time, the longer-term future is even less predictable than the short-term. In fact, all long-term forecasting is somewhat presumptuous and absurd, unless it is of so general a kind that it merely states the obvious" (pp. 235–36).

Brown shares the same distaste for planning. As he told me, "Planning for effects that will really become visible ten or twenty years in the future is very difficult, and one should move slowly so as not to make it worse. And one of the problems I have with planning is that it takes today's information and locks into place tomorrow's reality. And that's a problem. Things change. So this planning is troubling."

• Both Schumacher (pp. 102–103) and Brown have been influenced by a book called *Topsoil and Civilization* by Tom Dale and Vernon Gill Carter (University of Oklahoma Press, 1955). During an interview in September 1976 with the *Sacramento Union,* Brown mentioned that he has the book in his office and said approvingly its thesis is that "all great civilizations have collapsed when their topsoil erodes beyond a certain point because the productivity of the land is destroyed."

• Schumacher called for a return to the simple agrarian life in order to escape the "intolerable" way of life in cities and suburbs and "to keep man in touch with living nature, of which he is and remains a highly vulnerable part" (pp. 113–14).

Similarly, at a press conference on June 5, 1975, Brown said he foresaw "nothing but good things over the long haul for those who work on the land. I think that is the way it should be, and everything I can do in this administration to support agriculture, I am going to do."

• Schumacher said that when millions of people live together in close quarters in cities like New York, London, and Tokyo, the result is "human degradation" and that the optimum population of a city is at most 500,000 (p. 67).

Brown on the same topic: "There is an elephantiasis that takes over when you get so big you can't function. I think if you look at the classical world, as the political entity expanded its role and responsibility, it ran into problems both in Greece and Rome that it could not handle" ("Firing Line," October 11, 1975). During an informal talk with reporters in Sacramento on October 30, 1975, Brown said of New York City's fiscal problems, "Any time you have eight million people situated in a small space like that without adequate jobs, you are going to be in trouble, and they are."

• Brown, who spent three and a half years in a Jesuit seminary and who occasionally retreats to the Zen community for meditation, has combined Eastern and Western philosophies in his outlook on life. The same can be said of E. F. Schumacher. The author of *Small Is Beautiful* was chief economist of Great Britain's National Coal Board for twenty years and was strongly influenced by the thinking of Mahatma Gandhi. Schumacher, who died in September 1977, advocated what he called "Buddhist economics," which would recognize

> one of the basic truths of human existence, namely that work and leisure are complementary parts of the same living process and cannot be separated without destroying the joy of work and the bliss of leisure. From the Buddhist point of view, there are therefore two types of mechanisation which must be clearly distinguished: one that enhances a man's skill and power and one that turns the work of man over to a mechanical slave, leaving man in a position of having to serve the slave (p. 55).

• Schumacher decried the idleness that modern technology has imposed by replacing people with machines. He advocated a system in which "even children would be allowed to make themselves useful, even old people" (pp. 149–52).

Said Brown during his National Press Club speech on June 18, 1976, "I don't think there's ever been a society where so many people have so little to do so much of the time. And each of us has a contribution, whether we're eighty or whether we're ten."

• Schumacher also stated that "modern technology has deprived man of the kind of work that he enjoys most, creative, useful work with hands and brains, and given him plenty of work of a fragmented kind, most of which he does not enjoy at all" (p. 151). Instead, Schumacher proposed an "intermediate" or "appropriate" technology, which would discourage mass production and concentration of resources (pp. 178–81).

In May 1976, Brown, by executive order, established a state Office of Appropriate Technology, and in April 1977, the first nine trainees in solar energy enginering completed a course run by that office.

The head of Brown's Office of Appropriate Technology is Sim Van der Ryn, who originally suggested that such an office be established. Van der Ryn, forty-two, a former professor of architecture at the University of California at Berkeley, a veteran of the People's Park struggle near the campus, and founder of the Farrallones Institute in Occidental, which studies alternative energy sources, has served as state architect since October 1975. He is a crusader for the development of solar energy and toilets that use little or no water. Van der Ryn would like to see human wastes used for fertilizer and said in a story that appeared in *New West,* September 27, 1976, "The flush toilet is the highest technical expression of Victorianism, but it should have gone out with the bustle and the hobble skirt." Aligned with Van der Ryn is architect Buckminster Fuller, who coined the phrase "Spaceship Earth" that Schumacher and Brown have often used to describe humanity's interdependence. Fuller once lamented, "I've visited four hundred seventy colleges around the world, [and] I can't get a single school to look at the toilet. We still use four gallons of water to get rid of a pint of pee."

In April 1976, Brown signed a bill that requires most new buildings in California to be equipped with toilets that use three and a half gallons of water per flush. Proponents of the legislation, which took effect January 1, 1978, estimate it could save 2.5 million gallons of water per day statewide. But Brown's and Van der Ryn's policies are subject to derision in some quarters. "What the hell is the Brown energy program, a three-[gallon]-flush toilet instead of a five-[gallon]-flush toilet?" asks Peter Finnegan. "Big deal. . . . I mean, if you can tell me what the Brown energy policy is, I'd love to know." Another critic of Brown, Bob Moretti, said, "You can bring on all the Sim Van der Ryns in the world you want to be your state architects, but you just really try and sell waterless toilets to the people of this state.

It's not going to happen. You know, go do it in your Zen temple somewhere, but don't try to make that a part of California life." (In fact, Van der Ryn designed a compost toilet for the San Francisco Zen Center's Marin County farm, which Brown has visited.)

Brown has brought other unorthodox thinkers to state government. Stewart Brand, publisher and editor of the *Whole Earth Catalog* and *CoEvolution Quarterly*—Brown reads both regularly—was appointed a special consultant to the governor. Wilson Clark, author of *Energy for Survival* (Anchor, 1974), is the governor's assistant for issues and planning. Brown also made two unusual appointments to the University of California Board of Regents: Theodora Kroeber-Quinn, who wrote *Ishi in Two Worlds* (Univeristy of California Press, 1961), and anthropologist Gregory Bateson, who gave a speech on peyote, snakes, and pregnant goats at Brown's 1976 Prayer Breakfast, and who has said his experience as a regent has convinced him that most of the issues the board considers are trivial and that the state is wasting its money on most of the students who receive a university education.

Brown's repeated calls for lowered expectations are not warmly received by some politicians and others who express concern for the "have-not" segment of the population. "I'm afraid that Jerry thinks there is still time to readjust the political philosophies," says George Moscone. "And there certainly is for people who are reasonably affluent. But there's just not time for a hell of a lot of people. And as a consequence, you've got to at least separate people so that the really impoverished are treated in what I used to know as old-fashioned liberalism: You put your money where your mouth was and just made sure that the programs were administered efficiently and effectively, but you certainly didn't say let them eat rhetoric instead."

According to Bob Moretti, "What he's in effect saying is, 'Listen, you guys, we're sorry, but the cars have run out of gasoline. We've got ours, and there just isn't enough room for you to get yours.' He's not talking about giving what he has to the poor. He's saying there's no room for anybody else on the bus. There's nobody I know . . . that wouldn't be very happy to settle for forty-nine thousand dollars per person in their family. They'd manage somehow to buy the groceries and pay the rent. . . . This whole business of lowered expectations is alien to me, and I

think it's alien to the American political and economic system.
You sure as hell never hear lower-income people suggesting that
we ought to lower our expectations."

Frank McCulloch agrees with Moretti that "it's very easy for
that young bachelor to talk in those terms, and he doesn't
understand the aspirations and problems of somebody making
twelve thousand dollars a year with four kids to educate and so
forth." However, McCulloch added, "the undeniable fact is that
the resources *are* limited and that the expectations must therefore be limited. And that puts Jerry in the position of being the
messenger who brings the bad news. Somehow he's managed to
make good politics out of that, with the growing exception of
blue-collar workers, who see him as a threat to jobs."

John Tunney credits Brown with being the first liberal
governor and presidential candidate "to popularize the idea that
you could be socially liberal as well as fiscally responsible. He
really is representative of a majority of the people of the state."
According to Bob Gnaizda, Brown is "able to express what others
would consider unpalatable ideas and make them attractive to
left and right." Paul Halvonik believes Brown's views gave
direction to Jimmy Carter and the 1976 Democratic party
platform. "No matter what the economic experts wanted to tell
him [Brown], he could see that it was a world in which the myth
of our imperial power was gone to some degree. We're not going
to be able to exploit the rest of the world the way we have in the
past." Even environmentalist John Zierold, often a critic of
Brown, lauds the governor for his desire to symbolize "a shift in
state history from all-out consumption to prudence and to living
within all of our economic and ecological means."

Brown has rejected charges that his philosophy implies writing
off the less fortunate members of society. "Those at the bottom,
who are even below the minimum wage, certainly you can't ask
them to take less. I always like to say that those with the biggest
belts ought to make the biggest sacrifice and tighten them up the
most," he declared on "Meet the Press" on October 5, 1975. He
has expressed similar sentiments many times since.

Here is Brown's application of *Small Is Beautiful* to the
problems of 1978 and the future: "I think we can all clarify our
expectations to conform to the possibilities that the planet makes
available. We want a culture that is compatible with the
ecological and political realities that we face. And certainly there

are some at the bottom who have to be given more opportunity while all of us try to live more ecologically, politically, and psychologically sound lives. I'm asking everyone in society to measure their demands against the possibilities and the limits of the political, economic, and ecological structure."

Brown said he is "trying to find the common thread that can pull all of us together. I don't see it in just quantitative terms that there are a certain amount of goodies on the table, and there's one group on the left that has to be given more goodies from the other group on the right. That undermines the democratic fabric. I'd rather try to inspire and communicate the possibility of a shared future that everybody can gain from. That's not easy, but I think it's possible."

In February 1977, during a tour of the United States six months before he died, Schumacher visited Sacramento and, at Brown's invitation, lectured state employees, including Brown, on his *Small Is Beautiful* theories. On November 30, 1977, Brown traveled to London and attended a memorial service for Schumacher at Westminster Cathedral. During the service, the governor eulogized Schumacher as a man who "made a very important contribution at a time when bigness had overstepped itself."

By 1977, Brown had started to aim his sights higher, into outer space. His new interest in planetary exploration and colonization caused him to diverge from Schumacher, who had criticized "the pursuit of supersonic transport speeds and the immense efforts made to land men on the moon. The conception of these aims was not the result of any insight into real human needs and aspirations, which technology is meant to serve, but solely of the fact that the necessary technical means appeared to be available" (p. 51).

On August 11, 1977, the day before the U.S. Space Shuttle made its first solo flight near Los Angeles, Brown staged a day-long space symposium in Los Angeles to publicize and glorify the new quest into outer space. A month earlier, he had written to the state's congressional delegation, "Space exploration is critical to our future here in California and throughout the world," and had declared that "the Space Shuttle will inaugurate a new era of possibilities for the planet. The exploration of Jupiter will push our understanding to new limits. In addition, the possibilities of converting the sun's rays to electricity by means of space solar-power satellites is a challenge that ought to be taken up now in a bold way." Not long afterward, Brown suggested that California might even launch its own satellites someday.

In September 1977, Brown became the first governor to have a house astronaut. Apollo 9 veteran Rusty Schweickart, who had helped put together Space Day the previous month, joined Brown's staff as a special assistant for science and technology. Schweickart was on temporary leave from his $37,620-a-year job with the National Aeronautics and Space Administration (NASA), and Brown announced that California would reimburse NASA for half of his salary while he served on the governor's staff.

Brown's interest in outer space may have stemmed in part from criticism he had received earlier in 1977, when Dow Chemical had scrapped plans to build a $500-million plant between San Francisco and Sacramento and had blamed the state for foot dragging on the construction applications. Brown, anxious to patch his ties with labor and business as a reelection year approached, recognized that California industry holds half of all NASA contracts and that aerospace accounts for a third of the state's manufacturing output. Brown's shift from talk of limits to talk of new possibilities prompted an editorial in the *Washington Star* on August 15, 1977, that poked fun at him:

> Hey, is this the same fellow we listened to last spring and summer and into fall, solemnly proclaiming that small is beautiful, recognition of limits the course of wisdom, and similar pieties of scale? Surely it isn't the same Governor Jerry Brown—now ecstatic over the "everlasting frontier of space," contemplating the possibility that California may put its own satellites aloft and genuflecting publicly to the slogan: "California and the Space Age—an era of possibilities."

Near the end of 1977 Brown declared, "the exploration of space is inevitable, and everything reaches out for that—tall buildings, airplanes, rockets—so why not be a part of it? Let's focus it, encourage it." He said he had "no doubt" that people will ultimately live in space.

Brown pointed out that in Columbus's era, "People pretty well thought they were at the center. We're in the new world" now, he said, but "there'll be other new worlds. Let's explore them. It's interesting. There are certain inevitable evolutionary movements that we're not able to stop but [that] we can shape a little bit, work with, be part of. Space," he concluded, "it's a big place out there, a lot of room for people. Down here it's all pretty well accounted for."

On January 9, 1978, Brown submitted to the legislature a proposed $17.38 billion budget for the 1978–79 fiscal year. Included in the governor's plans was $5.8 million to buy communications channels on a satellite that is to be launched in 1980, as well as $500,000 to start a space institute at the University of California. Four days earlier, in his annual address to legislators, Brown stated, "I see the future of our species penetrating the universe." The governor added, "The space shuttle built in California marks the beginning, not the end. It has the same potential as the transcontinental railroad."

And so Brown, who has attacked the "Cowboy Ethic" for creating a "wasteful society," for "taking everything out and never putting anything back . . . everybody doing his or her own thing without regard to the earth as a spaceship," is now ready for a new era: the time of the Astronaut Ethic, when man will live within his means and use outer space to help enlarge those means.

CHAPTER THIRTEEN

...AND THE PHILOSOPHER AS GOVERNOR

Jerry Brown, about to take over the elective office that has the largest constituency in the country except for the presidency, looked at his friends, Carl and Betty Werthman, shook his head, and exclaimed, "Decisions!"

Three years later, Brown reflected on his role as chief executive and expressed his controversial attitude toward decision making with a question: "Why make a decision when you don't have to? So long as you can keep all the alternatives open, why not? That's always been my philosophy. . . .

"I maintain that a lot of actions that are defined as urgent and must be done today are not urgent and need not be done today." At what point does Brown deem a problem as requiring immediate attention? When "it looks like something has to be done today or something bad will happen."

He believes that "people invent crises in order to get things done, [just as] real estate salesmen say, 'If you don't buy at five o'clock today somebody else is coming over, and I'm going to sell them the house.' That's an old technique. I like to reframe the problem and say, 'Well, we'll take a longer look at this.' Otherwise, the executive becomes a prisoner of his own office."

Jerry Brown, the philosopher-prince, governs by asking questions, a process that drives many observers to distraction.

When has an executive asked enough questions? Brown and *Sacramento Bee* editor Frank McCulloch, among others, have widely different opinions on that point.

"Never," states Brown. "You have to keep asking yourself, 'What does it all add up to? What's it going to produce?' I think you have to continuously question and crossexamine, relentlessly scrutinize . . . your own assumptions. I like to redefine the problems. I like to ask the questions. I like to reach out to frontiers that haven't yet been fully plowed, fully opened and explored. That's what I mean by activism." Brown argues that the Korean War, the Bay of Pigs, Vietnam, Watergate, all might have been avoided if the president who had been in office at the time had stopped to ask more questions. For instance, Brown said, if President Johnson had put Vietnam on the back burner for a year or so, "as it turned out, it couldn't have been any worse." Although Brown's theory seems persuasive on its surface, the obvious response is that in each crisis he mentioned the president must have presumed either that he had all the information he needed to make a decision or that a decision had to be made whether or not all the data was in.

Frank McCulloch sits in his office a few blocks from the Capitol and declares, "Now we're at the nub of him, when you say what is Jerry Brown and how do you assess him? I would be really delighted to be able to walk around this newsroom and run it by asking questions. I can ask questions endlessly, and I can provoke and irritate and occasionally maybe even inspire and push people a little. But at some point I have to resolve things. I think the basic question about Jerry Brown [is], has he passed the point where the questions no longer suffice? There's a difference between being a philosopher-king, which is Socrates asking questions, and being a leader. Maybe he should be philosopher-king adjunct to the governor's office. But I'm not sure he ought to be governor and depend on that entirely." McCulloch said he was "petrified" at the prospect of a question-oriented president faced with the need to make an instant decision that might determine whether the world survives. He acknowledged that anyone making decisions "may be wrong. I make fifteen wrong decisions a day. But if I didn't make them, we wouldn't get a newspaper out. The alternative is paralysis. And that is what he's risking."

Jerry Brown would prefer to avoid mistakes by not acting at all. "When I try to slow government down, I see that as a very progressive idea," he declared at a news conference on March 31, 1976. A few months later, on July 25, 1976, he told the *San Francisco Examiner*, "I think to avoid major governmentally imposed disasters and inconveniences, avoiding the negative," is "the point of this place." An article in *Mother Jones Magazine* that same month quoted Brown as saying, "Sometimes it's better to do nothing. That's what I call creative inaction."

"He doesn't *do* anything," complains Bob Moretti. "He calls it creative inaction. I call it sitting on your ass. And the fact that he uses nicer words than I doesn't mean that he's describing anything different. You're either an activist governor and have some objectives, or you're a do-nothing, except you dress it up with some words you learned in a philosophy class somewhere."

Tom Hickey, former staffer for both Pat and Jerry Brown, said, "Jerry will wait until the level of suffering and the pressure has increased to a point where people are more willing to compromise and accept a solution, so Jerry becomes more identified with the solution than with the problem. I'm not sure that is good government, but it is good politics. The only certainty [is] that you will lose votes by taking action, but there is no certainty you will gain votes."

According to lobbyist Mary Bergan, "It's one thing to say there was a crisis and the governor solved it, but I think that's starting to catch up. People know one of the reasons the crisis is there is because he didn't take action that could have forestalled it."

A former lobbyist, Ben Bycel, commented, "Other than seeking the presidency, I don't think Jerry has a plan. I think he looks back over things and explains what the plan was."

Leo Wyler, Brown's finance chairman in 1974, explained why he supported Carter in 1976 and might back a Republican against Brown in 1978: "I'm disappointed in his performance as governor. . . . There isn't much substance. There's too much grandstanding and avoiding of any type of issue that has any possible political downside, regardless of the importance of the issue. . . . I would like to see a political stand for principles rather than just for votes even though I helped some of this grandstanding in the 1974 campaign. It was with the definite understanding that once in office there would be an activist governor looking at problems and taking stances, not necessarily always being right, but trying to find solutions to local and national problems."

Two former members of Brown's cabinet defend his refusal to involve himself in an issue until his presence is required. Don Burns said the governor feels "his direct participation is a limited resource, in terms of both time and authority, in the sense that you can't keep shooting your wad every day. There are a lot of problems that people freak out about that tend to go away." Alan Rothenberg, Burns's successor as secretary of Business and Transportation, said, "It's hard to judge the governor as administrator because he doesn't see that as being his job really. I think the people of the state expect him to see that the state runs, not run it himself."

Two other former members of the administration resigned in part because they disapproved of what they considered Brown's nonactivist approach. Larry Moss, who served as deputy secretary of the Resources Agency under Claire Dedrick in 1975, said he quit "because I didn't think Brown's administration was following through in the policy directions he'd indicated that he would take prior to the election. He's almost neurotic about wanting to keep his options open, not closing avenues of possible decision and so forth." Robert Gnaizda declared, "There were a number of reasons, but certainly one influential reason was because I saw a disparity between Brown's willingness to entertain ideas and his unwillingness to act on them." According to Gnaizda, Brown views government as "worthless." He recalled that at his farewell party he said, " 'I've never lowered my expectations [about what government can do], and, Jerry, you haven't, either, and you know it,' " and Brown responded with "a nervous smile." Gnaizda added, "One might have a healthy skepticism about government, but one must still see that action is possible." Brown later said he thought Gnaizda was the one with the more limited idea of government's role.

Justice Mathew Tobriner also finds Brown's attitude toward government disturbing. "I've urged him not to deprecate government," said Tobriner. "It's wrong to attack government too much because the public will pick it up and believe it."

Most of the criticism of Brown for failure to translate ideas into action comes from outside observers of the office of governor. But a similar view is also held by someone whom Jerry Brown occasionally refers to as "the governor before Reagan." According to Pat Brown, "I put my political career on the line time after time, far more than Jerry has."

Brown's theories of government may have evolved during his first three years in office, but the underlying principles have not changed. At a news conference on March 11, 1975, he declared that "I do propose to take a little more time in arriving at a decision, which is all part of my general philosophy, that you have to run very fast to slow things down around here." At another press conference a few weeks later, Brown pledged to "evaluate the evaluators" and "deprogram the programmers." Six months after becoming governor, he stepped up his attacks on the traditional ways government operates. On July 1, 1975, he said that "one of the few things the government does well is to send out checks. When it gets more complicated than that, watch out." And on September 26, 1975, he called government "the growth industry in this country. This is where the great job builders are today. They are not out there inventing new mousetraps, they are figuring out a new way to get a government grant."

Brown's remarks at a fundraising dinner for Assemblyman Lou Papan in Burlingame on November 20, 1975, may account, at least in part, for Papan's critical attitude toward him. "It isn't that I don't like to spend money," said Brown, but I think [it is best] to slow down and figure out what you get for it. And I don't think I'd call [that approach] conservative or liberal, I'd call it revolutionary." Citing problems that then faced the country, including the U.S. defeat in Indochina, Brown then told Papan's friends and financial backers, "So don't think that just because we have always been on top, we're always going to stay on top."

"What makes this man ignore the filling of responsible positions?" asked Papan, a burly former FBI agent who once scored a TKO over a former assemblyman who raised his ire. "Is it because he believes it's not important, and he's trying to prove that maybe government will function without this?" Or "does he believe government could fall on its face and this might be a factor to help it fall on its face?"

Then Papan proceeded to answer some of his own questions:

"The process, I think, is a lot sounder than he's willing to admit or understand, and all the time he works at the erosion of the process. He's the executive branch of government. . . . And he should be running the state along with setting policy and proceeding to solve some of the concerns. There isn't that kind of thing." Papan believes Brown's "take it as it comes along" attitude undermines the state government. Papan concedes, "He works hard, and he's bright. But somewhere he's misdirected and confused."

Brown considers his view of government positive but realistic. And he believes he handles his job the same way that "Everyman" would:

"What is anybody doing? What is any leader? That's my whole point around here. I mean, all we're doing basically is presiding and being the occasion for information and communication. So that's the point of that. I don't think my feelings and approaches to life are that much different from the average person. I'm trying to approach them [problems] as I think the average person would approach them if he were in my place. Everyman. I think that what I do is pretty ordinary. Work hard, deal with the issues, keep a diversity of people in here. It's not all that much different." If he is different, he says, it is because he is "open to what's possible. Basically, if someone can show me a better way to do something, I'm prepared to do it."

If a governor can do only so much, can a president do much more? No, said Brown, in the nationwide television speech his presidential campaign sponsored on June 25, 1976: "I look to the president not as someone who is going to solve everything all at once because the president [is] just a human being. He gets up in the morning; he works during the day; he goes to bed at night just as you do."

Brown also told William F. Buckley, "I don't think it fits very well for those in politics to be wining and dining and congratulating themselves in a ritual of affluence and excess when juxtaposed to the poverty of their performance. I think the modesty of our lives ought to match the modesty of our performance."

Few things frustrate Brown as much as grappling with government bureaucrats and bureaucracy. In a widely publicized move less than two months after he took office, Brown halted the

free distribution of attaché cases and briefcases to state employees, which he said had cost the state $153,000 in 1974. The
governor said his action would slow "the blizzard of state
paperwork. Too often, I find that the volume of paper expands to
fill the available briefcases. . . . The state should get out of the
briefcase business." At the same time, Brown disposed of three
paper shredders that had been used during the Reagan administration. He also ordered the removal of mechanical signature
devices that previous governors had used. If a document is signed
"Edmund G. Brown, Jr.," that means it was actually read and
signed, and quite possibly written or revised, by Edmund G.
Brown, Jr.

In a 1975 press conference, Brown described two unpleasant
encounters he had recently had with bureaucracy. In one, he
said, he had visited a state agency, "whose name I won't
mention," and learned that "in a lot of departments they just
write letters to each other and fill out questionnaires. . . . It just
goes back and forth, and nothing ever happens. All they do is talk
to one another." He also told reporters of the time he asked an
employee of one state agency, " 'How much money have you
spent this year?' And he told me he didn't know. They didn't
have that good of an accounting system." Brown expressed his
outrage at the situation.

On another occasion, Brown complained to reporters that he
had read a government report and found "nothing but mish-
mash, confusion, and utter gibberish, and that's why it takes so
many people to decipher it, because they are speaking in code.
This is basically a cover up, a cover up of what's going on that
only the experts, only the illuminati, can understand."

Llew Werner told about a meeting between a group of state
police chiefs and the governor to discuss obtaining federal funds
for such proposals as a PT boat to cruise San Francisco Bay, a
tank with a turret gun, and "all these mystical, walkie-talkie,
searchlighted, flying, intercepting, blue-helmeted, red-light-flash-
ing macho numbers, and Jerry couldn't believe it. So basically he
said, 'Hey, wait, something's wrong here. Show me that spending
this money has reduced crime.' And you know what? No one
could come up with it. He said, 'Well, if that's true, then why are
we spending it?' " Werner said that "a lot of these police chiefs
came out of the meeting shaking their head in disbelief. They
said, 'You know something, the fucker's right.' "

Brown has vetoed many bills that would have created new government bodies he saw as unnecessary. One such law would have formed a committee to nominate to the governor people to be considered for appointment as state college trustees. In vetoing that bill in September 1975, Brown declared, "I just don't see the public good to be accomplished by creating yet another advisory council with no binding power and therefore no final responsibility."

An early promise of "a top-to-bottom review of every department of state government" and "a very stringent scrutiny of everything we're doing" has led Brown to take a close look at virtually every line in the state budget and at many of the 1,500 bills that pass the legislature and reach his desk every year. According to legislative adviser Bob Williams, during Brown's first year as governor, he studied every bill "with a great deal of care and detail, and part of it, I thought, was an excellent learning process. You can gain a fairly good insight into the processes of government if you review fifteen hundred bills." In 1975, said Williams, "I don't think anything was a routine bill. There wasn't anything you could bring in that he couldn't find fault with. But that's his training, that's his interest. If everything were routine, he would leave." Furthermore, William said, at first "there was Socratic dialogue on every bill," with Brown asking volumes of questions each time. "Having experience with other governors [Pat Brown and Ronald Reagan], it was difficult for me to get used to the process."

Williams said that Brown has since become less concerned with insignificant bills and usually accepts his staff's recommendation as to whether to sign them, veto them, or allow them to become law without his signature. But Brown still goes over hundreds of bills himself, trying to learn all sides of the issue and answer his favorite questions: "Why?" and "What if?" Unlike Reagan, Brown does not rely on formal cabinet meetings for a decision on each bill. Instead, Williams and his staff are generally present while Brown ponders stacks of new bills, and Brown solicits any additional opinions he thinks may be helpful, including those of other members of his staff, legislators, cabinet members, and other state employees, lobbyists, and private citizens.

Brown occasionally calls for advice from Frank Mesplé, Pat

Brown's former legislative secretary who has since become a lobbyist for the county of Sacramento and an instructor in political science at the University of California at Davis. Early in Brown's term, Mesplé and others had convinced the legislature to pass a bill allowing the Camellia Bowl, a minor post season college football game, to be held in Hughes Stadium in Sacramento even though the stadium was owned by a school district and was potentially hazardous if an earthquake occurred. The Camellia Bowl had been held annually for several years, and the bill contained an urgency clause so it could take effect in time for the 1975 game. A law with an urgency clause cannot later be submitted as a referendum to the state's voters; it can only be repealed by an act of the legislature.

Mesplé related that Brown called him into his office and said, "Well, do you know what urgency clauses are to be used for? I remember your telling my dad about urgency clauses."

MESPLÉ: "Yes, I remember."

BROWN: "Do you know what the constitution says?"

MESPLÉ said, "I recited it fairly accurately," noting that under the state constitution urgency clauses are to be attached to bills only in emergencies that may affect the health, welfare, and safety of state residents.

Then Brown stated, "Well, I took the oath to uphold the constitution. Do you think not applying the Field Act [the earthquake hazard law] at Hughes Stadium [will avert] an emergency affecting the health, safety, and welfare of the people of the state of California?"

MESPLÉ: "No, governor, of course it won't, but it's the only way we're going to hold the Camellia Bowl. It's done all the time."

That something is "done all the time" usually carries little or no weight with Brown. In this case, he allowed the Hughes Stadium bill to become law—without his signature.

Mesplé still chuckles over the incident, and he has praise for Brown: "I think even the legislators who tend to deride some of his style or some of his approach admit that you go in to see him about a bill, and you're talking to a guy who probably knows as much about it as the author, in some cases more."

According to Don Burns, "It can be infuriating when he catches things you should have caught. And that's the quick-study thing. He doesn't necessarily see what is wrong with a bill, but he has a sense for saying, 'There is something funny about this: Would you please try to find out what it is.' " Burns said, "I think that effort warrants the time, although at times it's infuriating to deal with." He added, "The way to find out what Jerry Brown thinks is to read the veto messages. That's really where he says what he thinks. And they're almost all him, pure Jerry Brown."

A concern for detail implies a reluctance to rely on other people's opinions, and one of the most frequent criticisms of Brown is he is unwilling to delegate authority. In the opinion of Republican Assemblyman Mike Antonovich, Brown "keeps everything to himself and makes a lot of arbitrary decisions. It's not conducive to the healthy democratic process." Antonovich points out that President Nixon was often attacked for being a loner who mistrusted most people. "Well, Brown is more of a Nixon than Nixon ever was. His whole operation is very closed." Another Republican, Howard Way, who admires Brown much more than Antonovich does, says the governor "wants to know everything about every issue, and I've said this to him repeatedly, 'You just can't, the job's too big.' He's got to learn to delegate more. Every time I tell him that, he says, 'Yeah, I'm delegating more,' and I say, 'Well, you're not delegating enough.' "

Many Brown watchers believe that midway through his term he seemed to become more confident in his job and more willing to delegate power. Just at that time, however, some of the people Brown trusted most, including Marc Poché, Rose Bird, and Don Burns, left his administration, as had Robert Gnaizda previously. Their replacements do not have nearly as much stature with Brown, and as a result, Gray Davis and Tony Kline were left as the only aides he was willing to rely on to exercise authority on their own. In the words of Willie Brown, Poché, who was a tenured professor at the University of Santa Clara Law School, "played a unique role. He was one independent voice in the Brown administration that didn't have to eat as a result of Jerry Brown's generosity. And that was awfully important." The departure of that quartet appears to have negated Brown's evolving recognition that he had to relinquish some of his power.

Brown's friend Carl Werthman says, "There's an inner, inner circle, and that's Jerry Brown alone. Every decision has his own stamp on it. He has always run his own show. He ran the campaign, he runs the governor's office." Stephen Reinhardt explains that "Jerry feels somewhat uncomfortable about having people that he doesn't really know well in a position to do things in his name. I suspect a good part of that comes from his experience growing up under his father's administration and seeing a lot of people that he felt were doing things in their own interest rather than in his father's interest."

When Brown does delegate, he often acts in unusual ways. According to Reinhardt, "Jerry doesn't like people having titles." During the 1974 campaign, said Reinhardt, he and others "almost forced" Brown to appoint a campaign chairman for each county. Several days later, the chairman of one of the less-populous counties in Northern California defected to Flournoy. The loss was of little significance to the Brown campaign, but the incident convinced Brown he had been correct in his desire to avoid designating official titles, said Reinhardt.

Reinhardt added, "Jerry does tend to ask a number of people to do things without proper coordination," and power struggles have resulted. The best example occurred at the start of the administration, when Brown in effect asked both Poché and Paul Halvonik to handle his legislative relations. "It was a two-headed operation," said Halvonik. "Jerry never made it clear which of us was going to be doing what and really sort of invited us both to do the same job." Fortunately, chuckled Halvonik, "There were titles available for us of equal rank": Poché became Brown's assistant for programs and policy, and Halvonik was assistant for legislative affairs. In practice, Halvonik worked with the assembly and Poché with the senate.

Strangely enough, Halvonik said, the arrangement "worked out perfectly. I would never have believed it." The division of responsibility with Poché turned out to be "one of the best working relations I ever had with anybody." However, Halvonik said he resigned after a year partly for family reasons and partly because he decided, "It probably wouldn't be that smart for us to continue dividing it assembly-senate. Both Marc and I thought, 'You know, okay, this is fine for one year, but the second year, somebody ought to be able to do' " the whole job.

The experiences Reinhardt and Halvonik cited were apparently more the rule than the exception with Brown, who is not in the habit of telling his aides he wants them to do specific things for him. Said Richard Maullin, "Jerry's not the kind of guy that says, 'I'm telling you to go do this and then come back and report to me.' I mean, he puts the pigeon out of the coop, and it sort of flies away. And if it doesn't get shot down, he's still delegated it." Rose Bird says with a laugh, "You never have a specific delegation from him, which in a way is not a bad strategy because then when you get in trouble, he's never delgated it to you, so he doesn't have responsibility for what you've done."

Don Burns's experience was different: "I had a tremendous amount of freedom running my agency. The notion that Jerry doesn't delegate is really, I think, a mistake. Jerry sees how things are going, and he'll lean on you harder if he thinks things aren't going very well. So therefore there are varying degrees of rope that he'll give people." Burns' temporary replacement, Alan Rothenberg, commented, "I decided what to do, did it, and then told him, and he liked it." Rothenberg added, "The governor views his job as a sort of appellate body when the departments under him have conflicts or problems. He doesn't see himself as manager."

Daniel Lowenstein noted approvingly that when Brown was secretary of state, the interplay between Brown and his staff was: "Until the point that he went out in public on something, there was no rank. He was in charge in terms of a decision but in terms of what I was free to say to him or he was free to say to me, and this would apply to the others on the staff, we were equals." Unlike most politicians, who accept or reject ideas generated by their assistants, Brown often came up with various courses of action and asked his staff members for their opinion, said Lowenstein.

"The advantage in Jerry's rather personal approach is that the person you elected is actually making the decision," said Gray Davis. Everyone who is with Brown while he is reaching a decision "knows not only what the decision is but how it was reached. They are privy to his thought processes and can function as if the governor were present when they implement his policies, which is as it should be. If all Jerry did was choose item three on a piece of paper I handed him every morning" as his course of action, the people who must represent Brown would not know how he had reached his decision.

On the other hand, Davis continued, "the disadvantages are obvious: That approach requires you to focus your attention on the issue before you, and you can't range across countless issues. I tell Jerry this whole menu of government, this smorgasbord, is before you, and he chooses the issues which he thinks he should get involved in. In other words, 'Do what you do well.'

"In a sense, he delegates more than most chief executives," Davis said. "Decisions must still be made on other issues while he is occupied within one area. By default or by conscious delegation, he has carved out a part of the public's business for his own resolution and left the rest to his appointees. So what you get is fewer decisions resulting directly from the participation of the chief executive but hopefully a higher quality of decision making."

Brown's penchant for asking questions may be productive for him, but according to those who have participated in work sessions with him, it is also wearing. "I think you have to be extremely well prepared when you work for him," said Rose Bird. "It's foolhardy at best to try to bluff your way with the governor because he will crossexamine you until he finds out exactly what you know and what you don't know." Finance Director Roy Bell said that "in addition to being physically tiring, a meeting with Brown can exhaust you intellectually. He has that type of inquiring mind that demands the best of you at high speeds at all times. And you can get more worn out in an hour with him than in four hours with somebody else."

Frank Schober, head of the California National Guard, said he has instructed his staff to be prepared to answer any question during meetings with the governor, particularly on items that have been in the news. Similarly, Mario Obledo said that after an unfavorable news story, "I can almost tell you when the governor's going to call. If there's an article in the newspapers, I try to read it before he does early in the morning, and then I'll try to get the information because I know he's going to call. And generally he does. About ten-thirty in the morning the phone rings," and it will be Brown using the direct line that connects him with agency heads and key staff members, wanting to know about the story in the paper.

There is also such a thing as being too well prepared for a meeting with Brown. Claire Dedrick recalled an instance when she had the right answer for every question the governor asked. "About ninety percent of the way through I thought, *Goddamn it, I've made a mistake. I didn't leave him a spot to pick a hole in it.* And damned if I wasn't right. At the end of the thing, I said,

'Is that okay, will you sign the bill?' And he says, 'Let me think about it.' " Dedrick admitted, "I outfoxed myself."

One habit of Brown which Marc Poché says "would just drive people from the Harvard Business School to distraction" is that the governor "doesn't pay very much attention to chains of command and normal sources of information.

"His way of operating," Poché said, "is to phone out there into the bureaucracy and not necessarily to deal with the secretary [of the agency] but to deal with the assistant director or some little bureau chief if he's got a problem they can handle. People who had never seen a governor suddenly had this guy on the line screaming at them. And he'd say, 'This is Governor Brown,' and they'd say, 'Sure it's Governor Brown, my ass it's Governor Brown.' "

Rose Bird said when she was an agency head, her subordinates would often tell her the governor had called them. "At first, it drives you batty, especially if you're used to a more orderly structure," said Bird. But she added, "I can't fault it. He goes to the original source of the information, and then he can judge whether he's going to give credence to" the data, without having "a refinement all the way up the line."

When Brown arrives at his office, usually between 9 and 10 A.M., he finds on his desk a list of fifteen or twenty items suggested for his attention that day. This agenda, prepared by Chief of Staff Gray Davis, shows vacancies to be filled, meetings the governor might want to attend, bills that require a decision, public announcements and appearances to be made by Brown, and other matters. Some of the items are carried over from day to day until Brown acts on them.

Davis explains, "I try to alert the governor to a range of problems facing him and lay out which ones he should get involved in." Each morning, Brown and Davis go over the list and agree on how the governor will spend his day. Discussing the percentage of items on the list Brown elects to deal with on any given day, Davis said, "I've ranged from total failure to total success."

The daily agreement with Davis is the closest thing Brown has to a schedule. Said Davis, "Jerry operates through meetings rather than memoranda. He is reluctant to borrow some staff member's definition of a problem, much less their inventory of solutions. He's reluctant to leave a meeting until the problem that caused the meeting has been resolved.

"We would not have a Farm Labor Board if Jerry was scheduled like other chief executives," Davis declared.

Davis admits that Brown's inability to follow a schedule can be "the bane of my existence," particularly when people with whom Brown fails to keep appointments blame Davis. That is one reason Peter Finnegan, Don Burns, and others do not envy Davis his job. "Gray's role is a very strange one," said Burns. "It must be terribly unsatisfying for him. I kind of feel sorry for him. He's got a shitty job." Burns contrasted Davis's job, which he described as primarily administrative rather than substantive, to Kline's job, which includes a defined area of responsibility—all legal matters—plus whatever else Kline chooses to get involved in. According to Finnegan, "Gray has to eat shit every day. He is the no guy, the office hatchet man." Finnegan said even Brown realizes the difficulty of Davis's position.

People who must deal often with Brown and who are used to keeping to a timetable have the most trouble adjusting to the way Brown does business. Bob Williams is one such person. He is a technician; he advises Brown whether to sign each piece of legislation that reaches the governor's desk and explains his reasons. (The political aspect of Brown's legislative relations has been handled by Marc Poché and Paul Halvonik, then by Tony Dougherty.) Williams is in a unique position because he held the same job under Pat Brown and Ronald Reagan.

Williams said he could tell Reagan's personal secretary he needed a certain amount of time, and she would then schedule it. Furthermore, Williams said, he could usually depend on Reagan's following the schedule once it was made up. Jerry Brown, on the other hand, "rebels against" fixed schedules. "To my knowledge, he's never been anywhere in his life on time," said Williams. "I think if you told the governor he had to go on a precise minute-by-minute schedule, he'd probably dive out a window, and you'd never see him again."

William's way of arranging to see Brown is to "plunk myself down" outside Brown's office. "Your presence sometimes speeds up the process." Still, said Williams, "waiting is the most frustrating time I think a person can put in." And Williams has had more success in seeing Brown at scheduled times than have most other people because the governor must act on a bill within twelve days of the time it reaches his desk, or it becomes law without his signature.

Brown said he views his method of allocating time as a form of "uncommitted potential. This is the way one grows and discovers, and in order to do that, I don't like too rigid a format." He points out that he followed tight schedules during his campaigns, "but generally there's a lot of space on the calendar. I would say that's true. How to use one's time, that's a large part of what this job is, the setting of priorities."

Often, according to Brown, if somebody says, " 'Let's go do something,' I do it," and he gets results. As an example, he cited his dramatic last-minute trip to Colorado Springs in September 1977 to help convince the U.S. Olympic Committee to designate Los Angeles instead of New York City as the U.S. bidder for the 1984 Summer Olympics. Furthermore, Brown declared, his freeform schedule allows him to "spend more time on substantive matters."

At one point while I am in Brown's office, I learn firsthand how someone gets to see him. On being informed that a powerful member of the legislature has been trying to reach him to discuss some pending legislation, Brown responds, "Waiting all day? Tell him to come on down, and I'll talk to him." Another legislator, Assemblyman Howard Berman, observed that "the traditional way is probably the worst way of getting access to him, and that is to place a phone call to someone down there to get an appointment because he's not too good about developing effective schedules and keeping to them."

Wilson Riles, the state superintendent of public instruction, finds Brown hard to work with. Riles said that during Reagan's term, he could usually learn in advance what the governor's position was. He does not have that luxury with Brown, he said, because "he tends to not set his mind to a problem that may be coming down the road but to address each issue when it's before him, and he has to make a decision. It creates a difficult situation for me because the last thing I need is a conflict with the governor" on budget items, legislation, and other matters. "In this process, you need to know about where the governor is. If you can't find out, then you get up to the last moment of decision, and you can run into conflict."

                              *   *   *

If the tasks that federal and state government can perform are
finite and the needs of the citizens nearly infinite, who can
perform the necessary jobs that central government cannot be
responsible for? Brown's answer is a combination of local
government agencies and individuals doing both paid and
unpaid work.

The governor outlined part of his solution to the shortcomings
of centralized government in October 1975 at a meeting of the
state's county supervisors: "One of the first items on the agenda
is to try to recapture authority at the lowest possible level. At the
state level, I think we ought to be doing more of what the federal
government is now doing. And in the state, I think more ought to
be done at the county level instead of pyramiding a lot of these
new agencies that are unresponsive, unelected, and rather
obscure. . . . I'd like to devise ways in which authority and
responsibility can be left with those who are closest to the
problem."

On the same subject, Brown said in an interview with Walter
Cronkite on March 29, 1976, "I'd like to apply a ruthless
skepticism to everything we do in government. If social programs
don't work, let's try to change them. Let's try to bring them closer
to home, to the neighborhood, because that's where I think
everything begins." And at a press conference six months later,
he added, "As the state takes over more and more of the role that
formerly has been played by the church, by the family, by the
neighborhood, it will encounter extreme difficulties of management. I personally think that trend ought to be slowed down."

One area in which Brown favors more local control is in the
administration of schools. In July 1975, he declared, "Much of
school decision-making is top-heavy. It happens in Sacramento, it
happens at the centralized school board, and when you get down
to the teacher and the parents and the principal of the particular
school site, they're not really making the kind of immediate
human decisions that ought to be made."

After three years in office, Brown still saw the practice of
central bureaucracy dictating solutions as "a very big problem,"
one that he still wanted to resolve.

In 1977, volunteerism—encouraging individuals to take care of
their own and other people's problems—became one of Brown's
major programs. As long ago as April 1975, he had commented

that having San Francisco police take poor children on fishing trips was "a good idea" but questioned whether the public should pay: "I wonder why don't policemen just do it, why doesn't the mayor invite them to do that?"

Almost two years later, in his annual report to the legislature in January 1977, Brown said, "I want to ask the people of this state to also contribute their own individual resources, their time, their heart, their effort, because we can't do the job in this chamber. . . . There is just too much. The scope of human need in this state is beyond the thousand laws that will pass this year. It is beyond whatever program that we can fashion. . . . Volunteerism is something that has been a great mark in our history. We had it during the war. We had it in years past. I want to begin it again. . . . I don't think our problem has been that we have asked too much of people. I personally think we haven't asked enough." Brown announced a new volunteer program in state mental hospitals, promising that if it were successful, it would be expanded.

Three months later, the governor visited a mental institution in San Jose, then told a group of Junior Leaguers, "Volunteerism is not a luxury. It is a necessity for a civilized society that wants to truly meet its human ends."

In July 1977, Brown named Charles Baldwin as special assistant for volunteerism. However, Baldwin was not himself a volunteer; his job pays an annual salary of $32,000.

Brown's critics say he is a do-nothing governor, but the facts indicate otherwise. Perhaps Brown's style and personality account for much of the hostility toward him; or it may be envy on the part of those who would like to have his job.

Much of the criticism relates to his refusal to fill some of the jobs that are his responsibility. But the number of vacancies and the types of posts he has left unfilled show that such criticism is not justified. He has been faulted for not taking steps to cope with the state's drought of 1975 to 1977. Yet in practice, what could Brown have done? He cannot make it rain. The only solution to a drought is more dams to increase the state's water-storage capacity. But an extensive construction program would take five to ten years and would have no short-term effect. Much can be said for conserving or rationing water in the most severe drought years instead of spending hundreds of millions of dollars to erect dams that will not normally be needed and that will mar the environment. The end of the drought in the winter of 1977–78 showed that a hasty dam-building program would have served no purpose.

Brown's detractors can point to no catastrophes or even to any substantial problems that have resulted from his administration of state government. In fact, the state appeared to be in excellent shape after the first three years of his term. Cali ornia's unemployment rate, which was 9.1 percent when Brown took office and soon soared to 10.5 percent, had fallen to 7.5 percent by August 1977. And in June 1977, the California unemployment rate of 6.9 percent was below the national rate, 7.1 percent, for the first time in seventeen years. California's jobless rate is usually higher than the national average because so many people migrate to the state. Of course, unemployment must be dealt with on a federal level rather than by individual states, and the Brown administration did not take credit for the state's encouraging figures. But the fact remains that if Brown was not doing something right in fighting joblessness, he certainly was doing nothing wrong.

Over the same period, Brown's fiscal policies had succeeded in creating a multibillion-dollar surplus in the state treasury to save for emergencies.

Brown has also given new job opportunities to women and minorities; created the Farm Labor Board; secured passage of the coastline protection bill; and used executive orders to cope with redlining and many other problems.

Brown's employers, the people of California, have remained pleased with his job as governor. In the June 1976 presidential primary, the only time Brown's name has been on the ballot in California since he was elected governor, he received three times as many votes as the runner-up, Jimmy Carter. And the public-opinion polls, which Brown trusts so little, reveal that his popularity is unprecedented. He earned an 86.9 percent approval rating in March 1976, the highest for a governor in the history of the California Poll. A California Poll released in November 1977, almost three years through Brown's term, showed that 80 percent of those questioned still viewed him favorably, 15 percent unfavorably, and 5 percent had no opinion. By contrast, a nationwide Harris Poll released at the same time showed that after less than one year in office, President Carter received a positive job rating from only 48 percent of those surveyed, with 50 percent rating Carter negatively.

Brown's success in the public-opinion polls, in fact, constituted the main reason he decided to take his biggest political gamble to date: his entry into the race for the 1976 Democratic presidential nomination.

CHAPTER FOURTEEN

BROWN VERSUS CARTER: 1976 AND THE FUTURE

*In politics more than in anything else, you don't get oppor-
tunities very often. No matter how able or how bright or how
qualified you are, timing is the most important thing. When the
opportunity exists, you should take it, even if the odds are ten to
one or twenty to one against you."*
STEPHEN REINHARDT
member of the Democratic National Committee
and long-time political adviser to Jerry Brown.

Over Labor Day weekend, 1971, long before White House-
inspired "dirty tricks" helped undermine Senator Edmund
Muskie's bid for the 1972 Democratic presidential nomination,
Stephen Reinhardt and Jerry Brown, then California's secretary
of state, were on the campaign trail on behalf of Muskie. Late one
night, the two talked about the directions Brown might take in
life, and one of the possibilities they discussed was the presi-

dency, just as a young lawyer might say that if he got the right breaks, he might wind up on the U.S. Supreme Court, said Reinhardt. "I did not have the feeling at that time that Jerry had any specific program to run for president in a particular number of years."

During late 1975 and early 1976, it appeared that 1976 might offer the right opportunity: A nonelected Republican president was in the White House; the GOP was in disarray because of Watergate and President Ford's pardon of former President Nixon; and none of the many Democratic contenders—including long-time candidates, such as Hubert Humphrey, Henry Jackson, and George Wallace; veteran noncandidates, like Ted Kennedy; and newcomers, such as Jimmy Carter, Morris Udall, and Frank Church—had a clear lead over the others. Gray Davis, Brown's chief of staff, called 1976 "a kind of reshuffling year" within the Democratic party and said if Brown failed to run then, he might not be considered in the future.

The possibility of seeking the nomination was clearly in Brown's mind in October 1975 when he spoke at length with AFL-CIO President George Meany during the union's convention in San Francisco. Allard Lowenstein, an outspoken war critic and former congressman from New York, had spent the previous summer as a member of Brown's staff. One of Lowenstein's projects was to coordinate volunteers who were researching the various state laws about entering presidential primaries or winning delegates.

Many of Brown's advisers argued that he shouldn't try for the presidency in 1976. Among them were Tom Quinn and Richard Maullin; Jon Kreedman, who had been chairman of Brown's 1974 gubernatorial campaign; Assembly Speaker Leo McCarthy; and Robert Gnaizda, who had been deputy secretary of the Health Department during the first year of the administration.

In the late fall of 1975, Quinn advised Brown that he had reached "the go or no-go point." By early March 1976, Quinn was telling Brown, "I didn't think he'd win, so I thought he shouldn't run. I just felt it was too late." Quinn figured that either Carter would win the nomination, or the party regulars would throw it to Humphrey or someone else, but "I didn't believe for a second it was going to be Jerry Brown."

Maullin tried to lay out the negative case, that Brown might trip in 1976 and ruin his future career. "I tried to ask him to ask

himself whether he really felt capable of doing this. I was quite
equivocal in my own mind as to whether, just at this point of his
personal development, he would like being president and do a
good job at it." But Maullin said he could see that Brown's mind
"was already made up, even when he asked me the question."

Leo McCarthy advised Brown not to run, lest he jeopardize his
current public standing in California, where he was overwhelmingly popular. "He had a lot of credibility, and I thought
that running for president after being governor only sixteen
months would be damaging to him. "Even though Brown did not
follow his counsel, McCarthy agreed to be chairman of the Brown
campaign in California, as a symbol of unity among state
Democrats.

Gnaizda, who left the administration in late 1975 to resume
his career as a public-interest lawyer, remained in almost daily
contact with Brown. Early in his administration, the governor
had publicly called Gnaizda "the most qualified person to ever
walk across the street," and Brown continued to rely on his
counsel. Gnaizda told Brown "that he would remain the most
powerful political official in the country so long as he did not
seek higher office, and that if he chose to remain as governor, he
would be able to effectively espouse new ideas because of his
nonpolitical image. Consequently, Washington and the president
would have no alternative but to respond to his unique ideas in
affirmative fashion."

Public-opinion surveys taken by Carl Werthman in 1976
supported Gnaizda's view. "At that time, he was not perceived as
a politician," said Werthman. "He was seen as being above
politics. The citizens trusted him for that reason and enormously
distrusted" people who were viewed as ambitious politicians.
Werthman conveyed this information to Brown two days before
he announced his candidacy. Brown did not agree with that line
of thinking. "It's difficult to be a nonpolitician in a political
office," he now says.

Like Quinn and Maullin, two other members of Brown's inner
circle in 1974, Kreedman and finance chairman Leo Wyler were
not involved in his 1976 campaign. Jon Kreedman said he told
Brown he could not support him for president in 1976 because "I
didn't feel that he was ready, nor did we have the organization."
And Wyler watched Brown's performance as a presidential
candidate for several weeks, then decided to support Carter. "My

hope was that Jerry would enter into substantive discussions," says Wyler. "I was somewhat disappointed. He did not attack any substantive problems, he just talked about lowering expectations and offered slogans, slogans that I had helped create in the 1974 campaign." Wyler ultimately became Carter's California finance chairman. Brown's comment about the defections of Kreedman and Wyler: "This is a river. It flows, and I flow with it. Some stand on the shore, some dive in, and sometimes we meet them further down the stream," implying that they may be involved in his future efforts. Also missing from Brown's entourage in 1976 was Blackie Leavitt, who turned down a request from Brown for help. The only important aide from 1974 who was wholeheartedly behind Brown's 1976 candidacy was Gary Davis.

Brown's old friend Peter Finnegan thought 1976 was "a totally abortive campaign. I looked him right in the eye and told him, 'I ain't going to vote for you for president. You gotta be crazy. And furthermore, my mother isn't going to vote for you.' "

In late 1977, Brown explained why he decided to enter the 1976 presidential race: "It's very hard for the chief executive of a large state just to say, 'Well, this is an interesting exercise over here, this campaign for the presidency. I'll just sit back and wait for the summer, and then I'll become involved.' One has to either be a part of what's going on or be aloof. I thought what was going on was important. I decided to be a part of it and to take a leading part. I felt there was no clear leader at the point that I got involved and that I had something to say and that I had had some success in my year as governor, so I decided I would communicate my views to the rest of the country."

Brown announced his candidacy for president in an unorthodox way, while chatting with several reporters in his office on March 12 (described in Chapter Ten, "Facing the Press"). His entry into the race stirred little enthusiasm in the press. A month earlier, *America*, the publication of the Jesuit order in the United States and Canada, had editorialized: "Behind all the news stories is a promising but inexperienced young politician who should not enter national politics in 1976." *America* urged Brown to follow the advice of "his first spiritual master. '*Age quod agis*,' Ignatius Loyola told his distracted young novices. 'Do what you are doing.' " A political gossip column in the *Sacramento Union* gave a humorous treatment to Brown's background and ambition in a March 25, 1976, item that said, "We understand Jerry Brown is running for president because he thinks it would be a good stepping stone." In a more serious tone, the *Los Angeles Times* declared on March 17, 1976, "We believe that Brown is aiming too high, too soon."

Having decided to run, Brown had to put together a staff. Eleven days after Brown announced his candidacy, he signed on Mickey Kantor as campaign manager. ("Now that has to be a record, eleven days without a campaign manager," said Gray Davis.) Kantor, two years younger than Brown, had all the right credentials. He had managed Senator Cranston's successful campaign for reelection in 1974; he was a member of a politically active Century City law firm headed by Charles Manatt, the chairman of the California Democratic Committee since 1971 (John Tunney joined the same firm after S.I. Hayakawa ousted him from his Senate seat in November 1976); and during the five years he had worked as a poverty lawyer, Kantor had represented farm workers in Florida and had gotten to know Tony Kline and Bob Gnaizda.

Kantor said he was surprised when Davis asked him to come to Sacramento to discuss the job. "I just assumed Tom Quinn would be the campaign manager," Kantor said. However, Quinn not only had advised Brown against joining the race so late but also was unwilling to resign from his position as head of the state Air Resources Board. Quinn feared that opposition to his policies by business interests might prevent him from being reconfirmed for the job after the campaign.

Once Kantor agreed to become campaign manager, the next decision to be made was whether Brown should run only as a favorite son in California, as his father had in 1952, 1960, and 1964, or should enter other primaries as well. Initially, according to Kantor, the wisest course seemed to be for Brown to confine his efforts to his home state, given that the race for the nomination appeared wide open. As Kantor saw it, Carter would have to win on the first ballot or not at all, and Humphrey would eventually join the field. Brown had received an 87 percent favorable rating, the highest for a governor in the history of state public-opinion surveys, in a recent California Poll. If Brown campaigned only in California and scored an impressive win there in the June primary, "he would be a viable candidate on the second or third ballot, given the softness of much of Jimmy Carter's support among the delegates," Kantor said. That strategy fell by the wayside in late April after Carter won Pennsylvania, knocked Scoop Jackson out of the race, and became "a freight train going down the track," said Kantor. "There was a major change in perspective on everybody's part, not just ours, as to where Jimmy Carter was going and what he was doing."

The next question was where Brown should run in addition to his own state. Nancy D'Alesandro Pelosi, the Northern California party chairman, had one answer: Maryland. One month before Brown decided to run for president, Pelosi, whose father and brother had each been mayor of Baltimore, had coordinated a Democratic fund raiser at which Brown was the featured speaker. "While he was speaking, I was thinking," said Pelosi. Brown "really struck the chord that appealed to all Democrats" with his talk of finite resources and the limited solutions that government could provide. "He was able to win all of them despite the disparity of their roles within the Democratic party."

Pelosi pointed out the advantage Brown would have running in Maryland with its large Catholic population. She also introduced him to well-placed people there, such as her brother Tommy and Ted Ventoulis, the ambitious young Baltimore County executive. Their guidance persuaded Brown that Maryland offered him an opportunity to score some quick points. His name was placed on the May 18 primary ballot that also included Carter, Udall, Wallace, Jackson, Fred Harris, and Ellen McCormack, the antiabortion candidate.

Brown left California on April 28, 1976, for the first time since his inauguration almost sixteen months earlier to fly to Baltimore. One of the dignitaries on hand to greet him was Governor Marvin Mandel, then under indictment and since convicted on charges of mail fraud and racketeering.

"The irony was not lost on some people, the sainted knight on a horse from California teams up with the [machine] in Maryland," said Peter Finnegan. Fred Epstein, Brown's campaign press secretary, who accompanied him to Maryland, said, "It was a whole different ball game from what he was used to." Brown was "intrigued and fascinated," added Epstein. "Some of those characters in Maryland were straight out of *The Last Hurrah*. I think he was genuinely amused by that."

Said Nancy Pelosi, "A good campaigner is one who makes

believers out of people. He did that. His success in Maryland was
not attributable to anyone but himself." Pelosi said thousands of
people came into or called Brown's state headquarters, eager to
work for a candidate they perceived to be "smart, honest, and
willing to work for us."

In addition to his direct contact with the Maryland voters
through a heavy schedule of personal appearances, Brown was
reaching the media, which had been interested in him since he
ran for governor because of his unusual style and his family
background. As the charismatic newcomer in the presidential
race, Brown became the subject of daily reports in many of the
major Eastern newspapers. Coverage of his campaign was
frequently aired on local and national television and radio, and
he was written up in magazines ranging from *Time* and
Newsweek to *Rolling Stone.*

Although a Gallup Poll in early April showed that Brown was
the choice of 9 percent of the nation's Democratic voters, trailing
only Carter, Humphrey, and Wallace, Stephen Reinhardt said he
and others thought Brown would do well to finish second to
Carter in the Maryland primary and would more likely come in
third or fourth. Instead, "the reaction far exceeded anything
anybody expected."

By the time the polls closed in Maryland on May 18, Brown
was a true national phenomenon, having beaten the previous
front runner, Carter, by 65,000 votes and almost 12 percentage
points. Udall finished third, with one-ninth as many votes as
Brown.

Brown proceeded to make a virtual clean sweep of the
primaries he had entered, adding Nevada on May 25 to his
triumph in Maryland, finishing third in Oregon behind Church
and Carter with an astonishing 23 percent of the vote as a write-
in on May 25, persuading voters to elect uncommitted slates of
delegates who favored him in Rhode Island on June 1 and New
Jersey on June 8, also winning in California on June 8.

In Nevada, the Brown campaign enjoyed the support of an
unusual political activist: Beverly Harrell, owner of the Cotton-
tail Ranch, a legalized brothel north of Las Vegas. Harrell, who
narrowly missed being elected to the Nevada Assembly in 1974,
told the *Los Angeles Times* she was for Brown and had
contributed to his campaign because "he is fresh, has a lot of

energy, is honest, has a lovely disposition, and Nevada loves him."

Kantor considers Brown's showing in Oregon "the biggest miracle of all" because he was not even on the ballot. Oregon Governor Bob Straub, who had endorsed Frank Church, had a more mundane explanation for Brown's impressive performance: "I have no facts supporting it yet, but I have heard rumors that a number of young people from California registered up to the day before election and just voted on election day," Straub charged in a news conference the day after the election. Under Oregon voting laws, anyone eighteen or over could register and vote, provided he or she indicated a sincere intent to become a permanent resident of the state and had given up voting rights elsewhere. Straub called for an investigation of the write-in vote for Brown, but no wrongdoing was ever shown, and Kantor denied that the Brown campaign encouraged or knew about any illegal voting.

Judy Wiseman, an old friend of Brown who campaigned for him around the country, considers his showings in Oregon and Rhode Island the most remarkable. The Oregon primary was marked by the presence of many UFW sympathizers who had come up from California to help Brown. "It gave that feeling of mobilization. There just aren't campaigns like that anymore. We recreated our own era," said Wiseman, who had worked with Brown in the Eugene McCarthy campaign in 1968. As for Rhode Island, where the goal was to elect an uncommitted slate that favored Brown, "We had to explain nine moves on the voting machine to vote for Brown," she said.

As Brown's campaign for the California primary gained momentum, state political leaders who were uncommitted or who had endorsed other candidates had to make up their minds which way to go. Two who opted to back Brown were powerful members of the legislature, James Mills and Willie Brown. Mills later explained, "It would have been much too antagonistic an act to have supported Carter" or anyone else but Brown. Mills, who had been state cochairman for Jackson before switching to Brown two months before the primary, said he had endorsed Jackson in the fall of 1975, after Brown had told him he had no objections. However, aides close to the governor say the relationship between him and Mills has never been particularly warm and add that Mills knew Brown was seriously thinking about running for president when he endorsed Jackson.

Willie Brown's blessing was important to Governor Brown's hopes, both statewide and nationally, because of the articulate assemblyman's stature with blacks. A year after the primary, Willie Brown explained, "I endorsed Jerry Brown strictly out of the fact that I intended to remain in California politics. I suspect that if I had done the nationally politic thing, I would have endorsed Jimmy Carter," who made several requests for Willie Brown's support. "There certainly was not much difference between Carter and Brown, and I endorsed Jerry Brown simply because . . . I did not have any interest in doing anything in Washington, and it just didn't make any sense to do otherwise." Nevertheless, Willie Brown added, "I would not support Jerry Brown in 1980 against Jimmy Carter."

A leader of California's Democratic delegation to Congress, John Moss, said in an interview with the *Sacramento Bee* on May 22, 1976, that Brown was "flip" and "superficial" and added, "I have concluded that Brown is not ready for the office of the presidency. He needs to complete his full term as governor, and in this he has my good wishes. " Moss had previously been for Brown.

The most controversial endorsement of all came on June 3, five days before the primary, when Bob Moretti announced he favored Carter. Even though Brown and Moretti had been political foes, the governor had appointed the former assembly speaker to a $37,000-a-year job on the State Energy Commission. On June 5, columnist Earl Waters of the *Sacramento Union* noted the background of Moretti's action:

A grubbing politician who enjoyed a moment of transitory power as presiding officer of the State Assembly, Moretti's support of Carter has little sway. . . . Moretti assures himself of a place high in the ranks of political ingrates. For, having forsaken his seat in the Assembly in his disastrous attempt at higher office, Moretti found himself out in the cold and on the beach, all washed up. It was particularly bad for Moretti for he has no special qualifications for employment other than some political post. Yet, despite Brown's clear dislike for "professional" politicians and in the face of Moretti having done his best to thwart Brown's ambitions, Brown handed him a real plum. In appointing him to the State Energy Commission at $37,212 a year, he assured that Moretti would have more than margarine to spread on his bread. It is the best job Moretti has ever held at double what he made as speaker. If that wasn't enough, Brown also gave Moretti's sister [Marie] a job in the governor's office.

A year later, Moretti called his endorsement of Carter the most difficult decision of his political career. He said he had been hurting both "psychologically and financially" when Brown named him to the Energy Commission. "I needed a job. The day before he appointed me, I had to borrow fifteen hundred dollars from a friend of mine so I could pay that month's expenses, so that's why the job was so vital to me. I have four children and a wife.

"Because of my appreciation for the appointment, I tried to find every reason I could to be supportive of him [Brown]. And the more I saw, the less I liked, and it culminated in my endorsement of Carter." Moretti said he does not have "even the most remote regret" over backing Carter. "I was torn emotionally between wanting to get him out of California and caring for my own country. Well, I opted to care for the country. I just think he would be an absolute disaster" as president. "I think he's going to do enough damage as governor of California, and I just hope to God this country doesn't ever become saddled with him because we never will recover if that's the case. I think what Jerry believes is dangerous, I think it's elitist, and a very, very unhealthy thing. The world is a chess game to him."

Moretti also said that after he endorsed Carter, about 20 of the 120 state legislators told him, " 'Thank God there's one guy around here with enough balls to really say it.' They can't stand him. I guarantee you the day he goes down in those polls, they'll be coming out of the woodwork snapping at his heels."

Maullin and others who are still friends of Brown are critical of Moretti and his motives, but Brown voiced little concern. Referring to the appointment he gave Moretti, Brown said, "Theoretically the idea is that people are hired for a job because they are qualified. So I'm not sure that I have a right to personal gratitude. This is a public office." After serving on the Energy Commission for two and a half years, Moretti resigned to enter private business.

Although Brown made an impressive showing, Carter had the nomination locked up by the time the primaries ended on June 8. One reason for Brown's success in the primaries may have been that he far outspent Carter in Maryland, Nevada, and California, where his name was on the ballot, and in Oregon, where he was a write-in. Finance reports filed with the Federal Election Commission showed that in Maryland Brown spent $431,529 and Carter $175,450; in Oregon, Brown $169,710 and Carter $67,816; in Nevada, Brown $29,077 and Carter $24,808; and in California, Brown $860,774 and Carter $453,133. In retrospect, Brown concedes that running in just a few states may have given him "tactical advantages. I was a more isolated phenomenon." However, according to a subsequent survey made by the Democratic party, Brown spent money more effectively than the fourteen other major presidential candidates. The study showed that Brown received one vote for every fifty-one cents he spent, while the average for all fifteen candidates in both parties was $1.13 per vote. "We didn't lose, we just ran out of primaries" is the way Gray Davis assesses the Brown campaign. Many observers, from Pat Brown to teacher lobbyist Mary Bergan, believe Brown should have entered the race earlier, but Brown does not agree. He said he "arbitrarily" decided to serve a full year as governor before he started thinking seriously about running for president and added that he is not sure whether entering the race earlier would have enabled him to beat Carter.

Both Robert Gnaizda and Houston Flournoy think Brown made a mistake by running at all. Gnaizda believes that the race for president caused Brown to lower his own expectations because "he considers every action or nonaction in those terms. His great strength was that he was indifferent to being elected and had no higher aspirations, and therefore was untouchable. He had his moment of extraordinary greatness and grace," said Gnaizda, who added that Brown might be able to regain that peak "because he's a genius."

Said Flournoy, "I think it hurt him to run for president. It was a stupid thing of him to do." The attempt showed people "he really isn't any different than any other politician. I think he always was a very calculating bottom-line politician, but he just came in a different guise and fooled a lot of people for a long time." Flournoy thinks Brown is becoming more and more like former Los Angeles Mayor Sam Yorty, "who, I'm convinced, used to put his finger up in the air every morning and find out which way the wind was blowing."

But Leo McCarthy, who had not wanted Brown to run in 1976, now says, "As it turned out, he did extremely well in the half-dozen primaries he got in, and I don't think his entrance into the presidential race really did damage him."

The end of the primary season brought a new decision to be made: Should Brown drop out of the running and concede the nomination to Carter, as most of the other candidates had, or should he see the process through until the votes were tabulated at the convention?

"We could count as well as anyone," Kantor declared. "But at thirty-eight years old you don't want to look like a quitter." In addition, he said, the feeling within the Brown camp was "If you thought you had a new message for the American people, the only way to get their attention is to run for president." Therefore, in June and July, the inner circle, consisting of Brown, Davis, and Kantor, decided, "Let's continue to articulate the issues while we're here because we're not going to have this opportunity again, or at least not for a long time." Stating the issues was as important to Brown as being elected president, according to Kantor, who added that Brown felt obligated to his delegates and the people who had voted for him.

Remaining in the race until the bitter end may have been "unconventional, but that's Jerry," said Paul Halvonik. He said that staying in also let Brown expose Cesar Chavez, who made one of his nominating speeches at the convention, to a national audience.

Mary Bergan, a Brown delegate, agrees that Brown should not have dropped out, as had most other contenders, because his supporters "saw him as being different. A lot had never been active in politics except with Jerry Brown. They didn't like Jimmy Carter. They felt rightly or wrongly that a Southerner must be a racist, and they didn't want their votes to go to Jimmy Carter."

Leo McCarthy does not understand why Brown should have felt a greater duty to stay in the running than the other candidates had. However, says McCarthy, "Jerry Brown thinks differently from many other politicians on a lot of subjects." Others who shared McCarthy's view included Howard Berman:

"The last month of the campaign didn't accomplish anything for him" and Jon Kreedman: "I feel that although he had the national exposure [by staying in the race], it didn't help his image." Don Hoenshell, editor and vice president of the *Sacramento Union,* wrote in a column on June 15, 1976, that "Jerry Brown is still circling the bases a week after the Democrats finished the ballgame and turned out the lights."

Jeff Wald, using another baseball analogy to describe the situation, said it was as if "the Dodgers were ahead, eight to two in the eighth inning, and said [to the other team], 'Listen, why don't you guys quit?' " Wald said he was one of two Brown delegates who refused to accede to their candidate's request that Carter's nomination be made unanimous after the tally on the first ballot was Carter 2,238 1/2; Udall 329 1/2; Brown 300 1/2. "Why did it have to be unanimous? That's not part of the democratic process," reasoned Wald.

Brown rejects as "undemocratic" the notion that he should have quit the race before the balloting at the convention. "I wanted to run the process to the end," he says. "People who voted for me believed in what I was doing, and I just believed it was appropriate to keep going. There were still things to do, people to meet, points to be made, discussions to be had. Why give up until the counting begins?"

Brown's behavior at the convention, particularly after Carter was nominated on July 14, struck some people as ungracious. Gayle Montgomery, associate editor of the *Oakland Tribune,* wrote on July 16, 1976, two days after the vote at the convention:

The *real* Jerry Brown stood up at the Democratic National Convention and a lot of delegates frowned and shook their heads in disbelief. California Governor Edmund G. Brown Jr. swallowed the bitter pill of defeat yesterday with a tense and nervous half-smile as he introduced Democratic nominee Jimmy Carter to the California delegation, and his talk of "unity and convergency" was almost impersonal, with few references to the man who handed him his first real loss.

And columnist Chalmers M. Roberts of the *Washington Post* said two days later:

To some here—myself included—there was an unsettling edge to the Brown performance, an arrogance. . . . There were overtones of disrespect for the convention process. . . . There has been in his brief campaign a feeling of contempt for not just what have been past norms of American politics but a contempt for those who observe such norms and, as well, for the Democratic Party. . . . Brown reminds me of Huey Long, the anti-establishmentarian of Franklin Roosevelt's early presidency: not in the sense of Long's sheer demogoguery, though Brown could develop into a first-class demogogue, but in the overtone of contempt for others who may not be his idolators.

Carl Werthman thought the loss of the nomination might have been the best thing for Brown. "After it was all over, he told me he wasn't even sure he could have beaten Ford" because of his youth and inexperience. "People have slightly different expectations of a president than they do of a governor." Paul Halvonik agreed: "I don't think the country was ready to elect a thirty-eight-year-old bachelor who had just been governor for a year." But Kantor declared, "I don't have any doubt that Jerry could have beaten Ford, and I think he would have beaten him more easily than Jimmy Carter did." Kantor said President Ford might have done better in the South against Brown than he did versus Carter but that Brown would have more than made up for that by winning some of the large states Carter lost to Ford, such as California and Illinois.

A year after Carter narrowly defeated Ford, Brown said he did not know what the outcome of an election between him and Ford in 1976 would have been. Discussing his candidacy, he said, "I thought the whole campaign was a rather bold initiative."

Campaign director Kantor, who is from the South and knows some of Carter's aides, was gracious in defeat. "I think he [Brown] made an impact on Jimmy Carter and this administration" because of his message and his showing in the primaries. But "you can learn a lot from Jimmy Carter, too," said Kantor. "Not only did he have the best plan, he worked the hardest. His people were completely loyal to him and never panicked. He was the right person at the right time."

Throughout the convention proceedings, Brown made sure both the press and the public would keep an eye on him in the future. Syndicated columnist Mary McGrory observed Brown in action at the convention and wrote in the *Washington Star* on July 13, 1976, "Jerry Brown . . . has no idea of dying as a national figure. He has the taste in his mouth now. He'll be back."

And a month after the convention, while he was in Rockville campaigning for Maryland congressional candidates, Brown told onlookers, "I'm saving my [campaign] button. It may get better with age."

Between his entry into the presidential race in March and the general election in November, Brown spent much of his time traveling. Even after he lost the nomination, he remained on the road to campaign for Carter and for many other candidates, such as Allard Lowenstein, who was again running for Congress in New York; U.S. Senate candidates Bill Green in Pennsylvania, Paul Sarbanes in Maryland, Tom Maloney in Delaware, Frank Moss in Utah, and Donald Riegle in Michigan; Scott Matheson, who was elected governor of Utah; and congressional candidates in Michigan, Maryland, and Virginia.

Two years earlier, while campaigning for the nomination for governor, Brown had criticized Ronald Reagan for going to twelve states, Washington, D.C., and Acapulco during the previous three months. Reagan, said Brown on April 11, 1974, "finds it more interesting to travel throughout the nation campaigning for president than to remain in California and try and deal with the issues facing the people who elected him."

However, when Brown himself was running for president, his policy shifted drastically. Political editor Richard Rodda of the *Sacramento Bee* noted in a column on June 17, 1976, that "between April 28 and June 15 he [Brown] was in California 15 days, only 3 1/2 of them in Sacramento." By contrast, Brown had refused to leave the state even to attend governors' conferences or Democratic party functions during his first sixteen months in office and had agreed to appear on such national television shows as NBC's "Meet the Press" and William F. Buckley's "Firing Line" only if the shows were filmed in California.

Many of Brown's close associates say his travels as a candidate gave him a valuable education. During one of Brown's trips to New York, Dan Greer, a New Haven attorney who had been one of his best friends at Yale, met with him and said, "C'mon, Jerry, it's time you saw what the real world looks like." Greer took

Brown on a tour of the South Bronx and later said his old friend "couldn't believe it. I used to tell him, 'Jerry, you know New York and Pennsylvania may be decadent, but that's where the electoral votes are.' It was an educational process for him."

Moretti, who was raised in Detroit, offered a different description of Brown's learning process in 1976: "He's running for president, he goes back East, and alas! he found out there are slums in this country. Well, my God, he was just shocked. He came back and said, 'You ought to just see the terrible way some people live.' Well, goddamit, those of us who grew up in the streets knew that a long time ago. He's not trying to be malicious to people who don't have in this life. His problem is a little bit what Ronald Reagan's problem is. They don't know those people exist."

Gray Davis believes that Brown's travels enhanced his dealings with the state legislature. Senators and assembly members who received calls that Brown placed from car telephones and hotel rooms around the country were flattered and much more impressed than they would have been with a call from his office in Sacramento, Davis said. Also, "he was calling as a potential Democratic nominee and as a proven winner. Popularity is the currency of the realm in politics. I am convinced that he could contribute more effectively to the legislative process" because of his victories around the country.

That Jerry Brown and Jimmy Carter do not form a mutual admiration society has become a political fact of life since Brown undertook the race against Carter in 1976. Any antipathy that Carter feels for Brown may be due not so much to Brown's victories that year or his potential for causing trouble in 1980 as to remarks he made about Carter on the campaign trail, including:

• "Bible quoting has become part of the process, and I have my own text, that he who is last shall be first and he who is first shall be last" (Nevada, May 3).
• "Where is the real Jimmy Carter—there's the smile, but what's the person behind that? At the very time he say he's not seeking endorsements, he's on the telephone to the president of the United Auto Workers and Birch Bayh, trying to get the endorsement" ("Face the Nation," CBS, May 9).
• "I'm not going to smile away very difficult problems," and

"I try to be as truthful as I can . . . [but] to go around like George Washington seems a strange thing to me . . . I'm a little wary of people who claim to be reborn politicians" (Maryland, mid-May).
• "Look behind the smile. I've been listening to Carter for one and a half years, and that's why I got into this race. I can offer something better" (while campaigning in Maryland in May).
• Brown accused Carter of "running on a smile and a reorganization plan . . . which is a consumer fraud," and of using a "snake-oil approach which I'd like to see out of politics" (Los Angeles, June 2).
• Carter's government reorganization program "reminds me of the secret plan that we heard about Vietnam. It doesn't exist. And if it did exist, I challenge Jimmy Carter on this program, before he gets off," to reveal it ("Issues and Answers," ABC, June 6).

After Carter won the nomination, Brown pledged support and campaigned for him, but as late as two weeks before Election Day, the Californian's public statements about Carter were still lukewarm. Under the headline, "Brown's pitch is a curve," and the subhead, "Gives Carter qualified support on 3-state tour," an AP story in the *San Francisco Examiner* on October 18 quoted Brown as saying, while campaigning for Carter in Oregon, that he was backing Carter instead of Eugene McCarthy—who was still an independent presidential candidate—because "Carter has the Democratic nomination." In the same story, Brown was reported to have said that in diplomacy Carter "certainly can't do any worse than Jerry Ford," and that "I don't back up everything anyone says. But by and large, I'm supporting Jimmy Carter."

At a press conference on September 29, Brown was asked to explain why he was not going to appear with Carter at a campaign event October 7 in Los Angeles, the same night Ford and Reagan were to attend a GOP rally together in the same city. Brown responded. "I'm doing as much campaigning as I possibly can. . . . I'll try to be with Mr. Carter the following night." Brown added that he had committed himself to campaign for an assembly candidate on October 7. "If I could enjoy the virtue of bi-location, I would attend the [Carter] dinner, but not having been visited with that particular grace, I'm unable to do so."

Both during and after the campaign, Brown attempted to gloss over his attacks on Carter. When a *Sacramento Union* interviewer asked the governor on September 19, "How do you get along with Carter? You had some bitter exchanges in Maryland," Brown answered, "I don't think they were very bitter. I think they were gentlemanly and on issues and really not all that frequent." And when Brown visited Florida after the election, the *Florida Times-Union* reported on November 21 that he was reminded he had once described Carter as a "fuzzy fellow peddling snake oil." According to the article, Brown "smiled thinly and replied: 'I don't think we should get involved in a recycling of primary campaigns.' " A year later, Brown's assessment was that he had made "very minimal, very minimal" personal attacks on Carter. He added, "I think my comments were very positive."

Llew Werner, a Brown aide who was loaned to the Carter campaign in California, said that "Jerry Brown did everything Carter asked him to. I'm not sure Carter asked him to be as involved as perhaps other people would have suggested he should have been." Werner, a gregarious young man who helped found the Students for a Democratic Society (SDS) chapter at the University of Southern California and who also thrives on the Nixon Special, cottage cheese covered with catsup, was present when Brown and Carter first met in 1973. Werner recalled that Carter "was running for president then" and had said he would like to talk to the young secretary of state, son of the former governor and potential future governor. The meeting took place in a VIP lounge at San Francisco International Airport; the two men munched on peanuts, and Carter was accompanied by a black Georgia highway patrolman who served as his bodyguard. Other than that, Werner remembered little about the meeting because "at the moment it had no significance."

According to Alan Cranston, Brown declined at least one Carter request during the campaign: to film a joint television commercial Cranston had suggested. Gray Davis confirmed that Hamilton Jordan, Carter's top aide, had called him to ask that Brown make the advertisement. Davis said Carter then made the request directly to Brown, who turned it down because he had refused to do television commercials for any California candidates. Brown confirmed Davis's account, adding that he doesn't even like to make ads for his own campaign and that the only exception he made to his policy in 1976 was on behalf of Proposition 14, the farm labor initiative backed by the UFW.

According to Gray Davis, "Jerry Brown by his standards had made a rather unprecedented commitment to the election of Jimmy Carter" by campaigning for Carter for hundreds of hours in several different states. Davis noted that by comparison Brown spent only half a day campaigning for his sister Kathleen Brown Rice when she ran for the Los Angeles School Board in 1975. "You have to measure Jerry Brown against Jerry Brown, not against Hubert Humphrey or someone else," Davis added.

Cranston agreed that "Jerry did work hard" for Carter. "He went around the country. He said good things."

The press, however, was skeptical of Brown's efforts on Carter's behalf. Gil Bailey of the *San Jose Mercury* wrote on December 2, 1976:

> Brown, both California and Washington Carter staffers say, on the surface did his best for the Carter-Mondale ticket but underneath did little to help either Carter or Senator John Tunney, D-Calif., both of whom lost in the state. In fact, some Brown people with the approval of the governor, according to the Carter camp, did quite a lot to sabotage the Carter campaign with a number of stories in the national media.

The *Washington Post*'s Marquis Childs said on April 5, 1977, that "Brown gave Carter comparatively little help in the campaigning in his state [California] last fall and his indifferent behavior at the Madison Square Garden convention was hardly likely to make them bosom pals." And *Newsday* Washington bureau chief Martin Schram's assessment as of May 26, 1977, was:

> They [Carter staffers] think he [Brown] laid down during Carter's unsuccessful fall campaign in California, appearing with Carter whenever he came to the state, but doing little else to help the Carter cause on the days when the candidate was elsewhere. And mostly they think he was cool in his support for Carter because he wants, most of all, to be elected president himself, and eight years of a Carter administration might cramp the Brown timetable.

Willie Brown agrees with the three columnists. "Certainly there was no great effort by the governor on behalf of the president," he declared. "I suspect it will be very hard even for a born-again Baptist to be that forgiving so quickly."

And Gray Davis said of Brown and Carter, "I think the relationship could best be described as professional. Politics is the business of scarcity. The opportunities for advancement are limited."

Cranston said he "wound up doing some mediating" because of a "breakdown in communications" between the Carter and Brown camps. Each side was "tending to put the worst motives to the other. And I don't mean Carter, and I don't mean Jerry, I mean the people around them." Marc Poché shares this view: "I've never heard the governor say he doesn't like Carter. I think the problem maybe is with some of the troops or with people who thought they were troops. To the extent an intermediary is needed, Cranston is it."

Cranston, who has become one of the most powerful members of the Senate, said that some of Carter's top aides are "very suspicious of Jerry." He added that some members of Carter's staff wanted to keep Brown from playing too prominent a role when the president toured California's drought-stricken agricultural areas in May 1977, but that he had spoken to Vice President Mondale, who intervened and smoothed things other. Mondale and Brown "have a good relationship" even though they are potential rivals for the presidency in the future, according to Cranston.

Undeniably, a number of people close to Brown do take a dim view of Carter and the White House staff. "Look at Jimmy Carter, he's like Milton Berle, stealing jokes. The suit bag has one shirt in it," declared Jeff Wald. Carl Werthman said, "Jerry's just supplied Carter with a whole slug of political symbolism. He's just ripped them right off." Werthman was referring to Carter's taking an inauguration-day walk down Pennsylvania Avenue, ordering a reduction in the number of White House limousines, lowering the thermostats in the executive offices, and voluntarily paying several thousand dollars in income taxes that he did not owe. On January 23, 1978, President Carter stated on offering his first budget to Congress that "in formulating this budget, I have been made acutely aware once more of the overwhelming number of demands upon the budget and of the finite nature of our resources." He added, "The span of government is not infinite." His statement was an echo of Brown's

January 7, 1976, address to the California legislature, in which he said, "The country is rich, but not as rich as we have been led to believe. The choice to do one thing may preclude another. In short, we are entering an era of limits."

LeRoy Chatfield said that before Brown made a speech in North Carolina in April 1977, the sponsors had to clear Brown's visit to Carter territory with the White House "because we're not looking for problems." He added that White House fears of Brown's future plans might become "a self-fulfilling prophecy" by planting the idea that he is a force to be reckoned with in 1980. The smarter thing, he said, would be to "let sleeping dogs lie."

Llew Werner ridiculed Carter aides who started worrying about his reelection before he even took office. Werner's remarks came after a memo that pollster Patrick Caddell—who, ironically, had worked for Kantor as pollster in Cranston's 1974 campaign—wrote to Carter in December 1976 was made public. Caddell suggested that the GOP "seems bent on self-destruction" and warned that Brown "must be viewed as the single largest threat on the horizon within the Democratic party."

One of Brown's assistants said the governor "can't stand to see Carter's name" in the daily news summary he receives. "It drives him right up the wall."

As early as November 28, 1976, three weeks after Carter's election, journalists such as John McDermott, a *Miami Herald* political writer, were speculating that "if Jimmy Carter falters during the next four years in the White House, the Democrat most likely to pick up the pieces is the relatively young California chief executive."

Those familiar with the way Brown works are about evenly divided on whether he might challenge Carter in 1980. Joe Cerrell considers it likely that Brown will oppose Carter in the 1980 primaries. "He'll never be the crown prince, so why not be the pretender to the throne?" said Cerrell. He hypothesizes Brown's thinking as, " 'So I piss off Jimmy Carter. So what? What have I lost?' And I repeat, what has he lost? There's no great disgrace in losing elections, so why not challenge Jimmy Carter? I think they're nervous about it" in the White House. "And I think they ought to be nervous about it." James Mills, who has been in touch with some of Carter's key aides, said, "I think they're concerned about a possible primary challenge in 1980, and I think their concern is appropriate." Commenting on an April, 1977, California Poll revealing that two-thirds of Californians believe Brown will run for president in 1980, Democratic Assemblyman Lou Papan said, "No question of it. I'm sure he's hoping Carter will fall on his face, and he's watching closely, and he probably surprised himself at the success he met in the 1976 primaries. And he got to believing he should be president. And you know something? I don't think he's fully recovered from it. This fellow's really been bitten."

However, a veteran Democratic activist and long-time critic of Brown commented, "I don't think his star stays that long" to cause Carter any real problem.

Cranston and Howard Berman do not expect Brown to oppose Carter. "The facts of life are rather obvious," Cranston said. "A lot of people, including Jerry, would challenge Carter in 1980 if he's in trouble. Otherwise, no rational or prudent leader" would run against an incumbent president from the same party. Berman commented, "My own view is that one has to make quite a case to justify running as a Democrat against an incumbent president. I thought that case was made against Lyndon Johnson in 1968. But it simply can't be the ambition or the popularity of a particular political figure. There has to be a record of non-achievement and inappropriate conduct in office to really justify that." Marc Poché said in early 1977, " I would be astounded if he ran for president against Jimmy Carter. If Jerry Brown is anything, he's a very practical politician. And it would be an absolute exercise in futility. It would be a step toward political suicide." A year later, Poché had changed his mind and said he thought Brown is likely to run in 1980.

Brown has repeatedly refused to comment publicly on any plans he might have for seeking the presidency. During an interview on KNBC-TV in Los Angeles on July 23, 1977, for example, he was asked if he would commit himself to serving a full four-year term as governor, provided he is reelected in 1978. Brown's response: "I'm not prepared to make any long-range commitments."

Three months later, he told me, "Certainly, incumbent chief executives are generally well supported by their party." His only direct comment on 1980 was: "There's nothing I'm doing that is inconsistent with either not running or running."

However, one of Brown's political strategists pointed out that members of his staff make sure they read the *New York Times* and *Washington Post* daily. "And we don't read those papers so we can find out what is going on in California."

The best guess about Brown's future is that he will not run against Carter unless the president stumbles. Assuming, however, that Brown wins impressively in 1978, he and his advisers are likely to be watching closely for a Carter stumble, and they may be very liberal in their definition of what a stumble is.

In fact, as of early 1978, Carter already seemed to be in serious trouble. The year 1977 appeared to have been as bad for him as 1976 was good. On January 1, 1976, Carter was still virtually unknown outside of Georgia. Within a few months, he crushed his opposition in the early primaries, then went on to gain the Democratic nomination and the presidency.

The problem seemed to be that although Carter had a brilliant plan for grabbing the nomination, he did not have a clear concept of what to do afterward. Perhaps he and his campaign strategists were amazed at the success of their scenario. Clearly, Carter did not win the nomination because he was the most popular Democratic candidate; had Humphrey, Kennedy, Brown, and Church all been in the race from the start, Carter very likely would have been an also-ran. He was nominated because he had the best plan, not because the voters loved him.

The Carter strategy seemed to extend only as far as winning the nomination. Then for weeks Carter could not get going. More than a month after the convention, candidates for other offices in California who wanted Carter to campaign in their district learned from his California offices that scheduling was being handled out of Atlanta. Calls to Atlanta produced the information that scheduling for each state was being planned in the state. Carter finally won an unimpressive victory over an unimpressive Republican opponent.

After a honeymoon of several months, Carter was beset by problems. The resignation in disgrace of Budget Director Bert Lance tarnished Carter's image. The new president saw his energy program defeated in Congress, his Panama Canal treaties in serious trouble, and the stock market buffeted almost daily.

Newsweek, in its October 24, 1977, issue, asked the question, both on the cover and as the headline for the lead story, "Can Carter Cope?" Increasingly, observers were coming up with a "no" to that query.

Commenting on Carter's political problems, Robert Gnaizda compared the president to Brown. As evidence that Brown is a much more skillful politician than President Carter, Gnaizda cited Carter's New Year's, 1978, speech in Iran, during which he referred to the Shah as "my closest friend and ally." Referring to human rights violations that have taken place during the Shah's rule, Gnaizda predicted that "the extravagance and gross inaccuracy of this statement could come back to haunt Carter." By contrast, Gnaizda said, "Brown, who is very careful with his choice of words, would never be so inaccurate." Instead, he said, Brown probably would have said something to the effect that "*Iran* is a great ally," without specifically aligning himself with the Shah's controversial antihuman-rights record.

Meanwhile, where the Sacramento River meets the American, Jerry Brown is watching, waiting impatiently, and privately delighted over Carter's difficulties.

Unless 1978 and 1979 are substantially better years for Carter than 1977, Jerry Brown will very likely run for president in 1980. Of course, if Carter is still in trouble when the time comes for him to seek a second term, he will probably face opposition from other Democrats as well.

If the competition in 1980 is too stiff, Jerry Brown can afford to wait until 1984 or beyond. Of the other major candidates for president in 1976—Carter, Humphrey, Church, Jackson, Udall, Wallace, Ford, and Reagan—Carter was the youngest. Yet he is fourteen years older than Brown, which makes Brown closer in age to Carter's sons than to Carter. Even Ted Kennedy, who is still regarded as a young man, is six years older than Brown.

Yet Jerry Brown is in a hurry. When he was seeking the Democratic nomination for governor in 1974, George Zenovich introduced him to a group of Democratic women in Fresno, and according to Zenovich, one lady, who was for Alioto, said to Brown, "Why don't you wait? You're young. You'll be governor someday, and you'll be president someday." And Brown, then thirty-six, answered, "No, I can't wait, I haven't got time to

wait." Brown does seem to have a curious streak of fatalism. As
he has said, "Ten years from now, if I'm still alive, it may be
something else, who knows?"

At times, Brown talks about leaving politics, calls the job of
governor a "pain in the ass," discusses returning to the seminary
or becoming a missionary in undeveloped countries. But no one
who knows him well takes him seriously. In the words of one
observer, "It's not enough for him to be governor. I mean, his
father was governor. He wants to be an unusual governor. He
wants to be a great governor. And Jerry's expectations have never
been lowered. He had a long-term vision of what he wanted and
where he wanted to get. It was almost a sense of manifest destiny
that Jerry carried around with him. He gave the impression of
being a crown prince. And given that type of personality one
doesn't stop at being governor of California after two terms. But
Jerry knows the public doesn't like politicians who appear to be
overly ambitious, so he keeps his political candle burning
brightly inside but very much hidden by a bushel basket."

If Brown decides not to run for president in 1980, or if he
enters the race and does not win, he will most likely seek the U.S.
Senate seat now held by S. I. Hayakawa when Hayakawa's term
expires in 1982. By then, Brown would have completed two
terms, or eight years, as governor. In accord with the Jesuit rule
he is fond of reciting, he will have served long enough in one job.
Even if Hayakawa were to run for reelection, he would be
seventy-six in 1982 and would not present much of an obstacle to
Brown. Election to the Senate that year would give Brown a year
and a half to use the forum on Capitol Hill to reestablish his
credentials as a presidential candidate in 1984.

What kind of president might Brown be?

He would certainly bring new groups of people to power in
Washington, just as he has transformed Sacramento.

He would attempt to curtail federal programs and return
power to state and local government. Such a policy might make
an interesting experiment, but Brown will need to be flexible, for
the decentralization of authority might prove catastrophic. State
and local governments might not be able to take over all the
necessary programs; state and local taxes might climb much
faster than federal taxes would drop; and massive unemployment might occur among people who depend on federal pro-

grams for jobs. Brown would have to be willing to admit that decentralization of government does not work if in practice it turns out to be a failure. And there is reason to believe that he is not someone who would remain committed to a policy come hell or high water; he is pragmatic rather than dogmatic.

He would, both by policy and by example, inaugurate the development of new sources of energy, such as solar, wind, geothermal, and perhaps even tidal. He would not be locked in to any solutions but would be willing to investigate any energy source that looked promising.

He would pursue the exploration and colonization of space.

His style would be entirely different from the White House norm. Because of the demands of the office, Brown would have to follow a more rigid schedule than he has as governor, but even so, his timetable would not be comparable to that of any other recent president. Many analysts would insist that no president could possibly operate the way Brown would, but numerous observers said the same thing about his approach to the job of governor and were wrong.

The cornerstones of Brown's foreign policy would probably be a reaffirmation of U.S. support for Israel and the establishment of better relations with Third World countries. He would exchange ambassadors with any nation that wished to coexist peacefully with the United States. Among the countries with which Brown would begin full diplomatic ties would be China, Vietnam, and Cuba if a previous administration had not already done so.

Lou Papan speculates that Brown's lack of concern for protocol and his insensitivity to the feelings of other people would wind up involving the United States in wars. But Robert Gnaizda, who knows and understands Brown much better than does Papan, commented, "He is probably the person least likely to get us into a war of any major politician. There's nothing macho about him. He doesn't have a zealous ideological commitment. He's very adept at compromise. And very skilled when he wants to be at bringing out the best in other people."

In the words of Dan Greer, "Jerry would shake this country to its roots. His ideology is neither liberal nor conservative. He questions everything."

JERRY BROWN'S ELECTION RECORD

April 1, 1969: Los Angeles Junior College Board *

	VOTES	PERCENT
Brown	186,901	5.04
Mike Antonovich, teacher (member state assembly, 1973 to date)	134,010	3.61
Augusta Anderson, banker	106,857	2.88
Robert Cline, tax consultant (member state assembly, 1971 to date)	104,879	2.83
Joseph William Orozco, business executive	93,405	2.52
Marian La Follette, teacher	82,150	2.22
Frederic Wyatt, industrial consultant	76,277	2.06
Joyce Fadem, teacher	71,792	1.94

* 133 candidates ran for seven seats on the newly created board. The top fourteen vote getters qualified for a runoff election.

	VOTES	PERCENT
Kenneth Washington, college administrator	70,707	1.90
Irene Tovar, educational program developer	67,045	1.80
John Carmack, attorney	58,692	1.58
Alex Aloia, teacher	56,496	1.52
Odessa Cox, business executive	55,516	1.49
Allen Brandstater, political consultant	55,376	1.49

May 27, 1969: Los Angeles Junior College Board *

	VOTES	PERCENT
Brown	466,073	67.48
Mike Antonovich	405,014	58.59
Frederic Wyatt	376,465	54.46
Robert Cline	363,648	52.64
Kenneth Washington	355,918	51.52
Joseph William Orozco	352,027	50.96
Marian La Follette	349,613	50.61
Augusta Anderson	344,163	49.77
John Carmack	338,678	49.00
Irene Tovar	335,233	48.51
Odessa Cox	312,632	45.22
Joyce Fadem	309,747	44.80
Alex Aloia	276,410	39.97
Allen Brandstater	249,087	36.05

June 2, 1970: Democratic Primary for California Secretary of State

	VOTES	PERCENT
Brown	1,632,886	67.7
Hugh M. Burns	591,320	24.5
Jimmy Campbell	187,899	7.8

* Top seven elected

November 3, 1970: General Election for California Secretary of State

	VOTES	PERCENT
Brown	3,234,788	50.4
James L. Flournoy, Republican (no relation to Houston Flournoy)	2,926,613	45.6
Thomas Goodloe, American Independent	144,838	2.3
Israel Feuer, Peace and Freedom	110,184	1.7

June 4, 1974: Democratic Primary for Governor *

	VOTES	PERCENT
Brown	1,085,752	37.8
Joseph Alioto	544,007	18.9
Bob Moretti	478,469	16.6
William Matson Roth	293,686	10.2
Jerome Waldie	227,489	7.9

November 5, 1974: General Election for Governor

	VOTES	PERCENT
Brown	3,131,648	50.2
Houston I. Flournoy, Republican	2,952,954	47.3
Edmon V. Kaiser, American Independent	83,869	1.3
Elizabeth Keathley, Peace and Freedom.	75,004	1.2

May 18, 1976: Maryland Presidential Primary

	VOTES	PERCENT
Brown	284,271	48.3
Jimmy Carter	217,166	36.9
Morris Udall	31,340	5.3
George Wallace	25,414	4.3
Henry Jackson	13,556	2.3
Ellen McCormack	9,759	1.7
Fred Harris	6,880	1.2

* The remaining 8.4 percent of the vote was divided among thirteen other candidates.

May 25, 1976: Nevada Presidential Primary

	VOTES	PERCENT
Brown	39,649	52.8
Carter	17,538	23.3
Frank Church	6,775	9.0
Wallace	2,486	3.3
Udall	2,235	3.0
Jackson	1,895	2.5
No preference	4,595	6.1

May 25, 1976: Oregon Presidential Primary

	VOTES	PERCENT
Church	143,174	34.6
Carter	113,564	27.4
Brown (write-in)	96,486	23.3
Hubert Humphrey	21,917	5.3
Udall	11,368	2.8
Ted Kennedy	10,944	2.6
Wallace	5,700	1.4
Jackson	5,198	1.2
McCormack	3,693	0.9
Harris	1,332	0.3
Birch Bayh	722	0.2

June 1, 1976: Rhode Island Presidential Primary

	VOTES	PERCENT
Uncommitted (campaigned for by Brown)	19,066	31.4
Carter	18,171	29.9
Church	16,767	27.6
Udall	2,672	4.4
McCormack	2,369	3.9
Jackson	748	1.2
Wallace	534	0.9
Bayh	236	0.4
Milton Shapp	111	0.2

June 8, 1976: New Jersey Presidential Primary

	VOTES	PERCENT
Uncommitted (campaigned for by Brown)	194,673	42.1
Carter	129,455	27.9
Udall	59,365	12.8
Church	30,722	6.6
Wallace	28,944	6.3
McCormack	19,700	4.3

June 8, 1976: California Presidential Primary

	VOTES	PERCENT
Brown	2,013,210	59.0
Carter	697,092	20.4
Church	250,581	7.3
Udall	171,501	5.0
Wallace	102,292	3.0
Uncommitted	78,595	2.3
Jackson	38,634	1.1
McCormack	29,242	0.9
Harris	16,920	0.5
Bayh	11,419	0.3

☆INDEX

283